Coordinating
Community Care

Coordinating Community Care

Multidisciplinary teams and care management

JOHN ØVRETVEIT

OPEN UNIVERSITY PRESS

Buckingham · Philadelphia

Open University Press
Celtic Court
22 Ballmoor
Buckingham
MK18 1XW

email: enquiries@openup.co.uk
world wide web: http://www.openup.co.uk

and
325 Chestnut Street
Philadelphia, PA 19106, USA

First published 1993
Reprinted 1994, 1995, 1998, 2000

A catalogue record of this book is available from the British
Library

ISBN 0 335 19047 2 (pb) 0 335 19048 0 (hb)

Library of Congress Cataloging-in-Publication Data
Øvretveit, John, 1954–
    Coordinating community care: multidisciplinary teams and
care management / John Øvretveit.
        p.   cm.
Includes bibliographical references and index.
    ISBN 0–335–19048–0   ISBN 0–335–19047–2 (pbk.)
    1. Social service – Great Britain – Team work.
    I. Title.
HV41.09   1993
361'.0068'4 – dc20   92–46225   CIP

Typeset by Vision Typesetting, Manchester
Printed in Great Britain by St Edmundsbury Press Ltd,
Bury St Edmunds, Suffolk

CONTENTS

FOREWORD

The White Paper *Caring for People* heralded fundamental changes in the provision of community care. These are intended to produce a better planned and better integrated range of services which are more responsive to individual needs and which afford the user greater choice.

Their success rests crucially on the development of more effective working relationships between health and social care. Cooperation must replace the division and conflict which up to now has characterized many aspects of this relationship.

The publication of John Øvretveit's book *Coordinating Community Care* is therefore very timely. In it he suggests ways of bringing together a variety of different people to work cooperatively in small groups. He offers ideas and solutions to some of the organizational problems which make it difficult to realize the ideals of community care. The focus is on understanding the organizational structure and authority relations within teams and the incentive contradictions which can lead to conflict. He describes ten common types of team and examines communication between team members, as well as links between the operational and strategic levels of different organizations.

The ideas contained in this book are based on a continuing programme of development work undertaken with practitioners and managers over the last ten years. They build on the earlier work of the Brunel Health and Social Services Management Programme which since its inception has contributed greatly to our knowledge and understanding of health and social services organizations.

Andrew Foster
Community Care Support Force
Department of Health

PREFACE

Caring is giving understanding and practical help, *curing* is removing the causes of disorder. At times we all need both, and we all have to do both, caring and curing others freely and in unskilled ways in our families and neighbourhoods. There are limits to our caring and curing abilities, and some people who need care and cure do not have family or friends to help. At times we all have to turn to formal services provided by the state or voluntary organizations for more help, or for more expert help.

The 1990 UK health and community care reforms led to a greater variety of services, although many question whether the amount of services which people need has increased. More choice and competition often brings benefits for clients who need one type of service, but not always for clients who need many types. This brings us to the subject of this book: coordinating health and social care, and the incentives and organization to do so in the complex and changing world of the 1990s.

The history of community care is one of competition for finance between acute hospital care and primary health care, and between social care for those 'at risk' and others such as the 'disabled'. It is a history of division between health and social care, and of a few fragile alliances which have achieved much. Many feel that the reforms increase service fragmentation and that a mix of exhortations, punishment and care management models will not counter the financial and other pressures which appear to be creating greater divisions between services. This is certainly a possibility, especially if change is driven by short-term cost considerations and competition which sweeps aside the successful systems and relationships between services built over the last years. But reforms also have the potential to get to grips with long-standing coordination problems, and to introduce changes which make the most of the flexibility which is now possible.

This book is about how to bring together different people, who give different types of care and cure, to work together in small groups. These groups are to help one client, or to help many clients with similar combinations of needs. It shows how carers and curers can work out who does what, get more satisfaction from working with each other, and build services which they will be glad to call upon when they and their families need help.

It is easy to criticize community care policies and progress. This book offers ideas and some solutions to the organizational problems which make it difficult to realize the ideals of community care. The ideas were developed and tested with practitioners and managers over the last ten years, and have helped to overcome problems in teamwork and improve coordination in different settings. New ideas were necessary to prepare for and carry out the 1990 reforms, and most of this book draws on this recent work with teams and community service managers.

These ideas, and the best coordination in the world, will not solve problems of under-financing and split-service responsibilities. But better coordination makes resources go further, and cooperation rather than competition is often more efficient.

John Øvretveit

ACKNOWLEDGEMENTS

This book is based on a continuing programme of development research undertaken with managers and practitioners in community services and teams across the UK. The Brunel Health and Social Services Programme (BHSSP) has undertaken such research into health and welfare service organization for over 25 years. Its members carry out field research, consultancy and local workshops, and have developed and published a substantial body of knowledge about health and social services organization. The BHSSP is a self-financing applied research programme based at Brunel University.

My thanks to the many managers and team members with whom I worked for their help and contributions to the ideas presented in this book. My thanks also to Anna, Rick, and Mary, and the many Friends without whose support the book would never have been written.

Chapter 1
INTRODUCTION

Coordinate: *to bring into order as parts of a whole.*
(a. equal in rank, importance, etc.)
Collaborate: *to labour together; to act jointly*
Cooperate: *to act jointly with another; to unite for a common*
effort.

This book is about how people from different professions and agencies work together to meet the health and social needs of people in a community. It is about making the most of different skills to meet people's needs, and creating satisfying and supportive working groups. It is about the details of making community care a reality.

When we have a health or social need it is rare that one profession alone is able to meet our needs. We can usually benefit from the skills and knowledge of different specialists – so long as their help is well coordinated. Often these specialists are employed by more than one agency, making coordination even more important but the difficulties of achieving it greater. We see the consequences of failures of coordination every day in complaints and the law courts, but also in the hidden extra costs of duplication and staff frustration. The causes of poor coordination are many and well documented, and include under-financing, and fragmented responsibilities for health and social care, which the 1990 UK community care reforms did little to change. However, the reforms also created opportunities to overcome many of the long-standing problems – it is up to purchasers and providers to build on the lessons of the past and successful schemes and to use the new freedoms to benefit clients and carers.

Although critiques of community care are many, there is little published which is of practical use to managers and practitioners wishing to develop teamwork and care coordination. This book is mainly for practitioners working in teams and their managers, but also for students and other researchers, as well as for planners and purchasers of team services. The main purpose of the book is to enable practitioners and managers to improve their multidisciplinary team service and care management and to inform others about how teams work. It presents research carried out with a variety of teams before and after the 1990 reforms, and is of use to primary health care teams, and teams concerned with people with mental health problems, people with learning difficulties, with physical disabilities, older people, children and families, as well as special project teams. Although the focus is community teams and care management for specific client groups or populations, and most examples are from the UK, much of the book is of use to multidisciplinary teams in hospitals, and to teams outside the UK.

The practical issue addressed by the book is how to coordinate different professions and agencies to assess, treat or care for one or more clients or patients (hereafter called 'clients'). The trend in many countries is towards more community-based services, increasing specialization within professions to meet the specific needs of different client groups, and a wider range of agencies providing and purchasing services. There is a danger that these changes could result in less responsive and effective ways to meet clients needs, unless attention is paid to coordination. Multidisciplinary teams are one solution to the problem of coordination. Care management is another. We will see how these solutions can be combined or run in parallel.

One of the theoretical issues addressed is professional practice in modern welfare services, and the effect of changes in welfare provision and ideology on professions. Multidisciplinary teams are here to stay, and are the future context for professional practice. Social scientific knowledge does not sufficiently recognize that most professional practice is undertaken in multidisciplinary teams and in the community, and that consumer power is increasing. This, community care, and the 1990 UK reforms are changing the shape, structure and power of different professions. This book aims to contribute to an understanding of these changes on professional practice and power.

The rest of this introduction previews some of the themes of the book, and then describes the research method and sources. It then presents some of the history of community care and teams to give a context for the following chapters. It concludes by considering the implications of the 1990 UK health and social service reforms for teams, and by providing an overview of each chapter of the book. Practitioners who want to get a feel for the book might find Chapter 6 on team member's roles a good introduction. Managers of practitioners in teams might like to start with Chapter 7 on team leadership and management accountability.

THEMES AND ASSUMPTIONS OF THE BOOK

The following outlines some of the themes and assumptions of the book, and of the development research on which the book is based.

Personalities, problems and structure

The book shows how many problems of cooperation arise from poor organization and 'perverse incentives' rather than from the more popular explanation of 'personality conflicts'. For example, issues like a team leader not being able to get the information needed from a team member, or a team never confronting or making difficult decisions, are often explained in terms of the personalities involved. Or a legitimate concern about the quality of another team member's work is reduced to a 'conflict of personalities', when there were not agreed arrangements for monitoring and support, or arrangements for properly addressing and raising such issues without 'personalizing' them.

It is often more interesting and certainly easier to discuss problems in terms of personalities, rather than work at understanding the underlying structural and incentive contradictions and conflicts. Personalities are important, but the conditions under which many teams operate, and their organization, or rather lack of it, make it difficult for the most willing and cooperative of people to collaborate with others. In many teams and services I have worked with, the situation is often guaranteed to bring out the worst in people – so much so that it seems the aim is to prove that 'teams do not work'. In these conditions, setting up sensitivity groups to increase trust and respect rarely addresses the real structural problems which make cooperation difficult, and which remain after the group returns to work.

The book aims to put organizational structure back on the agenda of team development. It is fashionable to play down or deny the importance of structure, and especially of authority relations. The book considers the reasons for this, some of which are positive: over-emphasis on 'getting' the structure right, specification and bureaucratic procedures can be organizational suicide in the fast-changing world of health and social services in the 1990s. Sometimes organizational structure seems abstract and unrelated to what people do every day. This may be because when people talk about structure it is not clear what they mean. I mean the formal organizational position (organizational role) a person takes up when starting a job, in particular the responsibilities of the position and the working relations of accountability and authority to other positions and groups. I also mean agreed procedures and policies, for example about decision-making.

Certainly different people would interpret the responsibilities of the same position in different way, and would relate to other people in other positions in different ways. However, the way in which responsibilities and incentives are distributed, and the relations of accountability and authority, affect what people do as much as their personality. Certain problems and behaviours will be encountered if the structure is wrong, regardless of who works in the structure. People come and go, but the problems will remain. Problems of structure are not overcome by calling a group a team or someone a care manager – using these terms is the starting point for creating the details of the organization needed for coordination not the finishing point.

This book argues that we should pay as much attention to organizational structure as to the physical buildings and environments in which we work. Organization affects our life and the lives of others in much more profound ways. It influences how we act and feel and how we relate to others in ways of which we are often not aware. In developing team organization we are developing a social institution that outlives individuals, although paradoxically, it only exists through what individuals do – we create and re-create structure in our everyday actions. It is only by facing the more deeply-rooted structural problems that lasting solutions to everyday problems can be developed. Often it is only when the problems become so serious that people are prepared to work on the underlying causes, and it is this motivation which makes it possible to do the development research on which this book is based.

People working in groups need suitable organization if their constructive and creative potential is to be allowed expression. Where they are coping with anxious clients in pain and emotional distress, the group's structure and relationships are critical. The assumptions of this book and the research programme are that people are generally hard-working, well-meaning and conscientious, and that, given the right conditions, 'personality' factors play a relatively small part in problems of cooperation. Teams need to develop structures and organization which are not dependent on individuals and which provide an environment which survives the inevitable changes of membership.

Limited usefulness of the term 'team'

People use the term 'team' to describe a variety of groupings and arrangements – we see ten of the most common types in Chapter 4. If we want to improve teamwork or set up a team we have to be able to describe the details of how people work together. Some problems arise because different people mean different things by the terms 'team' and 'teamwork'. This book does not assume that there is a 'best model', but rather that, with the right tools and processes, people can build local arrangements which are workable, and improve them. The emphasis is on how to improve cooperation and collaboration, on how to recognize and overcome barriers to cooperation and on how to describe and discuss precisely the particular local arrangements which are necessary. This approach is particularly important to evolve care management systems which mesh with and complement the effective coordination which some existing teams have developed.

Multiple meanings

The use of the term 'team' is one example of terms used in discussions of organization which have different meanings for different people. Another assumption underlying this book and the research method is that conceptual explication and precision are the basis for science, and also for solving practical problems in social organization. Take, for example, the much-used term 'attachment'. I witnessed a furious argument between a GP and a nurse manager about whether health visitors should be 'attached' to the practice. The GP meant, 'have the same patients as the practice'; the nurse manager understood, 'under the direction of the GP'. Perhaps it would follow that having the same clients would mean that GPs would direct health visitors more than they did at present, but we were not able to discuss this. The 'discussion' deteriorated when the GP argued that he was 'accountable' and 'ultimately responsible' for the patient . . .

This is not to argue for a researcher imposing a particular 'legal' definition, but to argue for defining clearly the different meanings and options to make it possible to have a more productive discussion. If people do not know exactly what is proposed by a particular term, then they cannot properly examine what the implications are and whether the proposed arrangement is the best for the situation. Politicians know this, and sometimes it is appropriate to use terms in a general sense. However, for both scientific advance and for discussing and agreeing precise working arrangements for the future, it is important to define terms clearly and to agree their meaning. Research cannot be done if the subject of the research is not described and conceptualized.

Mutual advantage

Giving examples of how teamwork makes it possible to give a better service to clients usually leads to team members feeling that they really should cooperate more, but produces little real change. This book assumes that for change to happen people must perceive it to be in their own personal interests to cooperate – not just in the client's or patient's interest. Removing the barriers is not, of itself, sufficient to bring about cooperation; neither is exhortation and guilt. Practitioners and managers need to be shown the positive personal advantages of teamwork to be motivated to overcome some of the practical and attitudinal barriers and their fear of change. If people do not believe that teamwork saves time, is more satisfying and enjoyable, and more financially advantageous, as well as giving a better service, then they will not try to change.

Cooperation and the research process

One assumption of the research was that, if one is to improve collaboration, then the research process should itself be collaborative and aim to set up arrangements to ensure that collaboration continues. Other assumptions were that all relevant parties should be fully involved, should have the opportunity to express their views, and that each person's views should be valued, especially if they conflict – that solutions would work only if all agreed and wished the change to take place.

Much of the research drew on a team and service workshop programme. The assumption was that if these events could demonstrate methods for collectively recognizing and overcoming common problems, then the process could continue in everyday practice, if it was supported by structural changes and procedures agreed in the workshop. These events developed the notion of collaboration and cooperation, not just as a necessary organizational mechanism, but as a value central to working life. Chapter 8, on conflict and decision-making, says more about these assumptions.

RESEARCH METHOD AND SOURCES

> *There is nothing as practical as a good theory.*
>
> *To understand a social system and how it works, one must study how to change it.*
>
> (Lewin 1947)

The question is not whether to be guided by theory or by practical realities, but whether we are aware of the assumptions which influence our actions. While discussion of theories can be a way of avoiding action, to act without reflecting is to put oneself at the service of the worst theories. This book is based on research and development work with teams and service managers preparing for and following the 1990 UK health and social care reforms. The work was done using a distinctive method developed over the last 25 years at the Brunel University Institute of Organization and Social Studies (BIOSS). Earlier work with teams and services before 1986 was published in Øvretveit (1986b), and, before 1978, in Rowbottom and Hey (1977a; 1977b). The method, called 'social analysis', is an action research method for both applying and developing social scientific knowledge and enabling others to solve practical problems of organization. It is one of the more rigorous types of action research methods, with a well-elaborated methodology (Rowbottom 1977; Øvretveit 1984).

This practical and theoretical approach has its strengths and weaknesses when compared with traditional social scientific research methods, or with purely developmental or problem-solving consultancy methods. All the research for this book was funded by individual teams or health and local authorities, and some is already published in scientific books and journals. This is an indication of the benefits of a method which combines theoretical and practical aims, rather than emphasizing one at the expense of the other.

The features of the method reflect some of the themes and assumptions of the book:

- collaboration between the analyst and those wishing to resolve problems;
- a concern with conceptual definition, and explicating the models latent in the situation;
- testing of the logic of the models through a process of discussion testing, and then in practice;
- a concern to enable clients to clarify the options, be aware of criteria for choosing, and make their own judgements about what is best and workable;
- client confidentiality and control of dissemination;
- a 'grounded theory' approach to developing theoretical propositions.

The author's research reported in this book comes from two types of research using this method. The first source is a continuing two-day team workshop programme. Workshops are held on-site, either to help set up new teams by transferring lessons learnt from one team which already 'works well', or to help members of a team which is 'not working' to collaborate more closely. Follow-up workshops are held, making it possible to find out if the solutions worked. To date over seventy-nine of these workshops have been held across the UK. National workshops were also held at Brunel University for team members, team leaders and managers from across the UK.

The second research source is long-term collaboration with individual teams on different problems of team organization. This work involves helping the team to describe features of its current organization, and then to clarify alternative future options, such as for referral, case records, crisis services, or for whatever may be problematic for the team. The team and its managers then clarify, agree and operate the new arrangements and the researcher monitors its effectivenss. Two three-year projects of this type were undertaken (see Macdonald and Øvretveit 1987, and Macdonald 1990), two one-year projects, and one six-month project (Øvretveit 1991a).

We now turn to the policy context for community teams and care management and their part in community care for different client groups.

COMMUNITY CARE AND TEAMS

Care in and by the community

> *Community Care means providing the right level of intervention and support to enable people to achieve maximum independence and control over their lives.*
>
> Department of Health (DoH 1989b)

Care in the community is about helping clients and their carers in or near their homes, rather than in hospitals away from the 'community' in which they live.

Care by communities is about supporting and developing the help given by people other than service employees. It involves new methods of care and new types of services. It is usually planned, purchased and provided for 'client groups' of people with similar needs.

One underlying philosophy is that institutions, traditional services and entitlement to welfare create a 'dependency culture'. Community care is about supporting individual and family responsibility and about consumer rights and choice. This philosophy is criticized by some as justifying government withdrawing from meeting its traditional duties, as a way of cutting expenditure on health and social care, and off-loading responsibilities on to voluntary organizations and relatives, usually women. Others, sometimes the same critics, emphasize how care in the community can empower the disadvantaged and result in more flexible and responsive services, controlled by users.

Community care has a long history, and is something which each generation discovers and defines for itself. The 'ordinary life' and 'normalization' approaches (Brown and Smith 1992) were influential in the 1980s and gave ways to define community care, and a meaningful ideology for professional and other staff. Although there are some successful schemes which show what can be done, comprehensive community care is still more a philosophy than a reality, a potential for many client groups rather than a reality. In the UK the debate of the last few years, and the 1990 reforms, created the conditions for more widespread implementation of community care. We will shortly consider the implications of the 1990 reforms for teams, and the structures and processes for planning, purchasing and providing services for different client groups in the community.

Community care and multidisciplinary teams

> Too often teams are thrown together and expected magically to resolve problems of coordination and fundamental differences between agencies and professions. Just calling a group of practitioners a team has become a way in which managers and planners avoid the real problems and work needed to coordinate an increasingly complex range of services in the community.
>
> (Øvretveit 1986b)

> The coordination of assessment arrangements between agencies is undoubtedly easier where multi-disciplinary teams have been established at either the primary or secondary care level, but locating practitioners together is not of itself a guarantee of improved joint working.
>
> (Social Services Inspectorate/Scottish Office Social Work Services Group (SS/SOSWSG) 1991b: para. 67)

There are many ways of organizing the services which are needed in the community without multidisciplinary teams — an expensive and unnecessary way to organize in some situations. Care management is sometimes an alternative to teams: a care manager can be thought of as a 'team leader' of services for one client.

However, the history of teams is closely linked to the history of community care. Teams are often viewed as the way to start community care — as cornerstones for new types of services in the community, and the focal point for a locally based range of services.

> A general definition of a *multidisciplinary team* is: a group of practitioners with different professional training (multidisciplinary), employed by more than one agency (multi-agency), who meet regularly to coordinate their work providing services to one or more clients in a defined area.

Some hospital-based rehabilitation teams fit this general definition of a team. It excludes most multidisciplinary hospital teams, although the principles of teamwork covered in this book apply to these teams. It also excludes single-profession teams such as generic social work teams or single-discipline community nursing teams. From now on the book uses the term 'team' to mean a multidisciplinary team.

There are many different types of team for different client groups and problems. Here we consider the place of teams in community care, and how care management formalizes work which teams have tried to carry out: the work of coordinating the contributions of different professions and agencies.

Primary health care teams
The primary health care team (PHCT) is an example of the important part played by teams in one type of community care, and of the variation between teams with the same name. It is one of the few types of team considered in this book which bring together different professions for a number of client groups, rather than for the special needs of one group in the community. It is also an example of a very loose-knit grouping, which some would not call a team at all, but which I describe as a 'network team'.

The family doctor general practitioner medical service in the UK is one of the longest-running and most successful examples of community care. Before the 1970s there was informal cooperation between GPs and nurses working in the community. With community nurses becoming managed and employed by health authorities in 1974, the late 1970s saw them being formally 'attached' to GP practices and health centres. Other community practitioners such as community psychiatric nurses, therapists, and sometime social workers, linked in with or became 'members' of the PHCT. Often it was the availability of a base large enough, and especially a health centre, which provided the conditions for 'team' formation, or at least regular meetings.

Many reports refer to 'the primary health care team' (e.g. Edwards 1987) but none gives a usable definition, and I am not going to give one here. This is because it is more useful to consider the different ways in which primary health care practitioners and sometimes social workers working in the same area coordinate their work, and the different conditions which are essential for effective coordination. The PHCT can be characterized as a team with fairly high differentiation (a variety of different disciplines) and low integration (few, if any, formal common policies binding all in the grouping). There are, of course, exceptions such as 'patch teams' in Northern Ireland, with social workers and therapists managed by a 'patch manager'.

Although rarely planned and formally established, PHCTs have a central role in coordinating community services, especially for mothers and children and for health services to older people. The 1990s reforms and fund-holding for GPs may lead to more formal and integrated team organization and management, which we consider later.

Multidisciplinary community teams for older people, rather than for older people with special needs, are rare. (There are teams for older people with mental health problems.) Primary health care teams and generic social service teams have not always been able to coordinate their services for the elderly. Failures of the past, changing demographics, and rising costs led to the Griffiths (1988) proposals, and in particular to the concept of care management we consider specialist teams for other client groups, and their role in community care.

Community mental health teams and centres
Mental health teams are viewed as a specialist resource in the community, which can prevent hospital admissions and should be available for everyone with mental health problems. Mental health teams can also have an important health-promotion and illness-prevention role. In some areas these teams concentrate on supporting people returning from hospital, as well as people already living in the area with the most chronic and disabling conditions. Many were financed by hospital retraction or closure. In other areas, teams have neglected 'continuing care' clients but have pioneered a wider range of community services (Patmore & Weaver 1990a; 1990b). Teams sometimes pursue this latter role more effectively when the most disabled are served by separate services with care management. How the two relate or overlap is considered in later chapters.

Community mental health teams were influenced by community care programmes and Community Mental Health Centres (CMHCs) in the USA, and to a lesser extent by the Italian hospital closure 'experiment'. This book refers to CMHCs as buildings, and CMHTs as a form of organization of services. A CMHC is, in these terms, a *base* for one or more teams or services.

Sometimes CMHCs house CMHTs, as well as teams for day services, and user-run day areas. CMHTs vary in size and membership, but are generally teams with high differentiation and varying degrees of integration. Both CMHCs and CMHTs are discussed in Huxley (1990), Sayce et al. (1991) and in a pack issued by Good Practice in Mental Health and International Association of Mental Health Workers (1985).

There are a growing number mental health specialist teams for older people (sometimes called 'psychogeriatric community teams' (Lindsay 1991), as well as for people with addiction problems (Øvretveit 1987b), and for children and families. The latter are sometimes developed child guidance clinics.

Community teams for people with learning difficulties (community mental handicap teams)
Community teams for people with learning difficulties (CTLDs) also vary in size and membership. These teams, sometimes called community mental handicap teams, were established earlier than mental health teams. Most of their members only work in the community, do not have part-time roles or bases in hospitals, and are part of a range of services that are more developed in the community than for mental health. In part this is due to local authorities taking a fuller role in providing services for this client group, and in part due to the stronger influence of the 'ordinary life' and 'normalization' philosophy in services for this client group (Brown and Smith 1992).

It is these philosophies which also account for the high integration of some CTLDs: the ordinary life philosophy provides an over-arching set of principles which unifies members and allows professional differences to exist without undermining the team. Otherwise these teams are as highly differentiated as CMHTs.

The history and future of community care and teams in mental health is discussed in detail in Goodwyn (1990) and Huxley (1990), and for people with a learning difficulty in Brown and Wistow (1990) and in Brown et al. (1992). In all cases the purpose of these teams is to make it easy and quick for clients and carers in the community with special needs to access the specialist skills which they need. How teams can fulfil this role depends on how providers and purchasers make use of the opportunities and requirements of the 1990 reforms, to which we now turn.

THE 1990 REFORMS AND THEIR IMPLICATIONS FOR TEAMS

In the UK the 1990 government reforms to health and social services created a new context for community teams and introduced care management (DoH 1989a; 1989b; 1990b). Here we consider the changes which are of most relevance to teams, and some of the implications.

The reforms create a quasi-market with managed competition for both health and social services. Local state health authorities and local government authorities concentrate on assessing the needs of their population for health and social care, respectively. Their main role is to use finance allocated from taxation to purchase services to meet the 'most pressing needs' of the populations they cover, rather than to manage and provide services directly.

A plurality of purchasers and providers

The early 1990s saw an increasing separation between state authorities' purchasing and providing roles. Health authorities established purchasing or commissioning executives which, to begin with, agreed large 'block contracts' mostly with their own directly managed provider units. Authorities then cooperated and formally merged in order better to pursue their purchasing role.

The purchaser–provider separation increased with more provider units becoming NHS trusts, and staff being employed by a trust rather than by a purchasing authority. This reduced the bias purchasing authorities had to retain contracts with their own provider units, and opened the quasi-market to competition. While trusts are strongly 'tied into' the NHS, they have more freedom to sell, buy, borrow and employ (DoH 1989c).

Although prefigured in the earlier Griffiths Report (1988), reforms to social care and changes to local authority social services departments came later. The same principle applied of the statutory authority being an assessor, purchaser and also 'enabler', rather than a direct provider. Some social services departments were divided into 'purchasing wings' (sometimes also managing inspectorates and care managers) and 'provider wings' to encourage comparisons and competition (for example, Humberside, Berkshire).

Thus in both health and social services, state purchasing authorities control what is provided and how it is provided through contracts for services with independent providers, or with their 'own' increasingly independent providers. This is a change from control through management and employment relations. The provider's income, and ultimately staff employment, depends on getting contracts from statutory and other purchasers. Teams, as part of provider services, have to win contracts and then prove that they have met them. This was a major change for many teams, some of whom began to think of themselves as small business cooperatives. We consider in a later chapter how teams gather information about costs, quantity and quality, in order to meet purchaser's requirements.

GPs as purchasers and providers

General medical practitioners in the UK are contracted by Family Health Service Authorities (FHSA) to provide a range of primary care medical services. The reforms also introduced GP fund-holding for larger general practices. GPs can opt to become purchasers of a limited range of health services, mainly non-emergency acute hospital procedures, consultant out-patient sessions and some diagnostic services, and community nursing and therapy services. Fund-holding GPs can choose to provide some services themselves, or buy in from non-NHS or NHS providers. At present (1993) they have to buy most specialist community health services. As more practices become fund-holders there will be changes to the range of services which they can buy. There is debate about whether health authorities or GP fund-holders are the best purchasers of different services (Glennerster et al. 1992).

As regards the primary health care team (PHCT), new types of PCHT in GP fund-holding practices are emerging. More GPs are employing their own practice nurses, or contracting some nursing services from providers. It is likely that community health staff will continue to be employed by one or more separate providers and 'attached' to practices, but fund-holding GPs may employ more staff and two types of PHCT will emerge – a 'practice team' and a 'community team' – possibly meeting together for some purposes.

Care management

One of the most important changes of the reforms for teams is care management (previously 'case management').

> The rationale for this reorganisation is the empowerment of users and carers . . .
>
> (SSI/SOSWSG 1991b: para. 6)

> Care management and assessment lie at the heart of this new approach – 'the cornerstone of quality care'
>
> (SSI/SOSWSG 1991b: para. 2)

> All users and carers should experience the process of care management, whatever the type or level of their needs.
>
> (SSI/SOSWSG 1991b: para. 56)

Care management is a process for assessing and coordinating the care of any client in the community. Box 1.1 outlines features of the concept given in the specific guidance from the SSI/SOSWSG (1991b).

Box 1.1 Care management: excerpts from SSI/SOSWSG (1991b) guidance

What is care management?
Care management is a process of tailoring services to individual needs. Assessment is an integral part of care management, but it is only one of seven core tasks that make up the whole process:

Stage 1 Publishing information . . .
Stage 2 Determining the level of assessment . . .
Stage 3 Assessing need . . .
Stage 4 Care planning . . .
Stage 5 Implementing the care plan . . .
Stage 6 Monitoring . . .
Stage 7 Reviewing . . .

Care management is a process – a more complex concept than the concept of case management. The latter was a role proposed by Griffiths (1988) for undertaking a number of tasks in the process of care management. The original conception of case management in Griffiths (1988) was inspired by schemes in Kent and other areas of the UK, as well as in the USA. While care management is proposed for all clients needing community care, most schemes have been for social care for older people. To begin with, care management is being introduced for certain types of client, and the care manager may have a budget for social care – a kind of 'fund-holding social care GP'.

The reforms also require authorities to ensure that their providers have clear arrangements for cross-referral, and for cooperation to assess needs which are the responsibility of more than one agency (DoH 1989b). By 1993 all teams must be able to show their internal and external arrangements for doing this (Chapter 5). In time health practitioners, such as community nurses and GPs, may undertake care management and hold budgets for social care. The latter could mean GPs holding a budget for purchasing both health and social care for some clients, and this is easier to arrange where health and local authorities cooperate more closely (Chapter 3).

The important part of the SSI/SOSWSG (1991b) guidance for many teams is that:

> All or most of these tasks may be undertaken by a single practitioner, known as a care manager, or they may be performed by different practitioners.
>
> (SSI/SOSWSG 1991b: para. 8)

> Interagency working at the level of the individual user should be facilitated by establishing one co-ordinating practitioner across all agencies. Although local authorities have the lead responsibility, this coordinating function may be delegated to practitioners in other agencies according to the needs of the user. Where such practitioners are given delegated budgetary responsibilities and/or access to resources on a cross-agency basis, they are better able to cut through the usual difficulties of inter-agency co-ordination.
>
> (SSI/SOSWSG 1991b: paras 51–3)

Therapy services

In organisational terms, specialist staff who combine elements of both assessment and service provision may be regarded as either assessing practitioners or service providers, depending on the balance of their work. However, so long as they retain a significant service-providing role it would normally not be appropriate for them to be appointed as care managers.

(SSI/SOSWSG 1991b: paras 4.38)

Chapters 2, 4 and 5 consider care management, the implications for teams and give some examples. Chapter 3 considers models of structure for coordinating community care at different levels. While the guidance points to the 'considerable merit in local and health authorities developing systems for the joint-purchase of services that they specify, fund and monitor together' (SSI/SOSWSG 1991a: para. 4.19) there are problems agreeing what is health and what is social care, and the amount of finance for each.

Financing residential care

One change introduced by the reforms with implications for teams is financing arrangements for income support which were administered by social security departments. In 1993 local authorities took over payments for publicly funded places in residential and nursing homes. This gave local authorities incentives to finance more services to support people in their own homes, rather than in residential and nursing homes. The change increases the potential flexibility of case managers and other staff, as previously all the incentives were to transfer a person to residential care. This will have a significant effect on case management, and on community care services generally. It affects many teams because a combined health and social assessment is even more important, and new hospital discharge and homes admissions procedures are necessary (SSI/SOSWSG 1991b: paras 4.39–4.57). A long-running issue, now more acute with the new financing arrangements, is how fast hospitals can and should discharge clients into the community.

Implications for teams

Every minute of each team members' time is paid for by contracts with purchasers. The services which a team provides depend on managers and the team winning and keeping contracts to finance the team's services. Team members and their managers have to understand how the team is financed, and predict and prepare for changes in purchasers' requirements and provider competition. Teams that can offer and prove effective coordination and have good information systems will have a competitive advantage as community care markets develop. Chapters 2 and 3 discuss these issues in more detail – here we note some of the market and finance issues for teams.

In the early years of the reforms the finance for most teams came from the large 'block' or 'cost and volume' contract which a purchasing authority had with a provider unit, of which the team was part. This will continue for many multidisciplinary but single-provider teams, for example some integrated primary nursing and therapy 'patch' or 'locality' teams, and some mental health and learning-difficulty teams. However, over time more income will come from other purchasers (GP fund-holders, other authorities), and more contracts will be for one client or smaller numbers. Teams need to be aware of possible changes to the sources and ways in which their services are financed, and to develop information systems to give purchasers proof of what they have provided. They have to be able to cost their services, ultimately for parts of one client's care episode with the team (Chapter 10).

Many teams have members employed by other agencies, and all need to be aware of how the work which is done by these team members will change and how their time is financed. For example, mental health teams have social workers and other social services employees. For many, their role in the team depends on how the social services department introduces a purchaser–provider split and care management. Some departments require their social workers in such teams to become care managers and reduce the amount of care and treatment work which they can do. Others make such staff providers only, and their continued employment depends on their managers winning contracts, sometimes from care managers. Both options affect the work of the rest of the team, as do social services departments' arrangements for assessment and financing for residential care. These issues force clarification of the social workers' role in the team (Chapter 6) and raise questions about NHS trusts employing social workers.

Over time not only will more team services be purchased by different providers, but also more will be purchased for individual clients. GPs and care manager purchasers are setting the pace, wanting to buy services for one client, and often quite specific services such as an assessment or a specific number of therapy sessions. Teams have to be able to gather and provide detailed information and costs quickly and cheaply, clarify what they are prepared to offer, and be able to negotiate with an awareness of the issues for them and for purchasers. Team managers have to prepare teams for these changes and make sure that team members are aware of the changing market and the part they play in winning, losing and keeping contracts.

Teams also need to understand how changes in purchasers' organization and in providers' middle-management levels affect them. The degree of cooperation at these levels can limit or enable practitioners' cooperation. For example, a team for people with a learning difficulty is able to develop close internal cooperation if the team is part of an integrated health and social services provider trust, which has a contract with a purchasing agency which has a 'pooled' health and social services purchasing budget. Teams need to be aware of arrangements for cooperation and plans for integrated structures to avoid wasting time developing services and systems which are not compatible with future structures. Chapter 3 describes five models for services 'above' team level and shows how these structures affect team cooperation.

THE CHAPTERS OF THE BOOK

The rest of this chapter gives an overview of each chapter of the book. It shows how the book describes the structures and processes for implementing community care, and how it discusses details of team organization, care management and client and carer involvement in services and in purchasing.

Chapter 2: Needs and organization

A person's needs are the starting point for a team's service and for care management. A client group's needs are the starting point for team organization. Chapter 2 shows how needs assessment should decide what services and treatments are provided and how they are organized, rather than vice versa. Some aspects of the health and social services reforms ensure a needs-led approach, but other aspects work against basing services on a person's or a client group's needs. The chapter shows how to separate needs assessment from provision, and how to ensure that needs assessments are then linked to provision and resources through individual and community care plans.

Chapter 3: Markets, bureaucracy and association

Chapter 3 shows different ways of organizing needs assessment and of coordinating different services. It describes three 'modes' of organization, the bureaucratic mode, the market mode, and the association mode, and shows how people relate differently in each. It shows the variety of ways in which purchasers and providers are cooperating and competing and how this affects cooperation between practitioners at the local level. It then describes five common models showing different structures through which health and social services cooperate to purchase and provide services.

Chapter 4: Types of team

Chapter 4 takes us from the general principles and structures to specific types of team. Its purpose is to help decide which type of team is the best way to organize coordination for a particular client group or service at a local level. It describes loose 'network-association' team, 'formal' teams, and client-care teams for organizing care to one client, such as a care manager's provider team. It provides a way to define the type of team which exists, the type of cooperation or team which is needed, and a language to discuss and define specific changes to improve services. No assumptions are made about a single 'best' model, but the options are explained, and ways of choosing a model for a local area and client group are discussed.

Chapter 5: Client pathways and team resource management

Cooperation is about how much members work alone or together in receiving and processing work. Chapter 5 gives a framework for understanding how a team takes referrals and allocates, reviews and finishes work: it shows how a team can describe the one or more 'pathways' a client takes when 'passing through' the team, and gives examples of the five most common. It shows that everyday decisions about what work to take on and when to finish work are team members' 'priorities in practice'. It aims to raise awareness about how priorities are applied in team decision-making, the criteria which individuals and groups use and how they may better 'match' their resources to needs. The chapter raises the issue of the balance between each member's autonomy and the team's control over its resources.

Chapter 6: Team members' roles

Chapter 6 shows how team members can clarify their role by understanding the national and local requirements which rule out certain work and direct what they can do. This helps clarify the scope which each person has to negotiate his or her role, and helps teams understand the limits to cooperation and flexibility. It considers legal and managerial accountability, and common role problems such as overload, deskilling, and too much or too little 'role-blurring'. It also discusses informal roles and the influence of personality styles on how the team works.

Chapter 7: Team leadership

In my view, the most important role is that of the team leader. Chapter 7 describes different leadership roles, why teams need a leader and how to define and agree a leadership role. Profession managers frequently resist stronger roles for team leaders, and the chapter considers how practitioners are managed and managers' accountability. It describes three ways of managing practitioners to ensure the quality of their work, and to ensure that they get the support, supervision and development that they need.

Chapter 8: Decisions and conflict in teams

The point of teams is to make the most of differences within the team. Too often professional and other differences produce division and destructive conflict or are denied for the sake of unity. Conflict is to be expected and procedures for working through and reaching decisions are necessary in teams to make the most of differences for the benefit of clients and team members. The chapter describes different ways of making decisions about one client's care and about how a team works and is organized. It argues that the 'democratic ideals' of some teams are essential to effective working, but can also destroy a team if pursued in the wrong way. It proposes that the way in which teams handle conflict and authority is 'mirrored' in members' relationships with their clients.

Chapter 9: Communications and co-service

The subject of case records and client and practitioner access to records may appear a detail of team organization and not worthy of a whole chapter. Chapter 9 shows that it is not a dry subject and that record systems and policies reflect and themselves support relationships between team members and between team members and their clients. A true multidisciplinary team record system which everyone uses is one of the quickest ways to achieve closer cooperation. Professional control of records is an effective way to prevent teamwork. The chapter gives team members a way to judge whether this is the reason why such a system is opposed by some, or whether the differences in recording practices and policies are really insurmountable. It opens with a discussion of the differences between creative communication and two-way and one-way communication.

There are many types of client participation that teams carrying out community care policies are working to achieve. Chapter 9 describes different types, and shows how practitioners who find difficulty in changing to a more 'participatory approach' can be helped by the right type of record system. It gives an illustration of this approach in mental health terms in one area.

Chapter 10: Coordinating community health and social care

Chapter 10 lays the blame for many ineffective teams with higher management and their assumption that once people are in post they can take care of themselves. Carefully planning and setting up a team is not enough. Teams have to be managed, reviewed and evaluated if they are to continue to work well and continue to win and meet contracts. Especially in the first few years, teams face many problems which they cannot resolve themselves and which need to be resolved by higher management. The chapter argues that the maintenance of the team should not depend on one or two profession managers who 'believe in teams', or the luck of having an energetic and persuasive team leader, but on one manager or a very small group with clear responsibiity for the team's performance. The chapter describes how to plan and carry through improvements to different types of team and draws together some of the concepts and arguments of previous chapters. It gives ways for managers to 'check the pulse' and 'health' of teams and prevent predictable problems.

We now turn, in Chapter 2, to the subject of assessing needs at an individual and population level. This is the basis for the details of team organization which are discussed in later chapters.

Chapter 2
NEEDS AND ORGANIZATION

INTRODUCTION

Community services are criticized for being 'service-driven' and not 'needs-led': it is claimed that the services people get are a mixture of what providers can organize easily at low cost, and what providers think people should have. And it is true that some community services are a result of quirks of history, funding opportunities and personalities, rather than based on what people really need. However, it is not so easy even to define a person's or a population's needs. This chapter is about understanding needs, and linking this understanding to the services for best meeting needs.

Needs do not exist separately from the means of meeting need. Try to think of a human need, without at the same time thinking of a way of meeting that need. We usually describe need by ways of meeting the need. This chapter shows that to create needs-led services we have to overcome this difficulty of thinking about needs by thinking about our existing ways of meeting them. A 'needs-led' service is one which puts the emphasis on the 'needs' side of what I will call the 'needs–service' equation. It does this by separating an assessment of need from deciding the services to meet need. It then links the need assessment to the type and amount of services to be provided. A needs-led service also weighs the relative severity of different people's needs, and allocates its limited resources to those most in need. What makes this possible is organizing for needs assessment and coordination.

To create a more 'needs-led' service, both purchasers and providers have to address three problems in community service organization – what I will call 'linking problems'. The first is organizing to put needs first and arranging services to follow from needs assessment – the problem of 'sequence linking'. The second is coordinating different types of services so that a population or a person gets the combination of services which they need, without gaps or duplication – the problem of 'sideways linking'. The third is the problem of 'linking levels': making sure that there is a link between each level of assessment and planning: the individual level, the locality client group level and the population level.

This chapter shows a way to think about how to achieve these linkages. It outlines a model, and then shows how it applies in a community team. Later chapters use these ideas to show how to improve service coordination, team structure, 'client pathways' over time through teams, team priorities and team members' roles. The chapter is more theoretical than others, but the basic principles are necessary to understanding how to make practical changes to meet the aim of needs-led community services with limited resources.

THE NEEDS–SERVICE MODEL

The following separates needs from the services to meet needs. The purposes of this simple model is to help understand how to do two difficult things at once. The first is to assess needs without being over-influenced by ways of meeting needs. The second is to relate needs to services. The model helps to think about how purchasers and providers can organize to do this, and how their organization itself influences how they assess needs and make the links to services. We will develop this basic model, and refer back to it in many sections of the book. In its simplest form the basis of the model is:

Needs – Services

Later we look at both the 'needs' and the 'services' side of the equation in more detail, but first consider why we separate them and why it is difficult to do so.

Thinking about need without thinking about service responses

Some examples show how difficult it is to think about needs without at the same time thinking about ways to meet needs. 'You need a doctor' is our quick answer to someone who 'has not been feeling well for some time'. Another way is to spend time talking about exactly what a person is feeling, how long for, what she thinks might have caused the feeling and what she thinks might relieve her feeling of being unwell. Some doctors do this, or similar and start by asking 'what's the problem?' Some direct the patient to describe the responses they want from the doctor by asking 'how can I help?'

It is easier to think about responses to needs than about needs themselves. This is illustrated in the 'zeroing-in' approach: 'Are you hungry?' says the mother to the child. 'Yes.' 'What do you want?' 'I don't know.' 'Would you like a . . .?' The mother 'zeroes in' on the need, by offering different responses, but this is not the same as assessing needs separately and in their own right. If needs are only defined by responses, some needs might not be met, or might not be discovered. Health visitors and dietitians note that children soon learn to say that they want an ice cream or hamburger, and that they and their mother forget or never think about other nutritional needs.

The answer is not to completely separate needs from responses. Too great a separation can lead to abstract and inconsequential discussions about needs. If the mother is not too busy, she talks with the child for some time before remembering what is in the fridge. By then the child is either angry for having his expectations raised, or so hungry that he will settle for anything. However, as a result of the discussion the mother may have a deeper insight into the child's preferences, and may bear this in mind when she goes shopping.

Some argued that in the early planning for the All-Wales Strategy for People with a Mental Handicap, both problems occurred: discussions of needs were both too separate from discussions of responses, and too influenced by existing responses (Øvretveit and Davies 1988). In some places, discussions of parents' needs and of ideal services raised expectations and caused dissatisfaction when services took so long to materialize. By the time the services came, they were happy to settle for almost anything. Parents and clients sometimes saw their needs and 'ideal' services as the same: ideally they just wanted more of the type of services which already existed. They were not always made aware of new types of services, and where they were, they often wanted more of the familiar and traditional. However, some providers gained a greater insight into preferences, and did take this into consideration in their plans, and in what some called their 'shopping lists'.

This tension between needs and service responses, and the importance of holding them separate but relating them at the same, is an underlying theme in this and subsequent chapters. Let us look at needs assessment in more detail, before turning to how to relate needs to service responses and resources. We follow a client and carer calling on a service to see how their needs are assessed.

NEEDS ASSESSMENT

Perspectives on need

'Needs' can mean anything from what a client or carer says she wants from a service ('client demand') to professionals' judgements about preventive services which people may not want. Take, for example, Mrs Watkins, who forgot to turn the cooker off one night. Her retired husband, alerted by the smoke alarm, put out the small fire. The next day he called their GP because his wife was so upset, and he was growing concerned about how often she was forgetting things.

The 'client' (Mrs Watkins) just wanted something to 'calm her nerves'. Mr Watkins agreed, but he felt that more was needed – he wanted 'something done', he did not know what. The GP assessed Mrs Watkins's general medical condition. Her general health was fine, but her blood pressure was high, in part because of her anxious state (the GP did a 'profession-specific' needs assessment). Normally the GP would have left it at that – after all, Mrs Watkins apparently never forgot to put the cat out. But because of what Mr Watkins was saying about his wife's memory getting worse, and it being 'the last straw', the GP decided to refer the couple to the local social worker and to the consultant psychogeriatrician.

We stop the story here to draw out some general points. There are three different 'assessments of need': Mrs Watkins's ('nothing wrong really, just a bit nervy after last night'), Mr Watkins's ('. . . *and* she forget the name of the cat's favourite . . .'), and the GP's (Mrs Watkins's general medical condition, and Mr Watkins's 'unusual concern'). All three 'assessments' differ, but do not conflict, in this example. We will call these different assessments the client's perception of need, the carer's perception of the client's need (the carer has her own needs which are more specific), and the professional's perception of needs.

Note that these are all early assessments of need, and that each person's assessment changes in the discussion. The only 'formal assessment' is that of the GP, who also judges the urgency and severity of need. The GP also judges that a more detailed assessment of needs is called for: she takes things further because her response did not satisfy Mr Watkins, and because she suspects that there may be further needs which she does not have the time or skills to assess. She initiates a further 'level of needs assessment'. Note that she did not have to do an extensive general assessment to decide what to do next.

We now turn to the more detailed assessment of needs, and how it is done. To which agency did the GP make the referral? Was it to separate social work and medical services, or was it to the new community mental health team for the elderly? Our story goes back in time three years, to a Wednesday afternoon planning-group meeting. The subject, services for the elderly; item, population needs assessment. The background, both health and social services agreed to consider services on a client-group basis. They agreed boundaries to each community locality and the size and age distribution of the population in each locality. The meeting brings together their assessments of the needs of the elderly.

Definitions of need

At the meeting, different people put forward different estimates of need, each based on different ways of thinking about need. The community physician from the health authority predicts that, in the sector in which the Watkinses live, in each year, x people over 65 will suffer from 'functional mental illness', and y from 'dementia'. (This is 'normative need'.) Social services do not disagree, but they have their own assessments of the social needs of elderly people with mental health problems. They also make reference to research done in an area with a similar type of population. (This is 'comparative need'.)

The consultant geriatrician in the group draws attention to the number of people referred to specialist health and social services for assessment ('referred demand'), the numbers assessed, and the numbers treated and cared for ('utilization' or 'uptake'). Representatives from voluntary organizations and the community health council then give figures for people whom they said needed services, but were not referred (e.g. some ethnic communities), or did not get any service if they were ('unmet need'). The GP's representative nods, saying that GPs would refer more if the waiting list were shorter. With all these definitions and perspectives of need, confusion set in. As the tea came, someone was heard to say that confusion the point of the exercise as 'they have already decided what services they are each going to provide anyway'.

One of the outcomes of the meeting was a decision to pursue the idea of forming a specialist community mental health team for the elderly. This idea had been around for some time, but received a boost because people agreed that the planning group did not have much information about the needs of each locality – a team would make it easier to obtain more accurate information. A team would make it possible to 'channel' referrals to one point, and the team could also do a 'locality needs assessment'. As a result of this meeting, and many more, years later the GP was able to refer the Watkinses to the new team, rather than to separate services.

The general point is that each perspective and definition of need has a contribution to make to an overall assessment. This is true with our planning group at the level of the population, with the new team at the locality level, and also when it came to assessing Mrs and Mr Watkins. Organizing for needs assessment means ensuring that the different perspectives are presented and combined, at the level of the individual, and at the level of the population. In particular, it means that someone has a responsibility for getting and combining these perspectives and that there are structures and processes for doing this. The 'someones' in this example were the chairperson of the planning group, the leader of the new team, and the care manager assigned to the Watkinses.

Needs assessment, then, is not an objective scientific exercise, where someone takes a measuring tool and puts it up against 'real needs', reading off the amount and type of need. But neither is it an entirely subjective process. It is a social and political process, where different and sometimes conflicting perceptions are combined to form a more informed but always partial and provisional 'picture' of needs. The 'picture' is shaped by those who are involved, and by the process of forming it. Existing services, organization and resources influence the picture in different ways.

Service organization affects how needs are assessed: types and levels of population need

Although we should start by assessing need to decide services, the way services are organized influences how needs are assessed. For example, if professions are organized in a multidisciplinary team, they are more likely to do multidisciplinary assessments. A team reaches an understanding of the needs of people in a locality which is different from an understanding that comes from combining the assessments of separate professional services which serve the locality. How a service is organized, such as a community team, should follow from an understanding of the needs that service is to meet, but the way services are organized decides how needs are assessed.

This effect is reduced by separating purchasing from provision. This makes it possible for purchasers (and care managers in some places) to carry out assessments in new and different ways from the ways in which providers did in the past. However, purchasers still divide needs into categories of need to organize and carry out assessments. The way purchasers divide needs is in terms of their responsibilities. National and regional levels divide responsibilities between health, social and other services. At this level, needs are defined as primary health, secondary health (with 'community health' overlap), social, and other needs such as educational, housing, employment and leisure. Although these categories of need follow from how services were organized in the past, it does not follow that these purchasers define needs only in terms of the services which each purchases and provides. Note also that, even in a combined purchasing authority, the authority still defines types of need in order to organize its population needs assessments.

In many areas, where geographical boundaries are 'coterminous', each purchasing authority is responsible for assessing the needs of the same population, but assesses different needs, as defined by its responsibilities. In the same way that higher levels (national and regional) set the boundaries to each authority's responsibilities (both the population and type of needs to be assessed), so each authority defines or sets the boundaries to different types of need within its area.

In our exmaple of services to older people with mental health problems, health and social services agreed the boundaries to community localities. They also drew boundaries around different client groups: they decided that some people in the population had sufficiently similar needs to be grouped together and their needs assessed separately to the needs of other groups. The first division the statutory authorities made was on an age basis: children, adults and older people. The general needs of these groups were assessed first. Then it was decided that there were some people with special needs whose needs should be separately assessed and provided for. Older people with mental health problems formed such a group with special needs.

Thus the way services are organized affects how we understand needs, even though separating purchasing from provision reduces the influence of providers on how needs are understood. Purchasers themselves have different responsibilities and assess different types of need. The following describes how needs assessment at higher levels sets the context for needs assessment at lower levels, and how lower levels pass up to higher levels their more detailed assessments – the 'linking levels' issue. After this the chapter then turns, in the next section, to the service-response side of the 'needs–service' model.

Linking purchaser and provider needs assessments

The authorities in the planning group in the our illustration drew a boundary around a group of people within a community locality. They did so because they agreed that some people's needs were similar to and different from those of other people. These 'client-group categories' of need, and the purchasing plans that follow, influence how providers organize their services. Providers divide their services to coincide with purchasers' care group definitions, and, as we will see in the next chapter, in some places offer one service for both health and social care.

In our example, this care group definition set the parameters within which the new community mental health team for the elderly led a more detailed assessment of the different types of mental health need of older people in their locality. To do these assessments the team distinguished different types of need in this client group, and this in turn set the parameters within which team members and care managers assessed the needs of each older person referred to the team. This involved defining priority of need and level of need assessment, which we consider later.

To help develop a more detailed understanding of the needs of the client group in the sector, the team collected information about referrals, utilization of services and the needs of people whom they assessed. They also gathered information from people in the area about the needs of older people who were not referred to them. They passed this information on to their provider managers, who put it together with information from other sectors, and passed this detailed assessments of sector and population needs on to the purchasing planning group, as well as using it for their own business planning.

Thus, although higher levels set the boundaries to different types of need, lower levels assess different needs within these boundaries, and pass their assessments on to higher levels to build a more accurate picture of needs. More knowledge about needs comes from serving needs, at the level both of the individual and of the population. Organization for a needs-led service means ensuring that there is regular feedback between levels or 'links' between management levels, and between providers and purchasers, as well as links between agencies. It also means continually reassessing needs at each level.

Box 2.1 summarizes the points so far about separating needs from services and organizing to link needs assessment to services.

Box 2.1 The needs–service response dynamic

Separate and then link:

Separate	Link through
Assessment of need from services to meet need and update.	Care plans.
Level of need; assessment of individual;	Information systems.

community-sector; and population need.	
Different types of need (health and social needs; client group needs; individual needs).	Service organization for coordination.
Perspectives about needs (clients; carers; professionals; normative; comparative; met; unmet).	Care managers; team leaders; purchasing authorities.
Purchasers' and providers' assessments.	Information systems and relationships.

SERVICE RESPONSE

Service is what people give in response to their understanding of other people's needs. Some say that giving service is itself a basic human need, and that people need more opportunities to give voluntary service. Ironically, governments that most emphasize the self-interested pursuit of monetary gain also exhort people to give voluntary service – a contradiction arising in part because people give services less freely.

Scope of service and coordination

Here we are concerned with how service is secured and organized to help a person in need. Our focus is on formal organized service, and, in particular, on service given by more than one person employed to give service. We concentrate on services to an individual client and carers, and on services to between 15,000 and 90,000 people living in a 'community locality'. We touch on organizing services for general populations of 200,000 to 700,000, because how these services are planned and provided sets the context for services to localities and to individuals.

One dimension of service is the 'scope' of a service, in terms of how many people it serves. We use the following terms to refer to service managment for different size populations: strategic management for general populations, operational or locality management for community localities, and individual care management for a number of services to one person and their carer(s). Services to populations and individuals have to be coordinated because they are purchased and provided by different agencies. Most of this book is about how this is done for one person, or for a group of people in a locality with similar needs (a 'locality client group').

Response and resources

For the purpose of organizing service, we divide the 'service' side of the 'needs–service' model into two parts: responses and resources. We use the term 'response' to refer to a *method* for meeting need, rather than as a general term for everything that is done to meet need. A method of response is a treatment such as a drug injection or behavioural programme, or a social care programme. Responses to client needs at the level of a team are a weekly group for clients, or a regular clinic, or an information service. At the level of the population, a response is a home-help service.

These methods are 'types' or 'categories' of service. They are all methods for responding to the needs of one client or more. They do not include the second part of 'service', the resources for responding. 'Resources' are the sources of response, usually described in terms of amount and type. The resources to respond to a client's needs are mostly the people available – their skills, knowledge and the quantity of their time. Resources also include equipment, buildings and finance. Box 2.2 shows examples of responses and resources for one client's needs, for clients in a locality, and for a population.

Box 2.2 Examples of two elements of service: responses and resources

Level of need	Response (a method)	Resource (what is available to respond with)
A client	A treatment An assessment Practical home help	People (time, skills) Equipment
Clients in a locality	A weekly group Giving information	Team members Information 'library'
General population	Day centres Team services	Staffing Finance

---

Here we are mostly concerned with the resources purchased and made available by health and social services. We note that community care depends on other 'informal' resources. People giving service not only have to know about methods of responding, but must know about the variety of resources which they can call upon to resource themselves and the client. People giving service also have to know the limits to resources – in particular, the limits to their own resource of time and energy, and that of their family and friends. We now look at four ways to describe service in more detail.

Describing service: type, complexity, speed of response, and amount

Services are not only defined by the scope of the population they serve, but also by service type (category), its complexity, speed of response, and amount.

We saw above that there are different *types* of service responses – often these types of response are defined in terms of who provides the service, for example a home-help service or an occupational therapy service. To get the 'best match' between needs and response, the 'types' or 'categories' of service should mirror or parallel the types or categories of need.

The *complexity* of service to an individual is how many different types of service that an individual gets, and how often these change. Sometimes only one professional will give a complex service – carrying out many treatments or changing the treatments frequently. Complex services are provided by practitioners with higher capability and more skills and experience than junior practitioners. 'Matching' involves getting the right level of practitioner for the complexity of a person's need (Øvretveit 1992b).

More usually, service complexity is where a person gets services from more than one person or agency. The higher the complexity the more coordination is required to ensure that the types of treatment or service complement each other. Coordination is itself a service, which calls for a high degree of skill, capability, training and support systems.

The third descriptor of service, the *speed of response*, is how quickly a person in need gets a service. We see below that this aspect of service is linked to the urgency of need by priorities. The *amount* of service is the fourth aspect, describing how much service an individual or population gets, usually in terms of time, but sometimes in terms of finance. The next section further explains each of these aspects of service by showing how each is related to or 'linked' to parallel aspects of need.

LINKING NEEDS AND SERVICE RESPONSES

We have looked at each side of the 'needs–service' model. Now we consider how to link needs to services – through management. Management is about achieving the 'best match' between needs and services. Planning is central to management: a plan describes how services will be 'matched' to needs. Managers and others then use the plan to guide what they do, and to replan. Business planning describes how services will be financed to meet needs.

Care planning for linking needs assessment to service provision

Coordination is about achieving the best match between different needs and different services – it is management across services. Care plans are the main coordinating tool for organizing the best match between needs and services. A care manager formulates a care plan to link a person's needs to services. A multidisciplinary team formulates the client-group care plan to link the client group's needs to services they will provide. Purchasing agencies formulate community care plans to link the needs of the population to services each will purchase.

At each level, care plans coordinate and make these links in a number of ways: they draw together different people and agencies, and help structure negotiation and agreement about needs and about who will do what and when. We will see below how care plans link the different ways of describing needs and service: first, how care planners link types of need to types of service; second, how planners link complexity of need to skill; third, how plans link the comparative urgency of need to the speed of response; and fourth, how plans link the comparative severity of need to the amount of service a person or client group gets.

Linking types of need to types of service

The easiest way to explain how 'types' or 'categories' help link needs to service is to start the wrong way round – with 'types' or 'categories' of service.

We distinguish different types of service to think about what services could meet a person's needs after assessing types of need. There are different types of service for populations (housing, health services, educational services, social services), for a client group in a locality (GP services, community nursing, day care), and for an individual (practical home-help, therapeutic treatment, volunteer visiting). Often these service categories are a mixture of where the service is provided, which agency or profession provides it and what is provided.

Professional practitioners developing a profession-specific care plan use their knowledge of the types of responses they can carry out themselves. They use different types of treatment or intervention which they are trained to carry out, and select or adapt these in their plan statement. Similarly, a care manager formulating a care plan will think about categories of services and who could provide them. The same principle applies at the level of a team planning their services for a client group, and at the level of a purchaser planning services for a population. People plan using categories of service.

Where do they get their categories from? Practitioners, from their training in treatment and intervention techniques. Care managers, mostly from training and guidance from higher authorities. Purchasers, from guidance, but also using categories describing the services in the area or services which could be developed. But teams? Single-profession teams have a common language and set of categories to use together to plan their services. Multidisciplinary teams do not, and herein lies a problem for such teams which need to plan services collectively. We return to this issue at the end of the chapter when we look at how a team manages its services in relation to needs.

The second point about service categories is that they do not distinguish between different types of need. They distinguish between different ways in which providers can act, in order to make clear what is planned, and to choose ways of responding. To distinguish types of need, each provider or purchaser uses a set of categories of need. The professional practitioner defines need using diagnostic or assessment categories. For example, one group of nurses uses the following set of categories to distinguish the different types of mental health needs of older people: dementia, paraphrenia, acute confusional state, and depression. They use these categories when they assess a person in order to rule out certain problems, and to focus on more specific needs.

Needs categories are different from those describing the intervention, but they help link the person's needs to the types of intervention which the professional can make. The assessment categories and assessment methods are designed to direct attention to the presence or absence of certain signs, in order to make it easier to select or adapt an intervention method. The same principles apply at the level of a client group, and at the level of a general population.

Each professional service and agency service has developed categories for defining population needs to help it plan service responses. One difficulty in coordinating different services is that each has a different way of defining needs and responses. This difficulty is reduced at the level of a population, by agencies agreeing care group categories (for example, people over 65) and other agreed categories of need. Box 2.3 shows an example of different types of need, and of types of service response in a mental health team.

Box 2.3 Categories of need and categories of service response in one mental health team

Categories of need	Categories of service response	Sub-categories of response
Paranoia	Types of assessment	Contact assessment Profession assessment Full assessment
Schizophrenia	Types of treatment	Drug Counselling Therapy: behavioural, group, cognitive
Anxiety	Other types of care	Monitoring Practical assistance

Depression
Obsessive-compulsive
    disorder
Phobia
Personality disorder
Anorexia
Sociopathy
	Advice/consultancy
	Prevention/mental health
	    promotion	

'Pigeon holing' and 'labelling'

The general point is that it is impossible to think about needs without categorizing types of need, and similarly for responses. Some people object to categorizing need – they argue that we cannot separate, for example, social needs from educational or health needs. To do so is 'artificial', interferes with us seeing the person as a whole, and can dehumanize a person. However, when the same people assess need, they still use categories, just a different set, for example physical needs, physiological needs, companionship needs.

The objection is valid if the categories we use to assess needs are really categories of service, and services which have not successfully met needs in the past. Or, if the categories are developed only for the convenience of thinking about organizing existing services, rather than for understanding the nature of a person's needs and how that person and her carer understand her needs. The issue is not that we should not categorize, but that we should use categories which are the 'best' for the thing we are categorizing. We should categorize needs in ways other than 'home-help needs', 'medical needs', and so on, which pre-empt further understanding of a person's needs.

The dilemma is to develop categories which are not service response categories, but which help to make the links between needs and service. How to develop appropriate needs categories is not a subject we are able to discuss here. But note, first, that service innovation comes from thinking about and categorizing individual and population needs in new ways. Second, a practitioner, team or purchaser should select a way of categorizing need which is not a category of service responses, but which does enable the link to be made between the type of need and a suitable type of response. The last part of this chapter gives a practical example of how a team can use categories of need and of different types of services to link needs to their service response. We now turn to the second link between needs and service – linking complexity.

Linking complexity of need to level of response

Complexity of need is how many different types of need a person has and how frequently these change. Complexity of service is the number of types of service or treatment, and how frequently these have to be changed. A person in an intensive care ward has complex needs. There are two ways of linking complex needs to service: the first is by coordinating assessments and services (Chapters 4, 5 and 6 discuss care management and case coordination). This coordination is done after someone has made a judgement that a person needs a number of assessments: the service provider makes an early judgement about how complex someone's needs are, and about what type of assessment to do or arrange. This is the second way in which complex needs are linked to services, through someone recognizing that a person's needs may be complex, but not actually doing a full assessment.

The GP in our example thought that the Watkinses might have complex needs, and she referred them to a service for a more detailed assessment. Most services have arrangements for 'differential assessments' – they provide different types of assessment to match different types of need. They have a category system and methods for initial assessment (sometimes called 'screening') to help 'front-line' staff match complexity of need to the complexity of assessment. Often these arrangements also judge the urgency of need, the third link to which we now turn.

Linking urgency of need to speed of response by priorities

A need is urgent if it could increase dramatically if no one responds. Urgency is judged by a person in need – that person is desperate for help and fears the consequences of not getting help. It is also judged by others who think that a person is at risk or are concerned about them. Urgency is also relative – one person's needs are more urgent than another person's, their situation will deteriorate more quickly than another person's. On the 'service' side of the equation is how quickly a service responds to need. Waiting lists and service time intervals are measures of response speed that should relate to urgency of need.

The way we link urgency of need to speed of service response in care plans is through priorities. Priorities state which needs are to be met first – be it one client's needs (for example, arranging meals or housing), a client group's needs (those clients with given risk factors), or population needs (single mothers with children under five).

Some use the word 'priority' to refer to how many resources to put into something, and it is true that it is difficult to separate urgency of need from the 'depth' or 'severity' of need. For example, the priority of the mental health team in our example (Box 2.3) was clients who would have to leave their homes if they did not get a service from the team. Some in the team argue that the team should not spend all its time on clients with these needs, and that there are other needs that can and should be met by the team. The issue arises because there are so many clients who need the team's services to continue living at home, that the team does not have time for other work if it sticks to this priority. Hence some question the team priorities, and in so doing question what quantity of resouces the team uses for these clients. So priorities – what comes first when there are choices – are related to resources because resources are finite and choices have to be made. We set priorities after judging opportunity costs. This takes us to the fourth type of link made by care plans – linking relative 'severity' or 'depth' of need to the amount of finite resources by allocation and budgeting methods.

Linking severity of need to amount of service by allocation rules and budgeting

'Severity' or 'depth' of need is the amount of one type of need. Although severity and urgency often go together, severity (or depth) of need is different from urgency: there are some needs that do not grow more urgent if they are not met, but just 'deeper', and will need more resources to be met later – there is no rapid deterioration as there is with urgent needs.

Depth of need is sometimes difficult to assess, and we usually judge it in terms of the 'amount' of response, or in comparison to the depth of others' needs. An example of a set of categories for depth of need is nursing or social care 'dependency levels'. These categories of level of dependency help relate the depth of need to the amount and level of nursing or social care time. The deeper the need, the greater the amount of response called for.

The amount of service is measured by the amount of a service provider's time (hours, sessions, posts) or by the cost of a service. Care planning uses allocation rules and budgets to relate the amount of service to the depth of need. Note that the amount of any service is finite and needs are infinite, so that we can never fully match the amount of service to the severity or depth of need. What we can do is compare the relative severity or depth of different types of need, and then plan and allocate how much of our limited resources to provide. To do this we must know the limits to our resource, as well as enough about needs to judge differences in severity and depth.

For example, a care manager has a limited amount of time and finance for each client. These limits are themselves set by the care manager's manager, after she compares the relative needs of different clients. If no limits are set, the care manager knows that there are limits to the number of clients that can be served, and sets her own limits for each client.

The care manager judges the relative severity or depth of the different needs of the client, drawing on other professional assessments as necessary. She then judges, out of the total resources she can use for the client, what level of resources to allocate for each need. She also judges priority of need, and draws up a care plan. The care plan describes the best 'match' or 'balance' the care manager can make between the resources available and the severity of different needs. It also uses priorities to 'spread' resources over time.

Teams use similar principles to link their resources to the needs of their client group in a locality. They use priorities to link urgency to speed of response, and time allocation and budgeting to link depth of need to amount of response. To define priorities and time allocation, a team must have adequate information about the needs of the client it serves, about types of response and their effectiveness, and about the resources available to them. Box 2.4 summarizes these points about separating and linking needs and services.

Box 2.4 Summary: assessing needs and linking assessments to service

1 To get a needs-led service, separate the assessment of need from service provision to reduce the influence of existing services on how to understand needs.
2 Assessing needs and describing services:

To think about needs:
- bring together different perspectives about need

- categorize different types of need
- judge relative complexity of need

- judge relative urgency of need
- judge relative severity or depth of need.

To think about services:
- bring together different views about the effectiveness of different types of service

- categorize different types of services
- decide what types of assessment to offer, according to complexity of need
- consider speed of service response
- decide relative amounts of service for each need.

3 To link needs to services:
- develop and carry out care plans for individuals, client groups, and populations
- ensure different perspectives and types of assessment are brought together
- ensure higher levels set parameters within which lower levels do more detailed assessment and planning
- ensure lower levels pass details on to higher levels.

Later chapters show that some teams have problems setting and keeping priorities and time allocations. Members decide their own priorities and time budgets, and the team priorities are only the sum of each member's independent work management decisions. Chapter 5 shows a practical way in which a team can use these ideas to formulate, agree, and carry out priorities and resource allocation.

SUMMARY AND CONCLUSION

That services should be based on needs is a simple idea but difficult to realize. One reason why is that it is easier to think about a need by thinking about a ready-made way of meeting the need. We can sometimes work out a better way of meeting a need if we try to understand the need itself. This principle underlies separating an assessment of a person's or population's needs from providing service to meet the need. The separation makes it easier to define the need itself, rather than defining the need purely in terms of existing services.

After assessment, a person's or population's needs are linked to services by a care plan. The care plan makes the best match between needs and services. The match is never exact because needs are infinite and service limited. The 'best match' is made by care planners linking aspects to need to aspects of service. The plan links categories of need to categories of service, complexity of need to skill or level of service, urgency of need to speed of service, and severity of need to amount of service.

For a person to get a 'needs-led service' these links and care plans have to be made by care managers at the individual level, by teams at the locality level, and by community care plans at the population level. Different services, such as assessment, treatment and care services, have to be coordinated to make sure all of a person's needs are met. Organization ensures coordination – both of assessments and of service planning and provision. It is to the subject of organization and coordination that we now turn.

Box 2.5 Chapter 2: key points

A needs-led service depends on:

- separating an assessment of needs from deciding what services to provide to meet needs;
- linking needs assessment to service provision by care planning, priorities and resource allocation;
- performing needs assessments for different population levels – assessing the needs of a community as a whole, of a client group within a locality, and of a particular individual;
- linking different perspectives and types of assessment at each level (for example, health and social needs);
- linking needs assessments between each level – the higher levels defining the boundaries of assessments done by lower levels, and the lower levels bringing together individual needs assessments to pass this on to higher levels;
- deciding how sophisticated a needs assessment should be by differentiating levels of complexity of needs assessment ('differential needs assessment');
- organization to ensure that assessments are done, a plan is made, carried out and reviewed and that the links are made (responsibility and coordination).

Chapter 3
MARKETS, BUREAUCRACY AND ASSOCIATION

How can you meet needs when services are so fragmented? The market reforms did not solve the problems of split responsibilities, they just increased the problems of coordination by adding competition.

The market reforms allow us to solve long-standing problems of cooperation in community care by forming new alliances and organizational forms for needs-led service.

INTRODUCTION

It is a commonplace that organizations grow detached from their original purpose, and a frequent criticism that public services exist for their employees rather than for the public. In fact, public health and social services bureaucracies are able to provide cost-effective mass services, particularly where people only need one service from one agency. They are not so successful in tailoring a variety of services to meet the changing needs of each person, especially if the person needs services from different bureaucracies. Many people with special needs living in the community found that the only option was admission to an institution or hospital away from where they lived.

Some argue that the problem is lack of finance – that state services could provide 'individualized' services which are also equitable, if they had the finance. Some say that large bureaucracies cannot provide the variety, choice and innovative services that are needed. Most agree that large bureaucracies do find it difficult to work together and coordinate their efforts. The UK reforms aim to change bureaucracies to make them more responsive to needs. But there is no guarantee that purchasers know more about needs than providers, and the way that 'the market' is structured with different purchasers emphasizes different conceptions of need. Neither does 'the market' solve the problems of coordination. And coordination is essential for needs-led community services, especially as the variety of providers increases and clients come to expect a more individual service. The successful public services of the 1990s will be those that can respond to people's needs by coordinating services effectively – both their own and other agencies' services. Teams are one method of coordination, and care management another.

This chapter is about different ways of linking people in need to people giving service, and about ways of linking people giving service to each other. It uses the term 'organization' in a general sense, to refer to stable patterns of interaction and to relationships between people. It describes three 'modes' of organization: bureaucracy, market and association. It shows that the way people relate to each other is different in each. Each provides different ways of 'linking' needs to provision, and of linking separate providers to each other. In practice, community services involve a mixture of each, but to understand how things work (or do not) in a team or locality we need to understand these different ways of organizing.

The next chapter shows that one of these three modes of organization predominates in different types of practitioner team. This chapter describes the organization surrounding teams and how this influences how teams operate. It shows how decisions made by managers and planners, and how they relate across agencies, can make or break teams. Teams and their managers need to understand the organizational context to understand what type of teamwork is possible and appropriate, and why certain problems of cooperation arise. Because separate agencies have responsibilities for different needs, managers and planners in these agencies have to cooperate to predict needs and to organize providers. The chapter describes five different inter-agency models showing how cooperation can take place at different levels, and how this organization affects teamwork.

First we build on the discussion of the last chapter to show the part played by organization in a 'needs-led' approach to services, before then looking at ways of organizing to get this.

FROM NEEDS TO ORGANIZATION: THE THEORY

Health and social services are criticized for 'force-fitting' clients to the services which they happen to provide. Improvements to community care aim to make services follow from an assessment of each client's needs, as we saw in the last two chapters. In this chapter we add to the needs–service model the 'details of organization' that should follow from a decision about what type and amount of service to provide. In theory the sequence is:

Needs → Services → Details of organization

The example of the Watkins couple in the last chapter illustrates how organization, or lack of it, affects how needs are met. Mrs Watkins's 'loss of memory' made it more difficult for her elderly husband to cope. After the GP referred them to the community mental health team for the elderly, a social worker in the team did a social needs assessment. He also called upon other health professionals in the team for specialist assessments. The social worker, who was the care manager for the couple, brought together the assessments to produce a multidisciplinary needs assessment, and planned the services which Mrs Watkins and her husband needed. Not all these services could be provided, but the social worker arranged those that could be, and monitored how and when they were provided.

Even though the sequence was the right one – from needs, to services, to how they are organized – still the couple did not get the services which they needed. It was not because of lack of finance, but because some of the services did not exist in the area. The social worker was not able to arrange respite care (someone to come into the home, or a short period away). There were other services which the assessment showed were needed, and no amount of creative thinking by everyone involved could come up with alternatives. The problem was that neither the joint planning group nor any of the agencies involved had used their needs assessment to plan the range of services that people like the Watkinses would need. Even the services that were planned had run into problems because the agencies could not agree who should finance or provide them, and because the implementation was not coordinated. Although the right sequence was followed by the team and care manager, their managers and planners had not coordinated their plans and implementation to follow the sequence:

Population needs → Services → Details of each service's organization

The needs of a defined population have to be assessed, and services planned and then brought into being, by contracting providers, or by employing providers and managing them directly to carry out the plan. Otherwise the people planning one person's care will not have services which they can call upon. Indeed, it may not be possible to do a full needs assessment because a particular specialist professional is not available.

There is an argument that coordination is easier if one agency employs all the professions and provides all the services needed by a client group. But it would have to be a large agency, and what would be gained in ease of coordination could be lost in flexibility and choice. We will return to questions about whether to employ providers or contract services later in the chapter.

If clients are to get a full assessment and services which are tailored to meet their needs, many agencies and informal helpers are required at different times. Most clients need a variety of services which are purchased and provided by different agencies. These agencies, carers and clients must contribute in a coordinated way to each part of the sequence of assessment, planning and organizing the service, both at an individual level and at a population level. What is the best way of coordinating these different professionals, services and agencies? Before we consider five specific models of interagency organization, we look at the three 'modes' of organization in their pure form.

THREE MODES OF COORDINATION

Coordination for community care: to order together to form a whole, in a way which keeps the differences between the parts, but relates them to make the whole greater than the sum of the parts.

Coordination is aligning what you do in relation to other people. People coordinate through their relationships with each other. The relationship may be distant, as when a social security clerk receives a request to arrange a benefit payment before a client's electricity is disconnected. The way people relate to each other depends on the context and what motivates them to do so. Regardless of the personalities, the clerk will relate to his boss in a different way to the way he relates to a social worker on the phone, or to a shop assistant when buying something, or to friends outside work.

The following describes three different contexts for relationships: bureaucracy, market and association. These are all modes of organization. They provide different ways of linking people in need to people giving service, and of linking those giving service to each other. In describing these modes of organization features of certain specific organizations called 'bureaucracies' or 'associations' are emphasized. A market is not usually thought of as an organization, but it is a way of linking needs to supply. Relationships in a market are different to those in a bureaucracy or association.

These modes are also ways of coordinating whole organizations or parts of organizations to plan and provide services. An organization can be part of a larger bureaucracy, and relate to another part through direction, rules and policies (for example, a general manager requests that a psychology department and an occupational therapy department within an NHS trust agree a policy about how they will work together to provide a service). Parts of an organization can relate to each other through 'internal contracts', or through association which is not bureaucratic or contractual. Similarly whole organizations can relate through bureaucratic mechanisms or contractual relations or by association: partnership agreements, or implicit agreements based on trust and shared values, as in an association.

We consider these three modes of organization and relating because they are important to understanding how practitioners cooperate in teams. They help teams understand their place within a larger organization, and how agency relationships affect the type of teamwork which is possible. The context surrounding the relationship between practitioners and between agencies is important because it eases or impedes how they cooperate to assess and meet needs. People in a team where each is contracted to the team, as in some care management arrangements, relate to each other in a different way to people in a bureaucratic team, or in an association type of team. The client's relationship to team members is different depending on whether the service context is a market, an association or a bureaucracy.

The three modes of organization are not mutually exclusive: in reality a service shows a mixture of bureaucratic, market and association characteristics, as we will see when we consider types of team in the next chapter. The following describes each mode in its pure form, before then discussing coordination in community care through contracts, bureaucratic agreements, or forms of association. The three modes are summarized in Box 3.1 at the end of this section. The last part of the chapter shows how services are coordinated in practice, and describes five models of inter-agency cooperation which involve different mixes of market, bureaucratic and association modes of organization.

Bureaucracy

Bureaucracies employ 'service providers' to give service to people in need. The rules of the bureaucracy which employs service providers govern their relationships to each other and to people in need (clients and carers). A bureaucratic mode of organization is one characterized by hierarchy, sub-division of tasks, and control and coordination through rules and managerial authority. Typical bureaucracies are the army, the Church, the police, most public services, some large voluntary organizations and some commercial companies.

In bureaucracies the source of power to get people to coordinate their actions is authority. Authority is delegated by the employing body to managers, and is accepted as legitimate by employees who agree to be bound by rules and directions when they enter into an employment contract. Disputes and conflict are resolved by reference to rules, or successively higher rulings within the bureaucracy, or by courts of law. Relations between managers and practitioners are also characterized by accountability: the right of managers to call practitioners to answer for their actions and inactions.

Relations between practitioners are governed by rules, backed up by the authority of managers. Policies and employment contracts set sanctions for failures of coordination which can be applied by the manager to whom practitioners are accountable. With this emphasis on authority and accountability, coordination between practitioners is best when they are under one manager, who makes the rules and gives directions. When they are employed by the same bureaucracy, but under different managers, these managers need to agree rules and directions, or a 'cross-over' manager higher up has to arbitrate. Coordination between practitioners employed by different agencies according to a bureaucratic mode of organization requires that their managers enter into bureaucratic agreements, typically joint policies.

Bureaucracies have clear boundaries: if a person is not employed by a bureaucracy he is not part of the organization, apart from a few exceptions like honorary positions. Critics of the bureaucratic mode of organization argue that services based on these principles are inflexible, slow, unresponsive to client need and not able to adapt to a fast-changing environment. This view influenced the 1990 UK NHS and community care reforms, which introduced elements of a 'market' mode of organization within and between health and social services bureaucracies.

Markets

Markets link needs to supply by exchange mechanisms. In simple markets, people in need give something in exchange for a service which they believe will meet their need. Usually the item exchanged for service is money. In public service markets a 'third party' exchanges money for service on behalf of people in need. People pay for the service by paying tax to the government which then allocates finance to the 'third party' to buy services. In markets the activities of independent units (people or firms) are coordinated through price signs. Needs are related to provision by price signs: if needs are not being met, and those in need — or their agents — have money to exchange, the providers will offer services in exchange for money.

In many markets the relation between a provider and a buyer is often one where each tries to get the most from the exchange. Providers and buyers also try to change the market conditions to their advantage: providers try to remove competition, or form supplier cartels to fix prices. Buyers try to form large purchasing agencies, or to have market regulations put in place which work to their advantage. Buyers and providers are often the biggest enemy of the pure market, and government regulation is essential to maintain 'free market' competition.

A framework of laws is necessary for markets to operate. Chief among these is contract law, which governs the relations between otherwise independent agents. Coordination through contract involves specifying what will be exchanged and the conditions governing the relationship. Sanctions for failure are stipulated in the contract and enforceable by law. In public markets, contracts between public bodies are not enforceable in law but are subject to other regulations (DoH 1989d). Beyond the contract, markets allow purchasers and providers independence to pursue their own interests.

Contracts exist to guard against the tendency for each side to pursue its own individual interests at the expense of the other, a tendency which is accentuated by an ideology of competition and short-term gain. Markets are less efficient than other ways of linking needs to provision where the item to be exchanged for money is difficult or expensive to specify (as in many services), or where purchasers do not know enough about the type of service which is required to meet their needs. In theory, when an agency finds that the cost of specifying and monitoring the service to prevent its being exploited becomes too high, it considers employing staff to provide the service, and controlling it through management and employment contract. In fact an employment contract is a particular type of long-term service contract.

Markets need a number of conditions to operate as effective ways of relating needs to provision, and to coordinate the activities of different agents. One group of theorists argue that markets work best when there is unregulated competition and there are many providers and buyers. Providers compete to offer what buyers want, and those that do not will go out of business. If there are many buyers, then providers are not exploited by a sole buyer. Other theorists argue that regulation is needed to ensure that many suppliers and buyers exist in the first place. Finally, we note that in many countries, bureaucratic organizations operate within a market context, usually for labour, and often buy and sell goods and services through a market mechanism, and relate to other organizations through contracts.

Association

There are ways of meeting needs and of coordinating people and agencies other than through bureaucracy or markets. The term 'association' is used here to describe a third mode of organization, and a context for relationships characterized by trust, respect and shared values.

In contrast to bureaucracies and markets, relationships in associations are informal, unspecified and characterized by equality and mutuality, rather than by authority or resource differences. People relate to each other in associations because of common interests or values – they form partnerships without contracts. Relationships exist within a particular culture, with norms, customs and rituals which create and maintain obligations and rights. Examples of associations are cooperatives, special interest groups of professional practitioners, some voluntary groups, most religious associations, and information networks. In recent years there has been a growth in the number of self-help groups of people in need associating with each other exchanging information.

Coordination in association is by informal agreement to pursue valued objectives. Sanctions are mainly those of losing the respect and valuation of others, losing the right to expect things of others in the association, damage to one's reputation, shame, and the possibility of exclusion from the association.

In contrast to markets, the relationship in associations is more important than a particular exchange. People do not 'calculate the balance' of the relationship as they do in a market-contract relationship. Association is long-term, and parties recognize mutual interdependence, and that each can best achieve its own objectives by cooperation or by pooling resources.

Some theorists criticize simple market concepts as inadequate descriptions or prescriptions for relations between practitioners or agencies. They note that some transactions between commercial organizations do not aim for maximum short-term advantage, but recognize that both parties' interests are best served by stable long-term relations and 'partnership' contracting (Øvretveit 1992c).

Associations are effective where exchange relationships are difficult to specify, or the relationship is damaged by doing so, or where absorption into a bureaucracy is not an option (for example, a purchaser directly managing a provider). Some argue that the association mode of organization is more suited to community services in the 1990s than bureaucratic market modes. This is because association modes may be more appropriate where there are an increasing variety of providers and purchasers, a need for flexibility, political and cultural change, and more participation for clients and carers and other community members.

Box 3.1 Three modes of coordination: summary and comparison			
	Bureaucracy	*Market*	*Association*
Key features	Hierarchy, division of tasks, control through rules and managerial authority	Coordination of independent providers and purchasers through price signals. Short-term, opportunistic, extract maximum advantage. Low trust. Unequal	Common interest or values, trust and respect between members, formal or informal, not time-limited. Equality
Boundary	Clear and stable membership	Clear and variable participation	Fuzzy. Degrees of membership
Norms	Rational-legal: 'proper procedures'	Competition, individual advantage	Recognition of mutual dependence
Coordination by	Directions, rules sanctions	Price competition Contract	Trust and cooperation
Exchange	Long-term exchange of labour for pay	Short-term exchange of specified items	Long-term mutual obligation
Power	Authority of position	Resource imbalance	Common interests or values. Influence
Sanctions	Withholding organizational benefits	Penalties (legal enforcement)	Disapproval, rejection shame
Key issues	Flexibility and speed of response	Type and amount of regulation	Creating and sustaining trust and cooperation
Examples	Most local authority services pre-1990	Most labour markets. Stock exchange	Partnership. Cooperative. Collegiate

DISCUSSION: AGENCY COOPERATION IN COMMUNITY CARE

These descriptions of the three modes of organization help us understand the complex mix of relationships in community care, and to consider better ways of coordinating services. They help us to establish the best way to coordinate practitioners and agencies in a locality or larger area to ensure that their efforts are combined effectively to meet the needs of a client and a client population. We start by looking at the strengths and weaknesses of each mode, before describing five models of how services coordinate their activities in practice.

Coordination becomes more of a problem the more people's interests and values diverge, and the more they pursue different objectives. An assumption underlying the bureaucratic mode of organization is that employees need to be controlled and monitored to ensure coordination. In markets the assumption is that payment incentives will ensure coordination, backed up by contract penalties. Association assumes that cooperation comes from common interests and values, and the desire to reciprocate out of free will.

Coordination through bureaucracy is the most common within and between health and social services. Separate bureaucracies coordinate their own employed community practitioners, and form bureaucratic coordination agreements with other bureaucracies at different levels of the hierarchy. Bureaucracy is much criticized for inefficiency, inflexibility, slowness of response, and for not encouraging creativity and variety. One modern theorist argues that bureaucracies can meet the challenge of the 1990s and has mounted a sustained defence of bureaucracy, arguing that: 'The problem is not to find an alternative to a system that once worked well but no longer does; the problem is to make it work efficiently for the first time in its 3,000 year history' (Jaques 1990b). Others have concluded that the time has come to try something else.

Regardless of its other merits, as a mode of coordinating community services provided by different agencies (lateral cooperation), bureaucracy has not been a great success. One solution is to encompass all services within one bureaucracy, and to coordinate through internal control mechanisms, as in Northern Ireland's Health and Social Services Boards (e.g. 'patch teams'). This solution to coordination was considered for the UK by the 1979 Royal Commission, and more recently in proposals for unitary purchasing authorities and integrated providers. A single bureaucracy providing community services is ruled out by the 1990 UK government reforms, which retain three separate purchasing agencies and GP fundholders, and encourage a variety of separate provider organizations. The thrust of the reforms is towards the market mode for coordination between agencies, with purchasers cooperating to contract different community services, and government or regional intervention to prevent large single-provider services.

A disadvantage of markets is the cost of transactions between purchasers and providers, and the need to specify what is purchased to avoid one party exploiting the other. For markets to be effective, the items exchanged must be tangible, there must be many providers and purchasers, low interdependence between purchasers and providers, and an ideology of competition. Without these conditions, 'transaction costs' theorists predict 'market failure' and absorption of contracted units into a bureaucratic structure. The market mode does not offer a solution to the problem of lateral cooperation between purchasers and between providers. Although planning agreements are possible, this is not a market type of contract. The only alternative within a market mode is for one purchaser to purchase all community services, and to coordinate others through contracts (for example a care manager forming contracts). One of the five models we consider later involves purchasers 'pooling' their finance for one or more community services.

Inter-organizational cooperation

In the 1980s a body of research emerged which questioned the bureaucracy–market categorization, and the notion of a bureaucratic–market continuum. This research describes other types of coordination within and between organizations: the clan (Ouchi 1980), collective (Butler 1980; 1983), association (Powell 1990), relational contracting (Macneil 1978), value-added partnerships (Johnson and Lawrence 1988) and many others. This research proposes that these forms are more suited to certain conditions than markets and bureaucracy. It shows that market contracts and bureaucratic agreements are only one type of a variety of inter-organizational relations between commercial and public service organizations.

The lessons from this research for needs-led community services is that purchasers and providers must recognize their dependence on each other, and work to build long-term relationships beyond contract. The relation between purchaser and provider is rarely an adversarial, transient relation, where each manoeuvres for maximum short-term gain, but often one of long-term cooperation to their mutual advantage. Purchasers and providers can relate purely through contract, but longer-term associations and partnerships are also possible, as well as direct management. Community care depends on forming the right types of relationship, and an awareness of the choices is necessary to do so. Figure 3.1 shows the spectrum of types of relationships between a purchaser and provider of a community service:

Contractual	Partnership	Part-ownership	Combination
Low volume, short-term, opportunistic	High volume, long-term, preferred supplier, open information, mutual dependency	Purchaser owns some of the provider	Purchaser owns provider, one management, e.g. DMU, GP hospital, some LA provider units

Figure 3.1 Spectrum of possible relationship between a purchaser and a community service provider

In addition, different purchasers have to cooperate, as each depends on other purchasers to achieve their community care objectives. Purchasers can coordinate in a variety of ways, ranging from information exchange, through joint assessment and planning, to merger (Figure 3.2).

Turning to relations between community care providers, in some instance these relations may be competitive – fighting for limited purchaser resources. Many community care providers in the early 1990s assumed that their only

Sharing information	Sharing a resource	Joint purchasing		Consortium	Merger
e.g. population profiles and data, contract specification	e.g. staff, facilities, equipment, same inspection unit, overlapping board membership	Agreed purchasing plan	Pool finance for some or all services	One agency purchases, but each purchaser remains an indpendent entity	New single purchasing body

Figure 3.2 Possible types of purchaser cooperation for community care purchasing

option was to compete with other providers, and held mistaken notions of how competitive commercial markets worked. In some cases these misunderstandings of commercial markets led to providers actually creating the inappropriate and unnecessary competition they had feared. Research shows that many commercial companies in fierce competition in some areas form cooperative joint ventures and provider associations for other markets. Providers can often better meet their objectives by cooperating with other providers, even if they compete fiercely in other areas.

Community service providers, be they publicly owned, voluntary or private organizations, can cooperate through a variety of types of relationships: bureaucratic agreement, merger, market contracts, joint venture, or mergers (see Figure 3.3).

Sharing information	Sharing a resource	Joint venture		Consortium	Merger
e.g. community needs, client data, contract specifications	e.g. staff, facilities, equipment, overlapping board membership	Aligned, e.g. agreed plan	Joint-owned Pool finance for some services	Providers each keep status, but form one agency for relating to purchasers, or other purposes	New single-provider corporation

Figure 3.3 Cooperative relationships between community care providers – the alternatives to competition

We now turn to examples of five models of coordination between agencies and services. Each model involves a mixture of the three modes of organization. How the purchasing and provider agencies relate at higher levels sets the context for how a team or care manager coordinates services, as we see in the next chapter on types of teams.

COORDINATING COMMUNITY SERVICES – EXAMPLES

For comprehensive and needs-led community services, agencies have to coordinate at a strategic level (both purchasers and providers), at an operational management level, and at the practitioner level. The following describes examples of coordination between agencies in broad terms. It considers ways of coordinating populations needs assessments and service provision. Arrangements for coordination at these strategic and operational management levels affect how practitoners cooperate to assess and meet one client's needs.

A service to a particular client group in the community will involve a mixture of forms of cooperation and relationships: the following describes just five of the most common combinations.

Model 1: Parallel, directly managed bureaucracies

This arrangement was common in the 1980s for mental health services and for services for people with a learning difficulty. It exists where purchasing authorities directly manage health and social services provision. Coordination is most effective where each bureaucracy has managers at similar levels, with similar responsibilities and authority (see Figure 3.4). Coordination is typically through jointly developed plans, formal and informal agreements, and joint management groups at each level.

An example was the structure for the All-Wales Strategy for people with a learning difficulty in Welsh counties in the 1980s. Here social services took 'lead responsibility' and there were joint management groups at local and county levels which combined managers from health, social services and education and others (Macdonald 1990). Practitioners were managed by profession managers

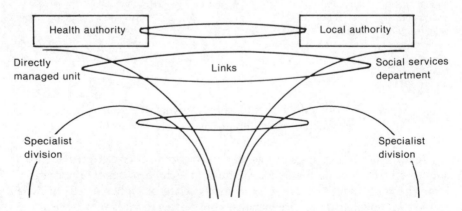

Figure 3.4 Two bureaucracies coordinate at different levels

or general managers who coordinated policies with their counterparts in other agencies.

Model 2: Parallel purchasing from single providers

This model evolved out of Model 1, where a local authority has clear purchasing and provider wings, and most community health provision is within one NHS trust (see Figure 3.5). At the strategic level, purchasing managers cooperate to form community care plans which are agreed by purchasing authorities. Provider managers cooperate at the strategic and operational levels.

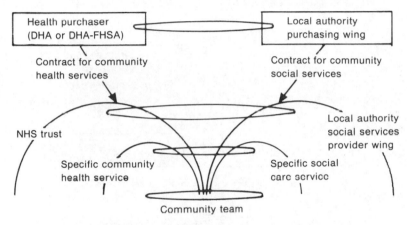

Figure 3.5 Purchasers and providers coordinate at different levels

Model 3: Pooled purchasing from one provider

In this model, purchasers establish a single purchasing agency, and pool their finance to form a single purchasing budget (see Figure 3.6). Many services are purchased from one organization, such as an NHS trust, which provides health, social and other types of services. Some services for people with a learning difficulty are close to this model.

Model 4: Pooled purchasing from many providers

This model is similar to Model 3, but with a purchasing agency which contracts many providers (see Figure 3.7). Purchaser and provider managers agree contracts for large-volume services. Care managers employed by the purchasing agency buy some services for individual clients using delegated purchasing budgets. The purchasing agency and care managers coordinate services through contracts.

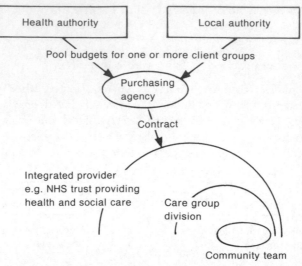

Figure 3.6 Coordination by contracting an integrated provider

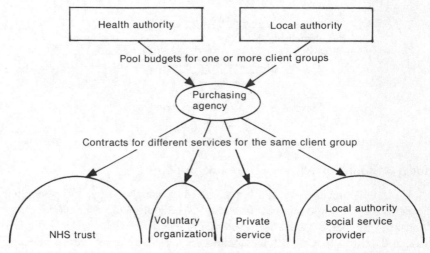

Figure 3.7 Integrated purchasing and separate providers

Model 5: Parallel purchasing from many providers

This model is the most complex and coordination the most difficult, although choice is greatest. It is similar to Model 4, but without a single purchasing agency. The separate purchasers (which may be many, if there are fund-holding GPs) agree definitions of the client care groups. They coordinate their plans and purchasing through agreements and meetings, and they each contract a variety of providers (see Figure 3.8).

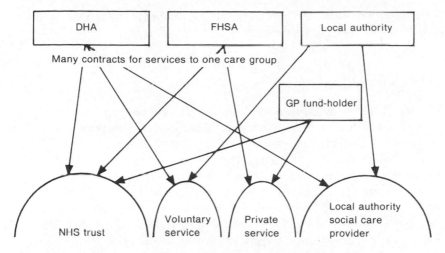

Figure 3.8 Many purchasers and many providers for services for
clients from one care group

Box 3.2 shows that increasing provider variety and client choice often means
making service and purchasing coordination more difficult, which causes
problems planning and providing for clients needing many types of service.
Gains in choice and variety are offset by losses in ease of coordination and
higher administrative costs. Are choice and variety only possible through many
different organizations, and is the sort of choice worth the benefits?

	Box 3.2 Coordinating purchasing and provision, and variety and choice for clients	
	One provider	*Many providers*
Many purchasers	Low choice	Maximum choice and variety
	Easy provider coordination	Coordination most difficult
	More difficult purchaser	(Model 5)
	coordination (Model 2)	
One purchaser	Lowest choice	High choice
	Easiest to coordinate	Provider coordination difficult
	(Model 3)	(Model 4)

Each model shows different ways of coordinating how client group needs are
assessed and how plans are formed and implemented. The overall structure of
the service influences how practitioners cooperate, and the type of teams that
can be set up, or are appropriate. If all practitioners are employed by one
agency, then close-knit teams are possible. If many purchasers have many
contracts with different providers, then stable teams for one area are more
difficult. The next chapter describes different types of team and cooperation

between practitioners and considers which are more suited to each of the above models of inter-agency cooperation.

CONCLUSION

Meeting client needs involves assessing needs, and planning and arranging services – at the level of the individual and at the level of client populations with similar needs. Organization ensures that needs are linked to services and that service providers are laterally linked to each other. These links are different in the bureaucratic, market and association modes of organization.

The bureaucratic mode links needs to services, and links services to each other by rules and managerial direction. Cooperation between service providers is easier if all providers (practitioners and managers) are within the boundary of the bureaucracy, and under the rules and direction of one manager. Then the drawback of the bureaucratic mode is that providers have less flexibility to respond to needs, and there is a tendency to fit clients to the service provided, rather than vice versa.

In theory, the market mode is better than the bureaucratic for linking suppliers of simple products to people with need for that product, so long as people in need have something to exchange for the product. Market modes are more flexible, allow producers and purchasers more independence, but become less efficient with complex services. Contract relations specify what services are to be provided in exchange for payment, and there are clear sanctions for failure. In the market mode lateral relations between providers for cooperation are less easily organized: a purchaser coordinates providers through contracts which require providers to cooperate, even though they may be in competition with each other. However, providers may combine in different ways to offer better lateral cooperation, and hence gain advantage in the market.

Association is a mode of organization that is effective for lateral cooperation, and efficient where services are difficult to specify, or not suited to bureaucratic organization. Cooperation is achieved through shared values, and recognition of common interests and mutual dependence. Client needs can be linked to provision by clients taking a part in producing the service in association with providers, as we see in 'co-service' in Chapter 9.

In practice, community services involve a mixture of modes of organization. The type of cooperation between agencies at the strategic and operational levels has a major influence on how practitioners work together in a community team. There are five common models of inter-agency relationships, and each affects how practitioners cooperate within teams in different ways. Chapter 4 describes these different types of team and methods for care management.

Chapter 4
TYPES OF TEAM

'But I take all my referrals from this meeting, like my manager told me to — I thought everyone did?' Angela looked upset. There was a silence in the team meeting, or at least it got as quiet as it gets in the annex next to main road and the boiler room. Where did the others take their referrals from?

Pete, as usual broke the silence — he saw some clients at the health centre when the GPs asked him to. Alan, the trainee doctor, said that GPs referred directly to the clinic and to the consultant but, 'we pass on many to the team, as you know'. Mary took referrals from the social work team, as she was in the same office and it was quicker, but she always let the team know — she thought that was agreed.

Angela looked confused, and some might say, betrayed. They were all doing it differently. No wonder they all had full caseloads before they came to the team meeting. She began to wonder what the meeting was for, especially as two members hardly ever came but still seemed to make all the decisions, or had to be there for a decision. It certainly wasn't like the last team she worked in. Dare she say it? That it was not really a team, just a meeting. Better not, she thought, they've all been doing this for years, so it must be working — they must know what's going on.

INTRODUCTION

This chapter is about coordinating people giving service to a person in need. It is about how people cooperate together to help this person, and how to make the most of their combined efforts. It concentrates on how practitioners and formal carers are coordinated in multidisciplinary community teams, and on how they cooperate in each phase of a person's care management. It shows how people relate and cooperate differently in different types of team.

The purpose of care management and community multidisciplinary teams is to get the best and quickest 'match' between a person's needs and the skills and resources available. The care management process and teams are ways of organizing this 'matching'. Predicting people's needs and making skills and resources available is the job of managers and planners – making the most of what is there for the person in need is the job of teams and care managers.

There are many types of team, each with different membership, and ways of 'matching' a client's needs to skills and resources. Understanding the differences between types of team is important to:

- planners, for deciding which type is most suited to the needs of a client population;
- managers, for managing the team in the right way, and making changes which improve coordination and hence service quality;
- practitioners, to understand their part in the team, and why certain problems occur;
- researchers, to contribute to knowledge about which type of team is most effective in a particular situation.

This chapter aims to answer a number of questions. What are the different ways of coordinating contributors to each phase of the care management process? Why have a team? What type do we need? What difference does it make for clients and carers, practitioners and managers what type of team we have? The chapter first explains the eight phases of the care management process – the phases that people in need are supposed to go through to have their needs assessed and met. Then it looks at teams as a way of organizing some or all of the phases of care management. It defines what a 'community multidisciplinary team' is, and shows how to distinguish different types of team. This helps team members and their managers recognize which type they work in or manage, and how teams vary in the degree of cooperation between team members.

The chapter then goes on to describe the first team category, the 'client team' which is all the people serving a client at a particular time. The second category is the 'network association', of which many primary health care teams are examples. The third category is 'formal teams'. The different types are described, with examples from mental health and learning difficulty services. One type of 'client team' which we consider is the 'care manager's provider group'. We see that help for the client is coordinated in this group differently than in the other two team categories, but also that care managers can be members of networks or formal teams. The chapter closes by looking at the advantages and disadvantages of each type, and at which might be best in a particular area.

WHAT IS A 'TEAM'?

A crowd at a football match is not a team, but most of the people running on the pitch are members of one of three teams. Unlike the crowd, the two football teams are small groups which, if they play well, coordinate what they do to achieve a specific goal. The referee and linespersons are in a different team, with a purpose that is different to that of either of the two football teams, although some members of the crowd doubt this.

Teams: a small group of people who relate to each other to contribute to a common goal.

Examples: football team, orchestra, uniprofessional team, multidisciplinary team.

People feel and act differently in small groups than they do in larger collectives, or when alone or with another person. This is true even when people are away from the group – the group still affects how they feel and act. All small groups have characteristics that we need to know about to understand how people in groups cooperate. We look at this in later chapters – here we note that one type of small group is a team, and that people in a team come together to achieve a purpose which they could not achieve on their own.

The main differences between health and social services practitioner teams and football teams arise from their different purpose, which is to meet the needs of clients. Their membership and organization should be designed for this purpose. Community multidisciplinary teams are a specific type of team.

Community multidisciplinary team: a small group of people, usually from different professions and agencies, who relate to each other to contribute to the common goal of meeting the health and social needs of one client, or those of a client population in the community.

This book uses the term 'team' to refer to a multidisciplinary community team. It emphasizes two features of these teams. First, the importance of relationships to the purpose of the group: relationships both between a client and a team member, and between team members and each other. These relationships are not secondary to the goal of the team, as they are in some project teams in industry, but are the means through which the client is helped. We will see that these relationships are different in different types of team. The second feature is that the combination of team members' efforts is greater than the sum of each person's contribution. A team is a way of coordinating each person's efforts so that the final result is of a different order than the sum of each person's efforts.

This chapter describes three categories of team. The first, the 'client's team', is the group of people helping one client at a particular time. They may not even know each other or meet, but they contribute to the same goal of helping the client. They relate to each other in doing so, even if it is only through a schedule. The second category is the 'network-association team', which is a more stable grouping, often for cross-referring clients. The third is the 'formal team', whose members regularly meet to organize assessments for a client population and to coordinate their work. Some share a responsibility for serving the population as a multidisciplinary collective.

Why have a team?

The argument for a 'client team' is strong: to coordinate different people's help to one client. It is not so obvious that different people should always meet together to coordinate their work with different clients, unless they all serve the same type of client. Put another way, why should different professions, employed by different agencies, and other formal carers come together in a team? What is wrong with them providing separate services in their own unidisciplinary teams, and only coming together when they all serve the same client and if they need to?

In some places, separate services are the most cost-effective way to organize services, so long as there are ways in which they can be easily brought together when one client needs a number of services. 'Client teams' or 'networks' are ways of doing this. More often, clients can get a quicker and better service if a permanent team of people from different services and professions is formed to serve a particular client population. We consider the advantages and disadvantages of each type at the end of this chapter. Next we look in more detail at how a client or a client's carer gets help, and how the different services that are needed can be brought together at different times.

THE CARE MANAGEMENT PROCESS

The care management process consists of eight phases for meeting client needs. This process shows the work to be done; after looking at this we look at ways of organizing people in teams to carry out each phase. Box 4.1 shows each phase and lists the different people who might contribute to one or more phases.

Box 4.1 *Phases in the care management process*

Phase 1	*Phase 2*	*Phase 3*	*Phase 4*	*Phase 5*	*Phase 6*	*Phase 7*	*Phase 8*
Publicity	Matching need to type of assessment (and simple response)	Full need assessment	Planning care	Starting plan	Monitoring	Review	Closure

People who cooperate in one or more phases:
Client
Carer

Care manager (who could be any of the following:)
Administrator/secretary
Social worker
Nurse
Therapist
Doctor
Care assistant, etc.

Source: SSI/SOSWSG (1991b) and Øvretveit (1992a)

Phase 1 starts the process by informing the public and referrers about what services are available, how to get them, and what amount and quality of help to expect (SSI/SOSWSG 1991b). Phase 2 is an initial assessment of a person in need to decide what type of assessment to carry out. Sometimes the person does not need a further assessment because his needs are simple and can be met by the person doing the initial assessment.

The third phase is a full needs assessment, involving the client and informal carers, and any other professionals or service-givers who could contribute to understanding the client's and carer's needs. Not all clients require a full needs assessment.

The fourth phase is concerned with planning ways to meet the person's needs and recording this in a care plan. It involves clarifying what services are available and the policies and priorities of these services concerning those they serve. A care plan will recognize that some of the person's needs cannot be met, and will note this. It involves agreeing who will give care or treatment and exactly what they will do.

Phase 5 is making sure that those contributing to the plan make a start, and that their efforts are combined in the best way. Sometimes phase 5 involves negotiating services from people who did not take part in the care planning, as well as getting resources, but this is usually done in the planning phase.

The sixth phase is monitoring and adjusting care or treatment. The seventh phase is formally reviewing what was done by judging if the original needs are met, reassessing needs, and deciding whether to finish or whether to replan further care or treatment. The process may start again with full needs assessment and then phase 4, or may move to a final closure phase.

The care manager role

A client should have a care manager for each phase of the process. In some services the care manager just organizes other people in each phase, in others she also provides care or treatment. The care manager accesses and coordinates people taking part in each phase, although she might only coordinate people for one phase: there can be different care managers for different phases, or the same care manager for most phases – this is better for continuity. A practitioner may be employed as a care manager and do nothing else. Alternatively, a practitioner may be a care manager for some clients, and provide profession-specific services for others (as in the case of some community nurses). Care managers can be in specialist care manager teams, or in a multidisciplinary team. Appendix 1 describes models of care management in more detail.

CLIENT TEAMS

The first category of teams we consider is the 'client team'. A client team is all those serving one client at one time. Care managers form a client team for each of their clients. Their client team may change in membership over time – specialists who contribute to the assessment might not be involved later on. This often-changing group of people 'surrounding' the client (Figure 4.1) is called a team because each member contributes to the common purpose of helping the client, and they relate to each other in doing so.

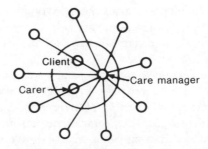

Figure 4.1 The care manager's provider team

We consider client teams as the first category of team to emphasize that community care does not have to be provided through permanent multidisciplinary teams, although it is often best done in that way. Some clients can coordinate their own care.

The particular 'client team' which we focus on here is the 'care manager's provider group'. A difference between this group and other teams is that the principle working relationships are between the care manager and each person in the group. The relationships are more specific and instrumental than in other teams – they are concerned with one client, and are governed by a combined care plan, which details exactly what each person is to do. Sometimes the relationships are defined in a contract, as when a care manager purchases a service. In addition, the group meets infrequently, if at all, and is more changeable than other teams – most members will belong to many other 'client teams'.

The care manager coordinates the group through specific statements in the plan or service agreement, rather than by members relating to each other. In other types of team, each person relates more to others in the team, and they also have a relationship with a stable entity called 'the team', to which they have obligations and from which they gain rights. In contrast, members of a 'client team' have no loyalty to the team – they are 'contributors' not 'members'.

The most extreme form of this type of team is the 'care manager's contracted provider group', because the relationships are closely specified through contracts and care plan. This group are all those contracted by the care manager to serve the client. It is a smaller group than the whole 'client team' because some members of the 'client team' are not contracted by the care manager, or do not have a service agreement with the manager. For example, a carer is often part of a client team and, although her relationship to the care manager is governed by the care plan, the carer does not have a contract with the care manager.

In this type of team the market mode of organization predominates, with relationships through contract. In some client team aspects of the association mode of organization may be present, if there are no contracts and a vague care plan. These two characteristics – the principle relationships are between members and the care manager and are specified, and the specific and instrumental nature of the relationship – mean that working in a client team is different to working in other types of team, especially for the care manager. Before looking at the other two categories of team – networks and formal teams – we note some of the different types of care management.

Models of care management

Care management was originally developed in the UK to provide elderly people with services in their own home instead of in a residential home. Central to the success of early schemes was that the care manager had a budget, which could be used flexibly to buy items from many sources to help support the person at home, for example, special aids, pay for volunteer's transport, and pay for a neighbour's help. Because the care manager could get others to respond flexibly to a client's needs, it was worth doing a detailed assessment to decide what type of help was most appropriate. Practitioners lose interest in recording service shortfalls when planners and managers do not use the information, or if services only materialize years later, if at all.

Current care management policies and schemes retain this focus on a person's needs and their care plan (Appendix 1). Care managers as purchasers and contractors are not so prominent, and need not be if they are able to get the services the client needs by service agreements and care plan agreements. It could be argued that care management was introduced because community teams failed, but community teams rarely had budgets which they could use flexibly, and had to rely on existing community services. Team case coordinators often found that they did not have sufficient powers to coordinate these services properly, even if they had a care plan.

The term 'care manager' is used to describe many different roles, some with budgets, some without, some as purchasers of blocks of services for many clients, and some as organizers of only part of the care management process (Appendix 1). Different roles and models are described in Beardshaw and Towell (1990), SSI/SOSWSG (1991b), and Øvretveit (1991e).

Care managers as members of permanent teams

A care manager may be part of a care management team, made up only of care managers. Alternatively, they may be part of a multidisciplinary team (network or formal) and provide a care management function within that team for those clients who need care management. Sometimes a member of a multidiscipliary team will act as a care manager for certain clients, as when a community psychiatric nurse has a budget and organizes services for a person with long-term mental health problems. Chapter 6 discusses these roles in more detail. Brown et al. (1992) note, in connection with their review of learning difficulty teams:

> To our way of thinking, the implication that care management should or will replace multidisciplinary teams is misplaced. Rather . . . it seems important to ensure that these two approaches to essentially similar problems should not proceed in isolation from each other.

In teams for organizing care managers, the care manager has relationships with other team members which are different to her relationships with the people she coordinates in her client teams. The people in the client team might not even meet as a group. Of course, in some places the same people may be helping the same type of clients, and may frequently meet together to discuss different clients. Here the same client team serves different clients, and members get to know each other because they meet more frequently than they would do if they were all only serving one client. The group then becomes similar to the stable formal team, with the care manager becoming more like the team leader in these teams.

We saw that clients with more than simple needs should pass through each phase of the care management process. Not all clients will need different professions and services for a full assessment, or for care or treatment. However, we can predict that some people in a community will have special and sometimes complex needs, and will need help from different professions and services. We can arrange for a care manager to bring together these professions and services for each new client. But where there are many clients who often need the same professions and services, it is better to have a permanent group dedicated to serving these clients, rather than have a care manager put together a different group or client team for each and every client. We now turn to the two main categories of permanent team, the network and the formal team.

TYPES OF PERMANENT TEAM

The rest of the chapter describes permanent teams for primary care, or for clients with special needs, such as mental health or learning difficulty teams. These teams differ in three ways: in terms of *integration* (closeness of working between members); *structure* (who is in the team and how it is managed); and *process* 'client pathways' – how a team receives clients and deals with them over time, through phases of the care management process).

The next chapter looks at different team processes and client pathways. This chapter describes differences in structures. Over the longer term, the team structure affects cooperation more than anything else, and is the most critical aspect of team organization for meeting client needs. First we consider the degree of integration in a team, in terms of differing types of cooperation between practitioners. This is a useful way to understand the main differences between types of team.

Degree of team integration: Types of practitioner cooperation

The last chapter showed that people can relate to each other through market and contract relations, through bureaucratic relations, or through network association relations. We will see how each of these modes of organization predominates in different teams. Here we note that there are different types of cooperative relations between practitioners, and that one or more types are necessary during each phase of the care management process. Box 4.2 shows how to clarify different degrees of cooperation between people who contribute to meeting client needs in each phase of the care management process.

Box 4.2 Degrees of cooperation in each phase of the care management process

Phase 1	Phase 2	Phase 3	Phase 4	Phase 5	Phase 6	Phase 7	Phase 8
Publicity	Matching need to type of assessment	Full need assessment	Planning care	Starting plan	Monitoring	Review	Closure

Type of cooperation between contributors in each phase:
No cooperation
Informing
Requesting
Consulting
Persuading
Mutual information exchange
Negotiating
Jointly performing
Seeking permission
Directing

What type of cooperation takes place between team members in each phase?

Degrees of integration

Teams vary in the degree to which team members cooperate with each other, and in terms of the degree of integration of the team or 'closeness of working'. If we concentrate on the structural factors which limit cooperation, rather than personal factors, we can place a particular team at some point on a continuum of degree of structural integration.

At the 'low-integration' end of the continuum is a group of practitioners, each of whom is a member of another service, often a uniprofessional or single-agency team based elsewhere. The group forms because each member serves the same or similar population, and meetings are a convenient way to cross-refer: it is a 'postbox meeting'. Many of these groups are 'profession-managed referral networks'.

More integration is possible if practitioners serve the same population. To the extent that they do not, they have fewer clients and interests in common, less reason to meet and more claims on their time elsewhere. Aligning practitioner's client boundaries therefore makes it more likely that they (and their clients) will benefit from their meeting in a group. Teams show even more integration when managers recognize that their practitioners should meet with others serving the same population, and assign their practitioner's time to the group. At the mid-point of the integration continuum we find that a number of team members are full-time, and often share the same base.

At this point further integration and closer working are limited by not having a formal team policy which defines agreed ways of working for all in the team, and by not having a team leader of some type. Without a policy and leader, team members' managers are able to take them out of the team, or direct them to work in ways which make it difficult to cooperate with others in the team. In addition, team members may choose to work in ways which result in lower cooperation, and there is no agreement or person in the team to correct this.

More closely integrated teams have an agreed policy and a team leader. At this point in the continuum we can talk of a 'formal multidisciplinary team'. The degree of integration then depends on how much cooperation over different issues is defined in the policy, and the authority of the team leader (Chapter 7). This is least where the policy only defines the general aims of the team and little about the specifics of work management, decision-making and referral procedures, and whether the team selects its own chairperson. The most structurally integrated team is where the team leader is the only manager of each member of the team, and where this 'team manager' sets the details of how the multidisciplinary team works.

This continuum also describes the degrees of formality in a multidisciplinary team's structure. The formality of structure is least in the profession network. With agreements, policies and then a team leader, the formality increases.

This is not to suggest that the degree of cooperation between team members depends entirely on formal agreements and on management arrangements. The next section shows that cooperation in networks is improved both by removing different structural barriers and by improving personal relations between team members. Rather, this continuum of integration aims to highlight how structural factors put limits to the cooperation which is possible. The most willing and committed of team members have difficulty surmounting problems of cooperating arising from separate bases, unenthusiastic line managers, and no agreed policies (e.g. see Øvretveit (1990a) and (1991g). The right structural conditions are a necessary, but not a sufficient condition for close teamwork.

We now turn to the details of the second category of teams at the 'loosely integrated' end of the continuum: 'network-association teams'. How do these differ from the other two categories of team?

NETWORK-ASSOCIATION TEAMS

In its pure form the network association (Figure 4.2) is a voluntary and informal grouping of practitioners. At one extreme there is the referral network, where one participant in the network knows some, but not all, of the participants in the network. The purpose of the network is for one member to refer a client to

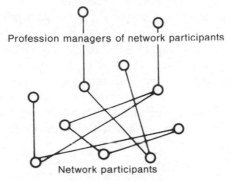

Figure 4.2 The network association team

another. At the other extreme there is a regular meeting of network 'participants' to exchange referrals, discuss cases in common, and plan joint work, such as a talk on prevention or setting up a client self-help group. Some primary health and social care teams are of this type (Øvretveit 1990a).

> *Network association team:* a voluntary association of service providers, relating to cross-refer, or to coordinate work with a client, or for other purposes. There is no agreed and binding common policy, and usually each network 'participant' is part of another team, based in a different place and managed by a profession or line manager.

Network-association teams differ from other types of team in that:

• participation is voluntary and not defined (if the network meets, participants do not have to attend);

- there are implicit customs and understandings, and no rules or detailed policies;
- there is no formal leader;
- relationships between participants are not specified;
- participants' loyalty is usually elsewhere (they are first and foremost a member of another team).

The advantages of a network as a way of coordinating practitioners is that it is flexible – it can expand and contract as necessary, it can change purpose, and it allows participants maximum independence. The disadvantages are that it lacks continuity, can be unreliable, and the implicit trust and reciprocity between participants usually is not sufficient to withstand pressures from outside. The association mode of organization, as described in Chapter 2, predominates in networks. The main mechanism which coordinates participants' actions in the network is their recognition of common interests and aims, and the trust and respect they have for each other.

Networks differ in terms of what people in the network cooperate to do. Some community mental health teams are a meeting of professionals from different services who come together to receive referrals and 'bid' for work. Beyond this, people work separately. Other networks involve frequent cooperation between participants over casework, as for example between doctors and nurses in a primary health care network team. Networks vary in terms of the type and amount of cooperation between participants at each stage of the care management process (see Box 4.2). Some networks develop into the third category of team – the 'formal team'.

FORMAL TEAMS

Formal teams differ from network-association teams in that they have stable membership, agreed and explicit policies and a formal team leader position. Usually the team has a shared base, which clients can come to, and referrals are made to the team rather than to a team member.

> *Formal multidisciplinary community team:* a working group with a defined membership of different professions, governed by an agreed and explicit team policy, which is upheld by a team leader.

The primary mode of organization is bureaucratic: there is a division of roles and tasks, rules and hierarchy. Relationships are specified and there is an explicit decision-making procedure. There are different schools of thought as to how to improve cooperation in such teams: one way might be to strengthen the bureaucratic mode of organization and increase specification; another way might be to strengthen the association mode of organization and improve trust and mutual understanding between current team members. Either approach affects hierarchy, leadership, decision-making and member autonomy, contro-.versial issues to which we return in later chapters. Another approach is to improve cooperation by introducing a market element, and contract some team members to the team.

The advantages of formal teams is that they ensure a continued multidisciplinary service, with a range of skills which should be suited to the needs of a client population. Paradoxically, the stability and specification of such teams can provide a context for non-bureaucratic associative relations and cooperation to grow. However, over-specification can prevent this and constrain flexibility.

Different types of formal team can be distinguished in four ways – in terms of: membership; the type of formal relationships between team members, especially between the team leader and each member; the type of cross-member cooperation; and the type of team policies. Looking at teams in this way, we often see more similarities between teams serving different types of client populations, than between teams serving the same types of client – some mental health teams are more similar in their organization to some teams for people with a learning difficulty than they are to other mental health teams. Teams can sometimes learn more about how to improve cooperation by looking at how teams for other types of clients are organized.

The following describes the most common types of formal team, concentrating on how they differ in terms of type of membership and in terms of the relationship between the team leader and team members. Which is best is the subject of the discussion in the penultimate section of the chapter. The next chapter looks at cooperation and client pathways in these teams in more detail.

Fully managed multidisciplinary team (formal team type 1)

The type of formal team which differs most from the network-association types is the fully managed team, because of its clear hierarchy and task division. These teams display, more than any other formal team, coordination through the bureaucratic mode of organization, and close integration. Apart from their multidisciplinary membership, they are similar to conventional single-disciplinary teams (for example, social work teams, community psychiatric nursing teams).

A fully managed multidisciplinary team (Figure 4.3) is one where:

- one team manager manages all the different professions in the team, and is accountable for each member's performance and has managerial authority in relation to them;
- the team manager decides team policies and procedures for cooperation, and directs team members;

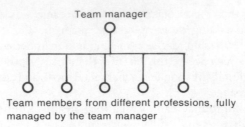

Team manager

Team members from different professions, fully
managed by the team manager

Figure 4.3 The fully managed multidisciplinary team

- a team member and the team manager may have access to a professional adviser, but the adviser has no authority over or accountability for the team member;
- usually all team members are full-time in the team.

An example is provided by certain primary care 'patch' or 'locality' teams in Northern Ireland (Appendix 3 and Øvretveit (1991a)). Here the 'patch' team manager is a general manager, who directly manages social workers, district nurses, health visitors, and occupational therapists in the team. The team provides primary care services to a similar population to those registered with GP practices in the area. Some mental health and learning difficulty multidisciplinary teams are made up of social workers and community nurses who are members of unidisciplinary teams, managed by line managers. These teams are combinations of two single-profession teams.

Fully managed multidisciplinary teams are appropriate where a client population can benefit from a team with a stable membership, and one service manager with accountability for performance and clear authority. Their success depends on the team manager's ability to understand and use different professions' skills to the best effect, and to be sensitive to and value professional differences.

This type of team is not possible in its pure form where a team requires practitioners who have case or practice autonomy, as they cannot be fully managed in the sense described above (Øvretveit 1985); see also Chapter 6 below). Neither are such teams possible where practitioners employed by other agencies are needed – their employers will not be able to agree to their being fully managed by another agency's team manager: the practitioner is accountable to his employing agency through his own profession or line manager. We describe below alternative types of team where some members are managed, and others are 'coordinated' or 'contracted' by a team leader. To describe these teams we first need to consider types of team leader other than a team manager, and types of team membership.

Team leader positions

Most formal multidisciplinary teams have a team leader, not a team manager. The team leader may manage some members of the team, but not all. They have defined responsibilities and relationships to members, even though their accountability and authority may be unclear in some areas.

There are two types of team leader other than a team manager. The first type of team leader is responsible for some aspects of a team member's management (so-called 'joint management'). This type is often called a 'team coordinator'. They have a formal agreement with other team member managers about who is responsible for which aspects of team member management. The second type of team leader coordinates team members through a contract or service agreement, rather than through an ongoing accountability and authority relationship. Sometimes they have a budget to buy in practitioners' help full-time or part-time, and can choose which profession to contract. Chapter 7 considers team leadership in detail.

Apart from type of leadership, the main difference between formal teams is who is a member and what type of membership positions there are in the team.

Team membership

The right number and mix of different professions and other staff in a team is essential for matching client needs to resources over the longer term. Formal teams differ in terms of which professions and staff work in the team, and in terms of the different categories of membership. Membership may be part- or full-time, core or associate, or of other types, such as 'honorary membership', 'link person' (for example, to an in-patient ward), or 'volunteer'.

The most common membership distinction is between 'core' and 'associate' (or 'extended team'), usually meaning full-time in the team or part-time. We follow this usage, but it is important to recognize that the terms 'core' and 'associate' can also refer to one or more of the type of membership listed in Box 4.3.

Box 4.3 Core and associate membership: different meanings

'Core' can mean:	'Associate' can mean:
Full-time in team	Part-time in team
All who are governed by the team policy	Those not governed by the team policy
All those managed by the team leader	Those with managers outside the team
Formal voting rights	No voting rights on team decisions

Type of formal multidisciplinary team

We now summarize other types of formal team apart from the fully managed team (type 1). Most teams involve a mixture of types of membership, and different formal relationships between the team leader and different members. Think of a team you know – which of the following type of teams closest describes the mix in the team?

The managed-core and coordinated-associate team (formal team type 2)
Probably the most common is the 'managed-core and coordinated-associate team' (Figure 4.4). Many mental health and learning difficulty teams are of this type, as well as some patch-managed primary health care teams. The team leader manages core full-time members, and coordinates part-time associates, according to an agreement with each associate's manager.

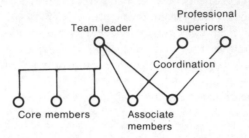

Figure 4.4 The managed-core and coordinated-associate team

The managed-core and contracted-associate team (formal team type 3)
The third type, which is becoming more common, is the 'managed-core and contracted-associate team' (Figure 4.5). Associates are contracted to work in the team part-time, or even full-time in some teams. The team leader manages core members, and monitors associates under contract. They may have authority to change or make service contracts for associates. Sometimes type 2 teams change to this type by changing the way they coordinate associates from a management agreement to a contract.

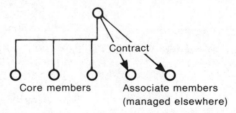

Figure 4.5 The managed-core and contracted-associate team

The managed- and coordinated-core, and contracted-associate team
(formal team type 4)
A fourth type is a more complex mix of 'managed- and coordinated-core and contracted-associate' (Figure 4.6). Some mental health teams are of this type: community psychiatric nurses are managed by the team leader. The leader coordinates the other core members such as social workers, who have a social

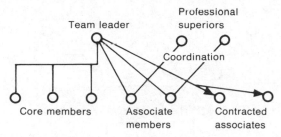

Figure 4.6 The managed- and coordinated-core and contracted-associate team

services manager. The leader also manages contracts for the therapist associates in the team.

The leader-coordinated team (formal team type 5)
The fifth type, which is less common, is the 'leader-coordinated team' (Figure 4.7), such as some drugs and alcohol teams of therapists and workers from different agencies. The team coordinator coordinates both core and associate members, under agreements with their managers and employers.

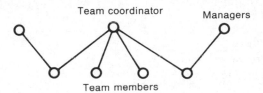

Figure 4.7 The leader-coordinated team

The leader-contracted team (formal team type 6)
If many team members work in the team under contract to a team leader the character of the team changes, and it becomes closer to the sixth type of formal team: the 'leader-contracted team' (Figure 4.8). In this type of team the market mode of organization predominates and the leader coordinates team 'contributor-members' through a contractual relationship. The way team contributor-members relate to each other (lateral team relations) is affected, if not governed, by their contractual relation with the team leader.

This type of team is classified here as a formal team because the team is set up to provide services to many clients, and contributor-members are usually semi-permanent. They may be contracted part- or full-time. The relationship of service contract between the team leader and contributor-member is similar to a bureaucratic coordination agreement, or to a management relationship which would exist with an employment contract. However, a contract for service

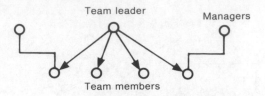

Figure 4.8 The leader-contracted team

makes such teams different to other formal teams, not least because the contributor-member's main loyalty is to his manager and employer elsewhere, or to his own business if he is self-employed.

Note that another type of contracted-contributor team is the team of people contracted to care for one client by a care manager. We considered this earlier as one type of 'client team'.

Box 4.4 Most teams have different types of member with different formal relations to the team leader

Team leader's
relationship to a team
member

	Core (full-time)	Associate (part-time)
Full-manager		
Formal coordinator (part-management)		
Contractor		

Type of team membership

Formal teams are often a complex mix of different types of membership, with different formal relationships between the team leader and different members (see Box 4.4). The more complex this mix, the more difficult it is to have a common simple and understandable team policy and clear arrangements for coordinating the care of each client. Many primary care teams are complex structures with a mix of members and relationships, and involve all three modes of organization (Box 4.5).

Box 4.5 Examples of 'complex teams'

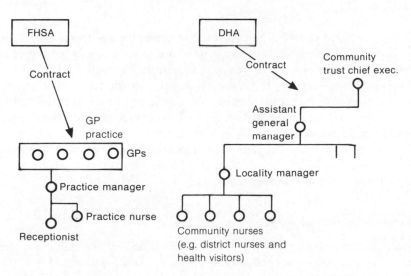

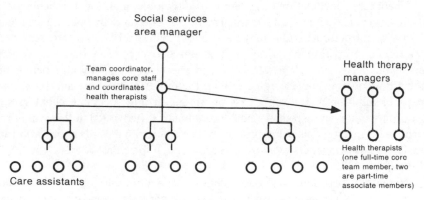

The primary health care team combines GP practice staff and community nurses.

(It may also include therapists, and if it is a fund-holding practice it will contract community nurses from the Trust)

Three 'zone teams' for sub-areas of team catchment

The Rhondda learning difficulties team

Source: Macdonald (1990)

IMPROVING COOPERATION THROUGH TEAM DESIGN: CHOOSING OR CHANGING THE TYPE OF TEAM

A number of problems can be traced to the wrong type of team being in place for the need of a population or to a type of team which cannot work given the way agencies are organized. Teams are for matching skills and resources to clients needs, and the way this is done is through coordination. At the strategic level this requires that team membership – skills and time – is matched to the need of the target client population. At the level of the individual client it means assessing and coordinating skills for each part of the care management process. This is done by forming the right type of team and by developing teamwork in ways discussed in the next chapters. Here we consider which type is appropriate in which circumstances.

Network or formal team?

Some managers argue that the costs of setting up and maintaining a formal multidisciplinary team are not justified. Certainly there is a dearth of research on the cost-effectiveness of formal teams, and too ready an assumption that formal teams are always the best way to service client needs. Where profession-managed services and agencies collaborate closely at each level, and an established network exists and works, a formal team may not be necessary to get effective matching and coordination.

Client care coordination can be improved by looking at how it is achieved at each stage of a typical care management episode, and by making changes. Removing structural barriers may be the most cost-effective improvement: each manager of practitioners in a network can agree to align his or her practitioners' area boundaries and clients to others in the network. They can define the practitioners' time allocation for serving the target population, and base them part- or full-time at the same base as others serving the same client group. Coordination in some primary health care teams is improved in this way – the profession-managed network remains but coordination and communication are easier because managers work together to remove structural barriers (Øvretveit 1990a).

Networks also improve coordination by team-building events, which strengthen understanding, trust and respect between network participants. However, there are limits to the degree of cooperation that can be achieved without introducing elements of the formal team, such as agreed explicit policies (for example, referral protocols) or a chairperson. Managers need to understand what type of informal cooperation happens and strengthen it, rather than weakening it with insensitively applied bureaucratic elements, such as a team manager when a team coordinator is appropriate.

Sometimes managers have to build a service from nothing, and the choice is between setting up separate profession-managed services which network and a care management system, or a formal multidisciplinary team and care management arrangements. We considered above the advantages and disadvantages of networks and formal teams above. Which type of formal team is most appropriate? Each has its advantages and disadvantages. If an entirely new service is to be created then the main consideration is how different agencies are organized.

Often services already exist, and the question is whether practitioner coordination would be improved by changing the structure of the team to another type, and if so whether it is worth the cost of doing so. The answer depends on the coordination problems which exist and how current services are organized. We consider improvements to formal teams in the next chapters.

All this tends to suggest that the choice is between network and types of formal team. What about the first category – client teams? Here one design issue is whether to establish a care manager role responsible for all or some of the stages of care management for a client group. If so, the second design issue is whether to create a separate specialist team of care managers, or care manager positions in multidisciplinary teams, or create a care manager role which members of a network or team can assume for some of their clients. Much depends on the definition and role of 'care manager' which one or more agencies develop (Appendix 1).

SUMMARY AND CONCLUSION

Meeting client needs in the community means arranging each of the eight phases of the care management process. It depends on getting the right people to contribute to assessment, and using a care plan to coordinating providers. Teams are small groups of people who work together to meet the needs of client and carer. Teams vary mainly in terms of how people in the group relate to each other (summarized in Box 4.7).

A 'client team' is all the people helping the client during one phase of the care management process. A client may have a different 'client team' for different phases of the process, and a different care manager for each phase, but this is bad for continuity. One type of 'client team' is the 'care manager's provider team'. Some care managers coordinate services to the client with service contracts with providers, while others rely on a care plan agreement (Box 4.6).

A 'network team' is a group of people who independently provide a service to a community, but associate voluntarily to cross-refer, or for other purposes. Networks are flexible, and involve different types of cooperation between network members which are not formally specified.

A 'formal team' is a permanent group with a collective responsibility for serving a client population. The group is more integrated than a network team, and has a team leader and a team policy governing members of the team. There are six types of formal team, ranging from the most integrated, where each member is managed by the team manager, to the coordinated team. Most teams are a mixture of different types.

Understanding the different types of team is important for deciding which type is best for clients in a community, and for improving cooperation in order better to meet client's needs. The next chapter looks at formal team organization in more detail.

Box 4.6 The care management process: key points

- Care management is a process for matching a client's needs to resources.
- There are different phases in the care management process.
- Teams are ways of organizing some or all phases of the process, usually for many clients.
- A 'client team' is a way of organizing the care of one client, for all or some phases.
- A care manager is a person who organizes one or many phases of the care management process for one client.
- A care manager may organize some services through a purchasing contract.

The 'care management client team' works differently to a network team or a formal team. Coordination is through agreement and specification in a care plan, and sometimes through a contract for service. Each contributor has little loyalty to the 'client team' and the care manager relies on the care plan agreement to ensure coordination.

Box 4.7 Summary of the three categories of team and variations

1. Client's team and care manager's provider team

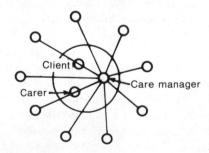

2. Network association teams

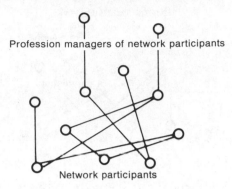

Profession managers of network participants

Network participants

3. Formal teams
Fully-managed multidisciplinary team (formal team type 1)

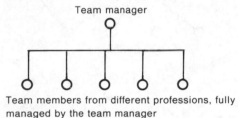

Team manager

Team members from different professions, fully managed by the team manager

The managed-core and coordinated-associate team (formal team type 2)

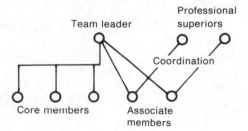

Professional superiors

Team leader

Coordination

Core members

Associate members

The managed-core and contracted-associate team (formal team type 3)

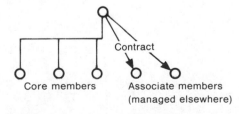

Contract

Core members   Associate members
(managed elsewhere)

The managed- and coordinated-core, and contracted-associate team (formal team type 4)

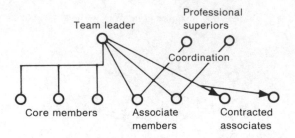

The leader-coordinated team (formal team type 5)

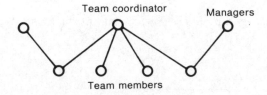

The leader-contracted-team (formal team type 6)

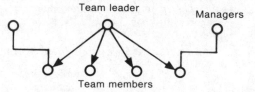

Chapter 5
CLIENT PATHWAYS AND TEAM RESOURCE MANAGEMENT

INTRODUCTION

The last chapter described teams with different membership and different amounts of interprofessional working. This chapter considers differences in 'process': how one team receives and responds to clients over time in a different way from another team. To help understand how a team receives and 'processes' referrals, the chapter shows how to map a 'client pathway' over time and 'through' a team.

I use the term 'client pathways' because it conveys an image of a client following a route laid out by the team. A team may have different 'pathways' for different clients, which may not be planned or 'mapped' in an operational policy, but are 'well-trodden' all the same. Teams have different 'gateways' for stopping some people from travelling further down the pathway and for conserving resources. Often the 'exit gateways' are built and operated by individual team members.

Team members will see that their team uses one or more of the five different client pathways described below. We see that some pathways are better than others for responding quickly to a client's needs, for the choices they give to clients and for 'matching' their needs to skills inside and outside of the team. Teams use this mapping method to improve the quality of their service because it shows where delays and mistakes happen.

Many teams have high workloads and do not manage their time effectively as a collective. Where the team is a network of separate services this is not a problem – workload is not a team issue but an issue for each separate service. For some teams with a 'collective service responsibility' for serving a client population, managing workload is a problem – they have not developed new ways to influence members' workload decisions to replace the old profession system. The result is that some clients with pressing needs do not get a service. The second half of the chapter is devoted to explaining the difference between these 'collective service teams' and coordinated professional services. It uses the pathway framework to show how such teams can better manage their resources. It shows how teams can influence team members' most important resource management decisions, and implement team priorities, yet also retain the autonomy which different members need. The chapter closes by describing six practical steps which such teams have used to formulate team priorities.

CLIENT PATHWAY FRAMEWORK

Chapter 3 proposed that, to meet client needs, managers have to organize services to carry out each of the phases of the care management process.

Phase 1	Phase 2	Phase 3	Phase 4	Phase 5	Phase 6	Phase 7	Phase 8
Publicity	Matching need to type of assessment	Full need assessment	Planning care	Starting plan	Monitoring	Review	Closure

We also saw that, for clients with special or complex needs, there are advantages to forming a specialist team which brings together the professions and services which such clients frequently need. A team makes it easier for the client to get help from different professions more quickly, and to arrange care management in each phase. In this chapter we build on this model to show a way of mapping a client's pathway through such a team (Box 5.1).

Box 5.1 Client pathways mapping framework for teams

Stage 1	Stage 2	Stage 3	Stage 4	Stage 5	Stage 6	Stage 7	Stage 8	Stage 9	Stage 10
Referral sources	Reception	Acceptance for assessment	Allocation for assessment	Assessment	Acceptance for longer-term care	Allocation for longer-term care	Intervention and/or monitoring	Review	Closure

Source: Øvretveit 1986b and 1991a

The purpose of this framework is to help team members understand how they respond to client needs and how they make decisions. This is why this framework is different to the care process model, but the two are closely related. The framework highlights decision points in the client's 'journey' which are critical for matching the team's resources to client needs. The later parts of the chapter look at resource allocation in more detail. First we describe each stage, and then use the model to show five different types of client pathway. Think about how a team which you know handles each stage, what a client experiences at each stage and whether the team has all the stages.

The first stage describes where the team takes referrals from. Does the team which you know take clients without a formal referral – can they walk in or telephone to ask for information or for help?

The second stage, 'reception', is concerned with how a referral is received – over the telephone, by letter or in person. It also describes who in the team receives clients, and what sort of help that person can give immediately – the team's 'first response'. This response may be taking down the details of the referral, giving information and advice, making an immediate visit for assessment, crisis intervention, or other responses. Some teams put a high proportion of their resources (in terms of staff time) into this stage in comparison to later stages.

The third stage concerns how decisions are made about whether to accept assessment, and what type and level of assessment is indicated from the 'reception' and other information. In a team you know, is it clear whether a team member or the team makes these decisions? This stage is closely related to the fourth stage, allocation for assessment', where the available information is used to match the client's needs to the person in the team who has the skills to carry out, or organize, the level of assessment which is called for. This is the ideal, but in practice 'allocation' is often simply a matter of whoever volunteers or who has space in his or her caseload. We will see later what prevents the best 'matching' for assessment in some teams.

The assessment (stage 5) may be a profession-specific assessment, done by one or more team members, either for the team or for a case manager outside the team. Alternatively, the assessment may be a 'team assessment', where one person follows a team assessment method. Asssessment may also involve care planning, or it may be a needs assessment only for the purposes of recommending to the team whether further team involvement is needed, and that someone else should do a care plan.

In stage 6 'acceptance for longer-term work', the person who did the assessment presents her recommendations to the team. She gives any details of the assessment which the team needs to decide whether the team should carry out more work for the client. Some teams receive an 'assessor's report', sometimes including a care plan which may outline services that the team (and others) should provide. These arrangements are changing as services separate assessment and provision. The choices are whether to accept for long-term work, and, if so whether to allocate immediately or put on a waiting list, or whether to refer on, or whether to move to 'closure' (stage 10).

This stage is closely related to the seventh stage of 'allocation for long-term work'. Now that the team has decided that it will carry out more work, it makes a decision from the assessment, and from a care plan if there is one, about who will do the work, or organize the work as a care manager. Again the ideal is the best match between the client's now fully assessed needs and the skills and resources of the team. This stage sometimes includes care planning.

An eighth stage of 'intervention' or 'monitoring' follows, before the ninth stage of review. Here the team member reviews his or her work with the client and others. Teams and practitioners have many different ways of doing reviews, which we consider later. Sometimes the team decides at this stage of review whether to move to the final tenth stage of 'closure'. We look at all of these stages in more detail below.

Note that some teams do not organize certain stages – these are dealt with by team members separately from the team. For example, the 'review' and 'closure' stages may be handled by each member without reference to the team or to a team policy. Note also that some teams combine stages. For example, in a team meeting for new referrals the team handles reception, acceptance and allocation for assessment all together. It may not be clear whether or how the team influences one member's decision to accept a case.

Note that I referred to 'the team' making key decisions, which does not always happen, if at all, and which assumes that the team has reached a certain level of integration. This was intentional, and aimed to highlight the differences between teams.

Teams, and team members use this framework for a number of purposes. The first is to understand better the difference between an integrated team and a looser network team. More integrated teams have team policies which describe these stages and influence the decisions which each team member makes. Network teams have little, if any, influence over network participants' decisions at any stage – there are no 'team decisions'. The second purpose is to understand how the team or a team member responds to one client's needs, and to work out how to organize a better response. By looking at decision-making for one client in each stage – especially the assessment and review stages – we can see what kind of multidisciplinary perspective, if any, is brought to bear on the client's problem.

The third purpose of the framework is to understand how a team is responding to the needs of the client population it serves. This assumes that a team has a collective responsibility for serving a client population, which is not always clear. The framework highlights stages and decisions which are critical for managing team resources in relation to client population needs. We consider how teams can better manage their workload and implement priorities later in the chapter. First, we look at typical pathways in different teams. This adds to the description of types of team in the last chapter by showing differences in process over time.

CLIENT PATHWAYS IN DIFFERENT TEAMS

Different teams 'handle' clients in different ways. The following describes five of the most common ways in which teams receive referrals and process work over time. It uses the client pathway framework to draw attention to differences between teams and to highlight issues that teams might consider for improving their service. Usually a team has one main pathway for most clients, but sometimes it will have two or more pathways for clients with different needs. The first type is the pathway in most 'network' teams. The fourth type shows a pathway in a closely integrated team where the team influences many team member's casework decisions.

Type 1: Allocation or 'postbox' teams

In this type of team (illustrated schematically in Figure 5.1) there are two pathways for clients to get to the team. In one the client is referred to a team secretary or a team leader, if the team has either, who then brings the referral to a team meeting. In the other the team member takes the referral and brings it to the team meeting, if he does not decide to take the case himself. At the team meeting, team members take referrals or are allocated them by a team leader. Then each team member goes his separate ways with 'his' client – he handles other stages without reference back to the team or to a team policy.

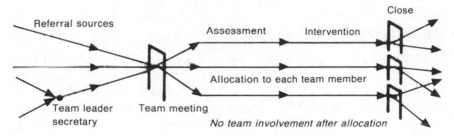

Figure 5.1 The allocation or 'postbox' team

Often the 'team' is a collection of individuals from other services who come to a meeting to 'bid' for clients whom they think they can help. The team meeting provides a focal point for referrals, and a convenient 'postbox' for otherwise separate professional services. Many network teams operate like this. In some teams, only the associate members of the team operate in this way. There is one 'gate' to the team, or rather to team members, and it is each member's decision as to whether to 'open' their 'gate' to the client.

Type 2: Reception-allocation teams

This pathway (Figure 5.2) is the same as the one for allocation teams, but teams using this pathway have a reception stage where the team organizes an initial response for all clients. 'Reception' always involves taking referral details, but it can involve giving advice or a 'duty system'. Teams with this pathway are able to get better information for later matching a client's needs to the most suitable team member in 'allocation'. They are able to give a faster response to clients, and sometimes meet simple client or carer needs for information or support. They do so at the expense of their time being used for later in-depth individual client work after allocation. Network teams can give a better service and

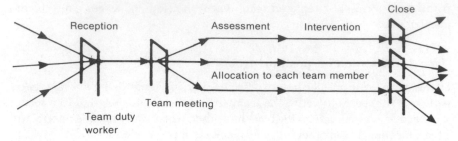

Figure 5.2 The reception-allocation team

improve cooperation by organizing a duty or rota system for a reception stage and an immediate response. These are 'two-gate' pathway teams: the first 'gate' is to the reception response, often locked after 5 pm.

Type 3: Reception-assessment-allocation teams

In addition to a reception stage, these teams have a pathway with two allocation stages, one for assessment (stages 3 and 4) and one for longer-term work (stages 6 and 7), as shown in Figure 5.3. Clients are not allocated to different members, never to be 'seen' by the team again, as they are in the first two types – they are allocated first for an assessment which is more detailed to that provided by 'reception'. This assessment is then used to decide whether to allocate for longer-term work, and who should do this work. It is not assumed that the person doing the assessment will do longer-term work, if any is called for, although for continuity it is better that it is the same person.

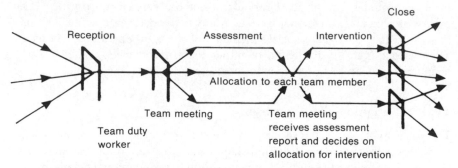

Figure 5.3 The reception-assessment-allocation team

The assessment is to understand more about the client's needs in order to decide what help to give, and to match the help available to the client's needs. By separating the assessment from the longer-term work, the person assessing is less likely to be influenced by what is provided and available, and more likely to concentrate on understanding the client's needs. The longer-term work usually starts with care planning. The team can also decide the level of assessment to offer (Chapter 2).

The team decision about allocation for longer-term work links to client's needs to team resources. Teams using this pathway are able to achieve a better match at allocation because they have better information about the client's needs. They also have more control over team resources – how team members use their time. These are three-gate teams – there is a gate to assessment, as well as one to reception and one to allocation for longer-term work. This third gate means that the team can serve more clients by providing an assessment-only service for some.

Type 4: Reception-assessment-allocation-review teams

Teams with this pathway (Figure 5.4) have a review stage (stage 9), in addition to the stages of the type 3 pathway team. The team sets a review date for a client when it allocates a client to a team member for longer-term work. At this date the team member presents a report to the team, detailing progress in carrying out the care plan and the client's current needs, and making recommendations to the team about any further work. Teams which are careful about managing their resources assume that team members have to justify 'keeping a case open' to the team – the team may be struggling to allocate other clients with greater needs. Some type 4 teams decide closure (stage 10).

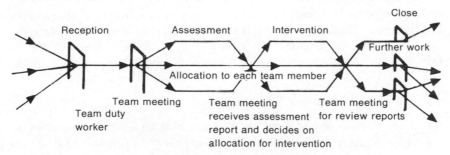

Figure 5.4 The reception-assessment-allocation-review team

This fourth gate to further team work after reviews makes it possible for the team to monitor client care, and to increase control over its resources. It also calls for closer team integration which requires a more bureaucratic structure, and reduces team members' autonomy.

Type 5: Parallel-pathway teams

In these teams there are two possible pathways. The first 'team pathway' is one of any of the four types described above (Figure 5.5 shows type 5). The second

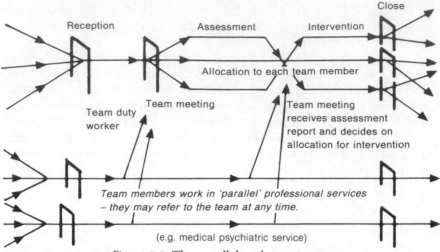

Figure 5.5 The parallel-pathway team

pathway is a member- or profession-specific pathway. Clients may follow this second pathway, and then be referred by the team member at any point to the team. Clients may either enter the team pathway (referral to the team) or the profession pathway (referral to the professional service), and may switch between each path at any point on their 'journey'.

Mental heath services often have parallel pathways for medical psychiatric service and for team service. The more pathways there are, the more flexibility and choice for clients – but also the less control the team has over its resources and the more complex the service becomes, sometimes leading to fragmentation. Client care coordination may suffer as a result. The extreme is a pathway for each profession, as in some network teams, or where there is no team at all.

The use of client pathway mapping

These descriptions of five types of pathways give an illustration of different ways of organizing work in teams. They help teams to think about the service which the team gives and how the team works as a group. These different pathways further highlight the differences between network teams and more integrated formal teams. They clarify to what extent a team is a collection of people, each making their own decisions, and to what extent a team is an integrated group, where each person's decisions are governed by collective policies and decisions.

Many teams are somewhere between these two extremes. We can see exactly where a team is, and understand exactly how much 'multidisciplinary working' goes on in a team, by looking at how decisions are made in each stage. Taking, for example, the 'closure' stage, does a team member make this decision without reference to a team meeting, or to a team policy? How does a team influence this decision, if at all? If the team has a policy about closure, how detailed is it? Is the policy related to a collective understanding of the needs of the client population? The answers to these questions also tell us the balance between member autonomy and team control. They tell us how a team manages its resources and workload, if at all. They tell us whether the team has collective priorities which it follows, and whether these are linked to client needs.

It is to issues of workload management that we now turn, using the client pathway model to look in more detail at decision-making in each stage, and to show ways of improving team service to each client, and to a client population. First, we consider whether members of a team share a responsibility as a collective to serve the needs of a client population, or whether they each provide separate services, with the team merely coordinating the care of individual clients.

TEAMS FOR CLIENT COORDINATION OR COLLECTIVE SERVICE

Most teams are formed to make it easier to coordinate care or treatment for clients. Coordination is often easier and more cost-effective if professions and services that care for or treat clients with similar needs are brought together in a team. Many network teams are of this type. In such teams the issues are who is care manager, what decisions do they make and what decisions do the people they coordinate make? The care manager makes resource management decisions about how much of which type of services the client gets – they relate the client's needs to the resources available. They form a 'client team'. (We saw in Chapter 2 how a care manager makes these links between needs and resources using priorities and resource-allocation rules).

Some teams are also formed to provide a combined service to meet the needs of a client group in a locality. This purpose is different from the first. In the first, people who often work together with similar types of client meet regularly to make it easier to coordinate their casework with each client. In the second people share a 'collective responsibility' for meeting the most pressing needs of that client group.

What does this 'collective responsibility' mean? Surely all teams share a collective responsibility for serving a client group? A team just for coordinating care does not worry about how clients get to the team, or whether it is using its resources to the best effect to meet the most pressing needs of a particular client group. The following discusses collective service responsibility in more detail because it is of such importance to team organization, yet is often not clarified by management or understood by team members. The chapter then shows how collective service responsibility teams can influence team members' decisions at each stage of the client pathway in order better to manage the team's resources.

Collective responsibility for a service to a population

Many network teams, with type 1 pathways, are separate profession-managed services. Practitioners are responsible for making sure that their skills and time are available to and used for clients who can benefit most. It is not their job to serve clients who have needs which are better served by others when there are already clients waiting for their own skills and time. It is the managers' job to get the right skills and time to the area by coordinating with other managers.

This pure profession focus is not open to practitioners in more integrated formal multidisciplinary teams. The practitioner's service is part of the team's service, and practitioners share with others in the team a collective responsibility for meeting the most pressing needs of the client population. Of course, this is more difficult to do if managers set up the team badly: there may be the wrong skill mix in the team for the client population, or other clients coming to the team in desperation because there is no service for their needs in the area. But such teams cannot turn away clients which the team was set up to serve because practitioners feel that their skills are better used for other purposes.

Although some practitioners in such teams may be part-time, in their 'team time' they have a collective responsibility in addition to their profession-specific responsibilities. In practice, this means that all team members contribute to discussions about how they as a collective respond to client needs. Being a member of this type of team means that your day-to-day decisions are influenced by the team, because this is how teams make sure that team resources are used to best effect. If the influence results in your skills not being used then something is wrong – but it is a team issue.

As we saw in the last chapter, most teams are mixtures, and it is not always clear whether some or all members share a collective responsibility, even if they feel that they do. In the fully managed multidisciplinary team things are clear: the team manager is accountable for using the team resource to the best effect. To do this they have the authority not just to influence, but to override members' decisions about how they use their time. In these teams members do not have a collective responsibility in a formal sense – their manager is accountable, but she will foster a feeling of collective responsibility.

In other types of formal team, where members have enjoyed a high degree of autonomy in the past, they are understandably reluctant to give up valued or familiar work in order to take on work because it is a team priority, especially if others in the team are not doing so. Achieving the right balance between team control over resources and member autonomy is an issue we touch on below and deal with more fully in the next chapter.

It is the job of managers and team leaders to make this collective responsibility clear, if that is what is intended for the team. Often it is only by recognizing that the team is not serving the clients most in need that managers confront this issue. Each profession or employment group is so tied up meeting its specific responsibilities that no one has time left to serve certain clients. The problem is less severe in teams that have the right mix and amount of professions for the needs of the community – each profession following their own priorities results in a reasonable match to needs. But needs and membership change, and needs have to be matched to resources week to week, as well as over the longer term.

Managers must clarify whether a team is for client coordination only, or for collective service (what I called elsewhere 'accountable service-provision teams' (Øvretveit 1986b), or for both. Managers have to agree changes to the responsibilities of their staff and to staff management if their staff are to contribute properly to a collective service-provision team. If managers do not, then the agency and professional responsibilities will always come before the team's collective responsibility to serve a population.

For example, social workers employed by a social services department are paid to carry out department policies and priorities. They may be assigned to serve a client group in a locality, but they provide a social work service according to these policies and priorities. If their manager does not modify their responsibilities to make it possible to take part in providing a collective service, then it is likely that their departmental responsibilities will take up so much of their time that they cannot take on clients that are a team priority, or even contribute to multidisciplinary case discussions.

In summary, if a multidisciplinary team is formed as an alternative to separate profession-managed services, and if managers intend the team members to manage their resources collectively to serve the needs of the population, then they must make this clear. Further, teams must then understand how members' decisions commit what is a collective resource, and must be able to influence these decisions. These collective service teams must manage their resources in relation to the needs of the population they serve. How they do this is the subject of the rest of the chapter. First, some questions to illustrate in practice what it means for a team to manage its resources.

Work management in collective service teams

There are two sets of work-management issues that collective service teams have to consider. The first is how best to use their collective resources to meet the most pressing needs of the population they serve. The second is how to get the quickest and best match between one client's needs and skills inside and outside the team. These decisions should follow from the purpose and priorities of the team – a subject we look at in the final section.

The first set of team decisions are about matching the collective team time and skills to the needs of the client population. Earlier chapters showed that this involves getting the right amount of the right skills in the team: team membership and structure. Here we look at how time and skills are 'spread along' the client pathway: at who spends how much time working in different parts of the client pathway.

Is everybody's time spent working with a few clients in the intervention stage (stage 8)? Is the work intense and in-depth, but limited in terms of time, with frequent reviews and closures (stage 10)? Or is it less intense monitoring work with 'longer-term' clients, such as those with learning difficulties or mental health problems? In some teams it is appropriate that the team time resource is distributed towards the end of the pathway because serving 'continuing care' clients is their purpose. But are there people with more pressing needs waiting, or not even known to the team?

At the other extreme, is most time spent on the first parts of the client pathway, serving many clients? Putting resources into crisis intervention and prevention and health promotion may be the most effective use of resources for client needs. A high proportion of team time on assessments (stage 5) may be appropriate for the purpose of the team. But teams setting up 'duty' systems, information services, or 'walk-in' direct access (stage 2) find that more and more teams time is drawn into this work, as referrers and others learn how to get a fast response, and play on the ambiguity of 'urgent' or 'emergency'. It can be very difficult for a community psychiatric nurse on duty not to rush out to a GP who says 'it's important', leaving other team members to pick up the 'duty' work. When this happens often, teams tend to increase time for the 'front end', at the expense of the more in-depth and sometimes more effective work.

In short, is the team's 'spread' right? Whether it is depends on the needs of the client population and the purposes and priorities of the team – the subject of the next section. Is the distribution of team time at each stage just a matter of chance, or by intention? Is it simply how each team member chooses to work, or is it something the team keeps under review? These questions take us to how the team influences how member's spend their team time. They take us to how to ensure that priority clients are recognized as such, that they get to the team, and that the team responds without delay. They take us to the details of each stage of the pathway and the second set of decisions, concerning resources.

The second set of decisions are about getting the best and quickest match between an individual client's needs, and team skills and time, at each stage of the pathway. Some of these decisions are made by the team at team meetings, but they are mostly made by each team member away from team meetings. The main ways in which the team influences members' decisions, and carries out its priorities, are through team guidance, policies and criteria for each stage in the pathway. Do team members follow team policies in each stage? We pursue this question in looking at how decisions in each stage of the client pathway commit team resources.

DECISION-MAKING FOR COLLECTIVE SERVICE TEAMS

Does a team manage its resources? What influence does a team have over the decisions which members make about the work they do, and when they finish work with each client? How many of the key work-management decisions which members make every day reflect team priorities and the needs of the client group?

This section draws attention to the way decisions made at each stage of the client's pathway commit team resources – they are the way team priorities are implemented. If a team has a high workload, suspects that there are more pressing needs which it is not meeting, and wishes to manage its resources better, it has to get to grips with how decisions are made at each stage and confront the issue of members' autonomy. The following shows how teams can influence members' work management decisions and manage team resources better. After showing the link between everyday decisions and team priorities, the chapter then turns to how a team can formulate collective priorities in the first place.

The two key workload-management decisions are whether to finish ('close') a piece of work, or to accept it. I put it this way around because people often think about the acceptance decision, but they forget that if they do not finish work they have no room to accept any. By not deciding to finish work we avoid having to decide about new work, even if we work all hours.

Practitioners make decisions about accepting and finishing three types of work: making an immediate response to a referral, doing an assessment, and carrying out longer-term interventions. If a team can influence these decisions, then it can relate the practitioner's time, which is a team resource, to community needs. That is, if the team's influence over the member's decisions reflects an understanding of community needs and team resources.

Teams influence practitioners' decisions in three ways: through client-pathway design, through decision criteria for each stage, and through team guidelines and policy. First we consider pathway design and how teams can improve resource management by adding stages, or by changing the order of stages.

Team resource management through client-pathway design

The key issues are, first, whether all practitioners or professions have their own client pathways, or whether there is an agreed team client pathway that all follow; and second, whether the team's pathway design reflects the needs of the community. Consider the design of the pathway in relation to needs and team resources.

Referral sources (Stage 1)

The key issue here is to ensure that people in the target population who are most in need get to the team, or that the team gets to them. The right publicity is important, stating, through different media and languages, who the service is for, how to get it, and what to expect. The aim is to get others to make the right decision. The dilemma for many teams is whether to accept only referrals from certain sources, or whether to do this and to have direct and open access, and perhaps 'walk-in' access. Although restricted referral can make sense for some new teams, it can make the team less available to some ethnic groups who do not use the 'authorized' sources, such as GPs. It does not work for drug and alcohol teams, where many users want direct access.

A team does not control its resources if team members make their own decisions about which referrals they take and from where, without reference to the team. Agreements are needed about whether and under what circumstances team members can accept work. The agreements should refer to the team's analysis of community needs and priorities. This may conclude that the team can best meet some of the most pressing needs if some members take certain referrals from sources other than the team meeting.

Reception (Stage 2)
The aim of this stage is to make an initial assessment of need to be able to decide, with the client or referrer, whether the team can help. It is the first response the team makes, and a speedy referral to another more appropriate service may be the most helpful response. It involves gathering information from the person about what they want and to clarify what they might need, and giving information to that person about what the team can do or arrange: a discussion to reach a joint agreement about what to do next (see Chapter 9).

One decision is whether to refer for further assessment, and if so, what level of assessment is indicated. Some teams have the option of arranging an immediate assessment. Most have the option of referral to a team meeting. The 'receiver' must obtain sufficient information about needs to help the team meeting ratify the decision to accept for assessment, and to decide the type and level of assessment and skills required.

Does the team have a reception stage for a team rapid response to urgent referrals, staffed by team members? If so, how much team time is spent on this work and is the time decided by the team after considering the priority and severity of needs in the community?

Acceptance for assessment (Stage 3)
This is the gateway to the rest of the team pathway, and a decision to accept is a decision to commit time from the team resource to do an assessment. That is why team members need guidance about the conditions under which they can accept for assessment in team time. Often the decision is made in a team meeting, and the decision is informed by the referral information and guided by the team policy and criteria for acceptance for assessment. The decision criteria should reflect the priorities of the team, and are built up like case law over time from decisions about past clients.

Teams which decide first whether the team will accept, and then discuss who will do the work (for assessment or for longer-term work), are better able to carry out team priorities and allocate team resources according to priorities. In some teams practitioner's decide whether to accept, and there is no consideration of whether the case, or other work, is a team priority.

Allocation for assessment (Stage 4)
Once the team accepts – or the person 'receiving' does, on behalf of the team –
the next decision is about who does the assessment. Criteria for deciding
include client or carer preference, the level of assessment indicated, who has the
best skills to do the assessment, who already knows the client, carers or
referrers, and who could do it soonest – it should not be just who has space in
his or her caseload at the time.

Assessment (Stage 5)
One type of assessment is a team member doing a profession-specific
assessment, which may be for a care manager outside the team, or for one inside
the team. A second type of assessment is where a care manager in the team
organizes others to do an assessment. The level and type of assessment are
usually decided before this stage, but it may not have been, or may need to be
changed as the assessment proceeds. The assessment may also involve
developing a care plan. The person doing the assessment is guided by the team
policy, and may be working to a team assessment format. In all cases the
assessment concentrates first on clients' needs and wants, and involves them
and their carers in the process (see Chapter 9).

The team's involvement may finish at this stage with an assessment, in which
case the assessor reports completion to the team. Often assessors report their
recommendations to the team meeting.

Acceptance for longer-term work (Stage 6)
This decision can commit considerable practitioner time, which is not then
available to the team for other clients' needs. Teams which separate the earlier
decision about assessment from this decision about longer-term work are better
able to manage their resources. Teams must be able to influence a practitioner's
decision about whether to take on a longer-term intervention. One point to
having an earlier assessment stage is so that this decision and allocation can be
made with sufficient information. Referral information is rarely sufficient to
enable a decision as to whether longer-term work is needed, or the best match
between the client's needs and skills in the team. It also separates assessing need
from the problems of meeting need, so that the latter do not overshadow the
former.

The team faces a decision about whether to refer on, to accept for
longer-term work, or to move to closure (stage 10). If the team decides to
accept, is an allocation made immediately, or is the client put on a waiting list?
Again, team policy and criteria guide each decision.

Allocation for longer-term work (Stage 7)
If the team accepts, the decision about who does the work depends on the work
which is indicated from the assessment, and perhaps a care plan as well.
Matching should follow similar criteria to those for allocation for assessment.
Giving the work to someone who has space in his caseload is not matching, but

dumping. However, if all could do the work equally well, then avoiding delays means allocating to whoever has time available. A team usually has a policy about when a client review is to be done, but, if not, this should be clarified at allocation, as well as what reports to the team the team member should make. Can any team members take on long-term work in team time, without reference to the team? Is there anything wrong with the term 'allocation' to describe how team members take on long-term work?

Intervention and/or monitoring (Stage 8)
In this phase the team member works with the client by carrying out any profession-specific work, and/or organizing others' work if acting as a care manager. The practitioner adjusts what she does according to changing circumstances and needs, and is guided by team policy about record-keeping, and when to report to the team.

Team review (Stage 9)
There are two main types of review: first, the team member's formal reappraisal of progress, current needs, and future actions, carried out with the client and carer; and second, the team's review of the team member's work and the need for any continued involvement. Without this the team has less control over its resources, and less control over quality.

Introducing a multidisciplinary perspective into a client's care is a separate issue. Sometimes teams try to do this and carry out the other two types of review at the same time: they meet to do an individual review, team review, and multidisciplinary review. None is done well if there are many clients to review – it may be necessary to arrange separate types of review for each.

Some teams assume that all cases will be closed after the review date, unless the team member is able to justify to the team why work should continue. Putting the onus on the team member in this way emphasizes that a decision is at issue about committing team resources to further work, and prevents 'casework drift'. There may be more pressing needs waiting to be met. Teams with good work management in earlier stages often loose control over resources at later stages. If there is no team review, and practitioners decide when and how to review, then the review may not get done, or the review may not relate a decision about doing more work with the client to other work waiting for team attention.

To emphasize that a practitioner's decision to continue work commits a team resource which is not then available for other clients, teams can arrange for review reports after they consider new referrals and assessment reports, and in the same meeting. Doing so makes it easier to see how a decision to continue working with one client is a decision not to work with another client who may be waiting for assessment, or some other help, and whose needs are greater.

Closure (Stage 10)
The closure decision is the most important resource decision a team member makes, and one of the most difficult. That is why the team must influence this

decision, although it may be impossible the team to overrule a member and directing him or her to finish work if the team member has a statutory responsibility or believes that the client is at risk. Team guidance and criteria about closure are critical, as well as the client's involvement in the decision, the client's knowledge of where to get further help, and closure information to the original referrer and GP.

By reviewing the client pathway that all members use and by agreeing a team pathway, teams can get a better match between client needs and skills and a better match between team resources and the needs of the client group they serve. They can also better manage their resources by developing decision criteria and team policies, which we consider next.

Team resource management by decision criteria, guidance and team policy

Teams influence practitioners to carry out team priorities and resource allocation rules by decision criteria, for each stage of the pathway. Decision criteria are principles for guiding decisions. For example, to guide a decision about who should do an assessment (stage 4), a team uses decision criteria to achieve the best match between client needs and team skills. Once criterion may be any indications from the referral and other information that one team member's skills would be best for the assessment. Another, whether the client comes from an area or referral source known to a team member. A third, the degree of urgency and length of time before a suitable person could do the assessment.

All teams have decision criteria for different decisions, and some are more explicit than others. Most teams develop these criteria over time by 'case law': looking back at how they handled different cases and decisions in the past. For workload management, a team needs criteria for the key decisions about acceptance and closure. The team leader must remind the team about the criteria, question whether the criteria should be changed if the team does not follow the criteria in making a decision, and keep questioning whether the criteria help the team match its resources to needs in the best way. These criteria should reflect team priorities from needs analyses, and not just past practice.

Box 5.5 Matching needs to resources in collective service teams

Collective service teams need information and procedures to ensure and to prove to purchasers that they match resources to priority needs. In practice, this means agreeing decision criteria, policies and guidance about:

- priorities between direct client work and other categories of work (i.e. how resources are used — should be informed by research);

> • priorities between types of client (propose what should be in contracts) and converting this into practical guidelines and decision criteria about such matters as publicity, receiving referrals, accepting for assessment, waiting lists, accepting for treatment/intervention, reviewing work, closure and recording and reviewing effectiveness.

Teams also influence practitioners' work management through team guidance and policies about any high-resource cost decisions made by practitioners away from the team. An example is a decision to visit a client, which may be costly in terms of time and travel expense. Teams with agreed guidance about these and other matters are more likely to influence how practitioners use their time. Again the team leader has an important role to play in reminding people, revising guidance, and taking action if people ignore the guidance.

Box 5.3 draws attention to the balance between practitoner autonomy and team control. The next chapter looks at autonomy in more detail, and Chapter 8 shows how to improve decision-making and handle conflict in teams.

Box 5.3 Work management decisions – practitioner or team?

Stage 1	Stage 2	Stage 3	Stage 4	Stage 5	Stage 6	Stage 7	Stage 8	Stage 9	Stage 10
Referral sources	Reception	Acceptance for assessment	Allocation for assessment	Assessment	Acceptance for longer-term care	Allocation for longer-term care	Intervention and/or monitoring	Review	Closure

Does the practitioner decide what to do at each stage, without reference to the team? Or does the team decide what the practitioner does?
Neither: for effective work management, the team influences the practitioner's decisions in different ways:

• by ensuring arrangements for each stage are agreed and defined;
• by team decision criteria;
• by team guidance and policy about practice.

Chapter 8 gives more details about decision-making.

FORMULATING PRIORITIES IN COLLECTIVE SERVICE TEAMS

In the following we assume a team with a collective service responsibility, rather than a team for coordinating separate professional services. We saw above that the former types of team carry out their priorities through pathway design, decision criteria and team policies. But where do the team priorities come from in the first place? Priorities in these teams are not the sum of each profession's and agency's priorities. If the team is to respond to needs, these priorities should reflect an understanding of the needs of the client group that the team is serving. Management has to approve these priorities, but teams have an important part to play in revising their priorities (Chapter 10). If management has not set any, the team must develop and propose its own. The following shows six steps for doing so, and draws on the concepts for linking needs to services presented in Chapter 2.

Step 1: Define the client group

The first step is for the team to clarify whom it is serving, and the needs it is there to meet. Teams do this, first, by exclusion: by ruling out the areas and clients it is not serving, and the needs it is not there to meet. To take our example in Chapter 2 of a mental health team for older people: this team does not serve people outside a defined locality, or people under 65. It does not serve people with learning difficulties, or with addiction problems, or people whose needs can be met by primary health and generic social services, or people with acute mental health problems who cannot live at home with some support.

The team is able to narrow its focus by ruling out the clients and needs it is not there to serve. Certainly there are 'grey areas' and overlaps with other services, and over time the team revises the definition of its client group and their needs, but it is impossible to prioritize unless the outer boundaries are defined. If these are not defined for the team by management, then the team has to define its own boundaries and propose these to management and to other services to help clarify gaps and duplication in services. Teams that are all things to all people end up being nothing to anyone: the only argument is how narrow the focus should be, and how precise the targeting.

Prioriphobia

Prioriphobia is the inability to decide or act on the decision that one person's needs are more urgent or severe than another's. It is common in professionals who are sensitive to people's needs, who understand the pain and suffering caused by denying services, and who refuse to judge degrees of need in people who all need help. Prioriphobia is made more acute by high demand and decreasing resources, and by having to reach collective judgements with other professions. In time it results in 'burn-out', and many clients not getting help whose needs are greater than those who are helped.

Step 2: Understand the client group's needs better

I stress 'understand . . . better' because so often teams put off setting priorities until they have 'accurate information' about needs. Teams already have some understanding of the client group's needs, and if they use this understanding to set priorities, then they have a greater incentive to obtain more information of the right kind so as to set more meaningful priorities. The thing is to get started with what you have. The difficulty is how to pool the collective understanding of the team about the needs of the client group.

One way is for each profession in the team to set out what it thinks are the needs of the client group and to compare notes. Think about referrals – which part of the locality they mostly come from, who refers, what types of problem and need are referred. Then think about which areas there are few referrals from, which types of problem and need are not referred, and whether this is because needs are less. Note the language or concepts you are using to describe needs – are you using different types of needs?

Next, having compared notes, agree a common set of no more than ten categories of need. These are categories which describe the main types of need of clients within the client group (Chapter 2). It is likely that different professions have different categories or some which look the same but which cover slightly different needs. Although it is difficult, agreeing a set of categories of need is important for a team to define collective priorities. This difficulty is one of the main reasons why teams do not agree priorities. Surprisingly, once agreement is reached, there is rarely disagreement about the priority of each category, or if there is, at least there can be a productive discussion. It may be useful to find out the categories of need used by teams which serve a similar client group.

This step finishes with a set of categories of need, and an estimate of how many clients in the locality have needs in each category, rated by severity and urgency. It also involves noting any statements by purchasers or management about which needs they think are the most urgent or severe.

Needs/problems categories	*Severity*	*Urgency*
NEED TYPE 1		
High	No. of people in area	No. of people with needs
Medium	with needs of type 1	of type 1 which are:
Low	high need, medium need,	very urgent, medium
	lower need.	urgency, not urgent.

Step 3: Team resources and responses

In this step the team takes stock of the resources it has, and the types of response it can make to meet needs. First the team clarifies exactly how much time each team member has as 'team time'. That is, how much time each member has for work which calls for his or her skills and knowledge and which the team has to do to meet the client group needs. This involves clarifying calls upon a team member's time which are already decided by his or her employers, and any preset requirements or priorities.

Probably easiest to determine is the time the team member has to spend on non-team work — for example a duty rota elsewhere, or sessions in other services which could not be considered part of the team's work. There are also responsibilities which could be considered to be part of the team's combined service to the client group, but which are set by employers and which make less time available to be used flexibly by the team. If too many members have these prior employers' responsibilities, then the team cannot manage its resources flexibly to provide a combined service.

This step also involves clarifying the skills and knowledge team members have to offer (see Chapter 6 on role clarification) and the types of response to needs which each can make, in terms of assessment, treatment and care services. Again each profession in the team clarifies this, before coming together to work out an agreed set of categories for team responses. As with step 2, the team needs to agree a common set of different types of responses. Although a few may be responses which only some professions can offer, most describe work which everyone can do. We saw above different ways of categorizing responses, for example in terms of treatments, or in terms of work categories. The conclusion to step 3 is laid out under the following four headings:

1 type of response;
2 team members who provide this;
3 proportion of team member's time on each type of response;
4 total team time on each type of response.

Step 4: Clarifying how we use our resources now

In this step the team compares its collective understanding of needs (step 2) with its estimates of responses and resources (step 3). Team members use the agreed set of categories of both needs and responses and consider how the team spreads its resources across the needs of the client group.

This helps the team consider two questions concerning the link between needs and their responses. The first is whether the types of response are the best way to meet needs. It may be that, after looking at these links, a team decides that it should use different categories of response to meet the different categories of need. This may just involve changing the way the team categorizes its responses, but more likely it will involve changing the way the team responds.

The second question is how well the team is responding to the most urgent and severe needs. In step 2 the team rated the urgency and severity of needs in each category. By comparing how much time the team spends on each category of need, the team can use the step 2 estimates to ask questions about whether it is spending enough time on the most urgent and severe needs.

Step 5: Future responses and time distribution: bringing practice into line with priorities

In this step the team agrees a better match between its responses and needs. Step 4 clarified the teams priorities-in-action: how the team spends its time every day. Step 4 also compared how the team spends its time with the team's earlier estimate of urgency and severity of need. In step 5 the team builds on this understanding to propose changes to the amount of time the team spends on different categories of need and on responses so as to achieve a better match between needs and responses.

Having clarified these changes, the team then has to think about how it will carry out the changes. This involves:

• clarifying the work which different team members have to reduce to give them more time to serve priority needs;
• new responses, or less time on some responses to give more time to others;
• deciding new skills needed in the team;
• defining criteria for allocation and closure, and changes to client pathways and team policy.

Step 6: Carrying out and reviewing priorities

The last step is applying these changes in everyday decisions, and recording and monitoring what is done to ensure that the priorities are put into practice. The agreed set of need and response categories can provide a basis for a team information system which it can use to manage its resources. If referral and record systems use these categories it is easy to monitor how time is being spent, and what types of demand are coming to the team. The team then has the accurate information that it was missing in steps 2 and 4 to review needs and its responses.

The purpose of these six steps is to help teams think about how to use resources as a collective. By working through these steps, team members clarify the extent to which they share responsibilities with others in the team for managing their resources as a combined service to meet the needs of the client group. They consider needs and responses as a group, and agree common categories to discuss and form priorities. They are forced to recognize that they have limited resources, and that for these to be used to the best effect, some lower-priority work will not be done and some clients who previously received a service will not get one in the future.

CONCLUSION

Clients follow one or more 'pathways' through a team. By understanding the pathways that most clients follow, teams can arrange ways to respond more quickly, offer more choice, and achieve a better 'match' between a client's needs and team skills. Team members can clarify who makes which decisions at each stage of the 'journey' and how the team works if there is no agreed description or policy.

Mapping pathways also highlights the difference between network teams of separate profession services, and collective service teams. In the former, each profession or service has priorities and resource-allocation rules govern what the practitioner can do. The team priorities are the sum of those of each profession and service – they do not allow scope for a team to develop and carry out collective team priorities.

If managers decide to form a team with a collective responsibility for serving a population, they and team members need to design a pathway which allows control over team members' work-management decisions. Such teams can develop team decision criteria for decisions about acceptance and closure, and team policy and guidelines for carrying out priorities.

Collective service teams must have priorities which link the needs of the clients they serve to their everyday decisions. Five practical steps teams can take to ensure this are to clarify the boundaries of their client population; understand needs in this population better; take stock of team members' skills and how they use their time; decide how to use team time to better effect; and finally, define decision criteria and policies and apply them in practice. One reason why these teams do not effectively manage their workload as a collective is member's fears of loss of autonomy, one of the issues we now turn to in considering team members' roles.

Chapter 6
TEAM MEMBERS' ROLES

Some common questions and problems raised by team members and addressed in this chapter are the following:

- What are the 'boundaries' to my role: what is my work and what should others be doing?
- Given that I could do certain types of work, what should I be doing?
- What if someone else in the team could also do this work – how do we decide who does it?
- I am finding that I am not using many of my professional skills and knowledge in the team because there is pressure for me to do other work.
- Who can tell me what to do?
- The team leader and my boss tell me to do different things. Then his deputy tells me something different again.
- What am I supposed to do if I feel out of my depth with a client?
- What should I do if I feel someone else in the team is putting a client at risk?

INTRODUCTION

New team members do not realize that 'old-timers' are still 'finding their place' in the team. Even if a team member's skills, knowledge and interests stay the same, other things change and alter that member's 'place' in the team. In fact, all team members make and re-create their place in a team – there is not a place that already exists, just waiting to be found. However, there are some formal requirements of each team member which are clear or easily clarified, and understanding these is the starting point for clarifying and explaining one's role in a team.

Most team members are highly skilled in their 'profession-specific' work, but are far less able to 'make a place' in a team. Professional and post-qualification education pays insufficient attention to 'role self-management' in professional practice, especially in multidisciplinary teams. As a result, practitioners' work and service to clients is not as effective in a team as it could be. As one psychiatrist wrote:

Increasingly for patients and GPs there are only good and bad psychiatric teams. The qualifications and academic standing of the psychiatrist has little relevance if he or she is unable to work with social workers, community psychiatric nurses, ward nurses, occupational therapists, psychologists, and other staff to provide a comprehensive and effective service.

(Harrison 1990)

The time has passed when community practitioners work alone, if such a time ever existed. Even teams that were relatively stable are now much more fluid. The speed and variety of change is increasing, demanding that team members continually review their role and priorities – in some teams membership turnover is more than 50% every three years, and each change of membership affects others' work and roles. The ability to clarify and negotiate a role is an essential skill that should not be something people 'pick up', often by making mistakes – this is bad for each profession and bad for clients.

The purpose of this chapter is to show how team members can make and remake their place in a team, and resolve or prevent common role problems in teams. It starts by describing some of the influences on a team member's role – the pressures and expectations that mould what a person does every day at work. The chapter shows how team members can clarify the formal infuences, their responsibilities and accountability, and understand the scope they have to create their own role. In particular, it draws attention to the importance of defining and assigning care-coordination responsibilities inside and outside a team so that all involved know who is coordinating a client's care. The chapter then uses these concepts to show how to resolve the more common role issues in teams, such as role-blurring, overlap, conflict, gaps, overload and skill dilution.

INFLUENCES ON ROLE

If you work in a team, how do you decide how to spend your working day? You may feel that you have little choice in the matter, and simply react to things as they happen. Consider some of the people and influences that affect what you do as a team member:

What you are employed to do
Team members are often employed to work full- or part-time in a team. If so, they have an employment contract and a job description which states what the employer expects, and the pay and conditions given in return. This is one influence over their work and relationships in the team. Volunteers in teams do not have employment contracts, but the team should have a statement of their rights and obligations (Øvretveit 1987b).

What your manager directs you to do
Employment contracts often have a general clause such as 'and such other duties as your manager may require'. In entering into an employment contract an employee agrees to accept the directions of a manager assigned by the employer. There are differences between professions, but within limits a person's manager can direct him or her to carry out tasks or to act in certain ways. We will see that these directions can conflict with other influences. Team members' employers and managers are themselves strongly influenced by the work which purchasers want done, and if the purchaser is a fund-holding general practice a team member may be subject to this influence directly.

What referrers want from you
Referrers can influence what a team member does in at least four ways. The first is by referring directly, rather than to the team, and asking for a personal and fast response. The second is by the number of referrals – too many can cause work overload, too-few may influence the team member to visit and talk about what he or she and the team can offer. The third is by the type of referral – the wrong type may cause unnecessary extra work. The fourth by being over-specific in what they want and not giving latitude to the team member to decide what he or she thinks is best in the situation – the referrer may prescribe a required response which is not appropriate.

What clients and/or carers want from you
The referrer can be a carer or the client herself. What the client wants is an important influence over a team member's work and over how they act. Chapter 9 shows that team members need to be able to adapt their role and the way they relate to different clients and to forge a 'service partnership'. Carers, too, have expectations that need to be met and often modified. Their expectations of the team member may be different to those of the client, and may conflict with the client's.

What other team members expect of you
Another influence is the formal and informal expectations of other team members. Everyone has an image of what people from different professions do, and other team members' ideas may be accurate, mistaken, or very vague. These expectations are often apparent in team meetings when it comes to allocating referrals. They can also be powerfully modified in case discussions or in co-working. A practitioner has to make sure that other team members know what they can do to help the clients which other team members are serving.

What you are able to do
There are two aspects to what a team member can do – what any qualified person from one profession is trained and competent to do, and what a particular person can do over and above this. Team members' work and

relationships are strongly influenced by their capabilities, which also limits what they can agree to do.

What you like doing and want to do
Last, but not least, is a team member's professional or work interests. People are often best at what they like doing, and preferences and special interests should influence what they do in the team, and be considered when a person is selected for a particular team. Too little of what people like doing causes morale problems and a low-energy team.

Some of these influences are explicit, as when someone makes a direct (or implicit) request. Sometimes we assume an influence when none exists – we may think that someone wants or expects something when they do not. 'Making a place' in a team is about understanding, clarifying and managing these influences, especially conflicting expectations. In the rest of this book we look at each type of relationship in more detail, in terms of the formal and informal aspects, and in terms of communication.

CLARIFYING A TEAM MEMBER'S ROLE – FORMAL REQUIREMENTS AND ACCOUNTABILITY

Although much of 'making a role' in a team is negotiation, it is important to recognize that there are formal requirements of a person working in a team which that person and other team members cannot ignore. Part of clarifying one's role in a team, and of finding answers to team role problems, is understanding and recognizing these requirements and the consequences of ignoring them. Team members need to be able to understand and explain their formal responsibilities and accountability, and be clear what scope they have to negotiate what they do. They need to be able to point out to their managers where these responsibilities prevent the kind of teamwork which is called for. Teams also need to be able to define certain roles, such as case coordinator, to ensure that the team is able to organize client care properly.

First we consider the formal requirements of a team member, then their formal work responsibilities, and then formal accountability relations. The following shows how to clarify, through successive exclusion, what a team member cannot do (what is proscribed), then what they are required to do (what is prescribed), and then their scope of discretion to decide their work – their autonomy or, more emotively, independence or freedom.

Formal requirements – limitations and exhortations

Formal requirements are set by higher authorities at the national and local level and rule out certain actions and put limits to what a team member can do. They also require a team member to act in certain ways in certain circumstances. Consider how different codes and policies successively exclude and call for certain behaviours.

Limits of the law

Team members clearly have to stay within the limits of the law, which are set at a national level. These exclude certain actions, such as acting outside one's professional competence, which can result in a lawsuit for negligence.

Professional codes of ethics

Professional codes of conduct and ethics are also set at a national level, and further limit professional behaviour. For example, many professional codes in the UK rule out some therapeutic treatments which are popular in California. Codes are also permissive and seek to promote certain behaviours, such as putting a client's interests before other considerations.

State registration requirements

Professionals with state registration risk loosing their license to practise if they breech professional codes or other rules set by state registration bodies (Øvretveit 1992b).

Employment contract and policies

At the local level, an employer specifies certain requirements of all employees in a employment contract and in other policies. The contract outlines the duties and responsibilities of a particular post. If these are not met, the team member could be judged to be in breach of contract.

Managers' policies and procedures

Employers authorize managers to delegate work to employees. Managers usually set policies and procedures for people working in their service. Team operational policies are agreed by managers, and further define how team members may act. Managers, and sometimes team leaders, may delegate specific tasks from time to time.

These requirements of team members are specified and enforceable by the bodies that specified them. Team members are formally accountable to these bodies for meeting these requirements. Knowledge of these proscribed limits helps to rule out certain actions – they de-fine (literally draw a boundary around) what a team member can do. Understanding these requirements is the first step in addressing such role problems as what work the team member should be doing and whether he or she is accountable for other people's work.

For example, a social worker's job description may require him to carry-out social work duties in relation to involuntary admissions under the Mental Health Act. If he has to be available for this work, this puts limits to what he can do in a team. Another example is a requirement that a consultant oversees and coordinates client care within a particular service. It is not stated in any national requirements that a consultant psychiatrist is accountable for the work of a qualified person from any other profession. However, an employing authority may require a consultant to oversee and coordinate care in its employment contract with the consultant. Consultants and others need to be clear about such requirements, and whether they conflict with other requirements.

It is true that these formal requirements are usually general and open to interpretation. If so, team members need to refer to legal or organizational 'case law' to help clarify what the requirements mean in particular instances. For example, an employment contract may state that a team member is 'responsible to the team leader for day-to-day issues and to his or her manager for professional issues'. The team member will need to find out from custom and practice what this means, and ask what happened in particular disputed cases in the past. Few requirements specify what a team member should do in any detail, or help with other role problems. To further clarify these issues we turn to the concepts of responsibility and accountability.

Understanding each other's strengths

'The idea that staff from different disciplines would relatively easily identify their spheres of competence and divide up work accordingly is, in retrospect a naive one. It was the experience of many teams that a long and arduous process of experiential learning had to take place before health and social work staff began to trust each other's respective skills and experience.'

Source: Brown et al. 1992

FORMAL WORK-ROLE RESPONSIBILITIES

Response-ability is our ability to respond, which is what we are capable of doing and what we are paid to do. Each employed team member has formal work-role responsibilities. People often feel responsible for more than what their work responsibilities require of them. Team members' feelings of responsibility will naturally guide them in deciding their role. However, we are here clarifying role through clarifying what is required and hence becoming clearer about what is open to individual team members to decide for themselves.

Formal work-role responsibilities: the work expected of a person by his or her employers; the ongoing duties, and the tasks which are delegated by higher management from time to time.

Work responsibilities are defined in a job description in terms of ongoing duties and specific tasks. Team members have four main types of responsibility.

Profession-specific responsibilities
Looking in more detail at a team member's responsibilities, we see that some can only be carried out by qualified people from one profession. A few of these responsibilities are specified by the state, which rules that only people with certain professional qualifications can carry out certain tasks – for example, prescribe drugs. Most profession-specific skills and knowledge are acquired by professional practitioners in pre-qualification training.

People from different professions are employed in multidisciplinary teams, in part because they are trained, qualified and competent to do, without supervision, tasks which people from other professions cannot do. These profession-specific responsibilities are relatively few, but do need to be clarified so that other team members understand when to refer to people from other professions, to help develop allocation criteria, and to publicize the team services. Teams can use the exercise in Box 6.2 below to clarify these.

Common responsibilities
Team members also have skills and knowledge which they have in common with one or more other professions in the team. For example, all qualified members of mental health teams have knowledge and skills in counselling, and if this work is called for anyone in the team could do it. To decide who does the work the team uses criteria other than skill and knowledge. Teams need to clarify which skills and responsibilities members have in common.

It is more difficult to understand and agree which profession is the most expert, or has the deepest knowledge. It is important to do so to decide whom to call upon for a complex case and to decide the best matching at allocation, and whether supervision may be necessary. It is best to agree common skills and then raise the question of differences in levels of competence, using length of training as an simple indicator of competence. How to handle disputes and conflict over such issues is discussed in Chapter 8. Team members also have responsibilities in common for work other than direct client work, such as for case recording, or for working as a 'team duty person', or for meeting other team policy requirements.

Common responsibilities are slightly different from shared responsibilities. A shared responsibility is working with someone to do something. In one team a nurse and a social worker share responsibility for managing social care workers – they both interview new staff and discuss and agree how to manage 'their' staff. They do not share responsibility for counselling – this is a responsibility in common which they only share if they are both counselling the same client or family.

Case coordination or care management responsibilities
Some members of multidisciplinary teams have skills and knowledge in case coordination or in care management, and are responsible for doing work to coordinate care. They have been given training to be able to draw together assessments done by other formal carers and practitioners and to formulate a care plan involving the client, and to use an assessment format for this purpose. This is different from training to do a profession-specific assessment and plan, which all practitioners are given. Assessment and planning for case coordination is a more highly skilled activity, as is care management, and calls for a high level of competence, experience and training.

Team members need to clarify whether they or others in the team have case coordinating responsibilities, and if so what these are. If more than one member of the team is likely to be involved with a client, then a team must have an agreed case coordinataor role with defined responsibilities, and a way to decide who will carry out this role, for example by agreeing this at allocation.

> *Team case coordinator role:* A role assigned to a team member, with defined responsibilities for coordinating other team members who are serving the same client. A team case coordinator does not coordinate other services outside a team.
>
> *Care manager role:* A role with responsibilities for accessing, coordinating and liaising with all the services a client needs for his or her assessment, treatment and care.

The responsibilities of a care management role are in addition to those of case coordination, which only describes coordination within a team. Some teams have care manager roles with responsibilities for coordinating services outside the team as well as within (Appendix 1). Later we consider problems which arise from unclear or conflicting definitions of the responsibilities of these roles. Note that case coordinators or care managers are not usually accountable for others' actions or inactions, although they are accountable for carrying out their coordination responsibilities.

Note also that an employing authority or manager can assign coordination responsibilities to any practitioner who is judged to be able to do the work. The practitioner might be employed to undertake case coordination or care management full-time and to do nothing else. Alternatively he or she may be given these responsibilities as well as other direct care responsibilities (for example, a district nurse or community psychiatric nurse). Employing authorities are required by community care legislation to make arrangements for care management. This involves assigning specific responsibilities for care management to suitable staff, and making arrangements for ensuring that all are clear who is care manager at a particular time for a client being assessed for or receiving multiple services. As well as giving a better service to a client, this also reduces the chance of a mishap and legal action.

The diagram in Box 6.1 gives an example of a team member's work role with all three types of responsibility — it represents 20% of their time spent on core-profession-specific responsibilities, about 40% on shared direct-service provision responsibilities, and 40% on case coordination responsibilities, where they coordinate the care of several clients served by other team members, and liaise with care managers outside of the team.

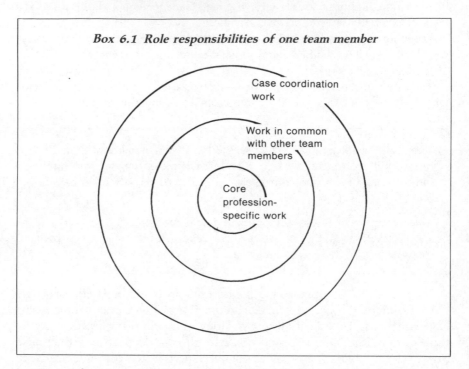

Box 6.1 Role responsibilities of one team member

Case coordination work

Work in common with other team members

Core profession-specific work

None of a team member's responsibilities discussed so far refers to responsibilities he or she might have for managing or supervising other people. Even care coordination only refers to responsibilities for agreeing services, and monitoring others' actions. A care manager is not accountable for what others do, only for meeting his or her care management responsibilities. The fourth set of responsibilities, which only some team members have, involves some form of accountability for another person's actions or inactions. We consider accountability after describing these responsibilities.

Management or supervisory responsibilities
These are responsibilities for overseeing and directing all or some of other people's work. We discuss the responsibilities of managers and team leaders in more detail in the next chapter. Here we note that:

- some team members may manage other team members (for example, a social worker may manager other social services employees in a team, or a consultant psychiatrist may manage junior doctors);
- management responsibilities are different in different professions (for example, a head psychologist has different management responsibilities for a qualified but junior psychologist to those of a social work manager for a social worker or a consultant psychiatrist for a junior doctor);
- a team member from one profession may have 'supervisory responsibilities' in relation to certain work done by another team member from another profession (for example, a psychologist supervises a nurse carrying out cognitive therapy with a depressed client).

It is the latter 'supervisory responsibilities' in teams which can be the most unclear of all the formal responsibilities considered so far. One reason is that these responsibilities are rarely stated in a job description, or assigned and explained by a manager, but are assumed by arrangement within teams. Some teams do define different 'supervisory responsibilities' in their operational policies, and this does help avoid problems. If you work in a team and 'supervise' others, or are 'supervised' by them, it is wise to clarify who is responsible for what, using the co-management checklist in Chapter 7.

Responsibilities for coordination, management and supervision take us to the last of the concepts for clarifying and defining roles: the concepts of accountability and authority for describing formal working relationships.

ACCOUNTABILITY

To understand and describe a team member's role we need to be able to describe his or her formal working relationships. There are many meanings to the term 'accountability' (Day and Klien 1987), some morale, some political, some religious. Here I use the term to describe formal accountability – a defined relationship with a person or body which has power to call a person to answer for his or her actions. Formal accountability is often confused with responsibility. People often feel responsible for things for which they are not formally accountable.

> *Formal accountability:* the person or body to whom you are answerable for meeting defined responsibilities, and for observing set rules and regulations.

With formal accountability, team members enter a relationship and agree the responsibilities for which they are prepared to answer. They agree that the person or body to whom they are answerable has authority to call them to account, and potentially to sanction them. They have formal relations of accountability with different bodies, as we saw earlier when looking at the formal requirements of team members.

There are two common accountability problems for team members. The first is the 'upwards' accountability problem – to whom they are accountable and for what. The second is the 'downward' accountability problem – whether they are accountable in any way for other team member's actions. The following considers the first issue – to whom team members are accountable – drawing on our earlier discussion of formal requirements.

When a team member applies for membership of a professional association, or she agrees to be bound by the rules of membership, which usually include codes of conduct and professional ethics. They are accountable to the association for observing these rules. Some of these rules define how members of the association should relate to clients. Clients can appeal to the professional association for redress against the practitioner. The main sanction available to the professional association is to withdraw membership. If membership is a condition for state registration, then this sanction is stronger than it would otherwise be.

If the team member applied for and was granted state recognition (generally state registration), or she is also accountable to the state regulating body (for example, the state registration council) for observing the conditions of practice set by this body. The sanctions available to this body are withdrawal of recognition, which may have a variety of consequences.

A practitioner in private practice is formally accountable to the customer for his or her actions and omissions. This accountability is not a felt moral obligation, but a defined relationship in law. He or she offers a service under laws which regulate any commercial exchange. The customer can call the practitioner to account through a court of law, and the sanctions available to the customer are defined in the Sale of Goods and Services Act, and in other Acts. This is the only relationship of formal accountability for the practitioner who is not a member of a professional association, or regulated by the state in any way, apart from his or her accountability in law as a citizen (for instance, some psychotherapist team members).

Some teams contract private practitioners to give a team service. Private practitioners' accountability changes because they have a contract with a contracting body rather than with each client. They are accountable to the contracting body for fulfilling the contract.

Team members are likely to be employed by a state employing authority, a private hospital, or a voluntary organization. They decide whether or not to agree to the terms of employment, which in effect puts their services at the disposal of the employer. They have a 'contract of service' with their employer. Typically professions do this because employment is not incompatible with their other accountabilities, and there is a commonalty of purpose between them and their employer. Having agreed an employment contract, they are accountable to their employer for meeting the responsibilities laid down in their contract, and for observing the employer's rules and regulations. The sanctions available to the employer are laid down in employment law.

The employment contract states to whom team members are accountable for their employment responsibilities — usually to one manager. Sometimes problems occur because they are accountable to a manager and a team leader, or because managers change — we discuss this further in the next chapter. Here we turn to the first of a number of role problems which the chapter considers below — medical accountability.

Accountability of consultant medical practitioners in teams

The consultant has direct responsibility to see that the variety of disciplines caring for patients are coordinated and used effectively to pursue the best treatment of the individual patient in his medical care. *This implies leadership of the multidisciplinary team dealing with clinical problems and accepting the responsibilities of leadership.*
(Bulletin of the Royal College of Psychiatrists 1977; emphasis added)

The concepts of accountability and types of responsibility help clarify uncertainties about whether a consultant medical practitioner is accountable for some or any of the work of team members from other professions. The short answer is that consultants are accountable for meeting their responsibilities, which are mostly profession-specific medical responsibilities. If they have a contract with their employer which includes responsibilities for directing staff from other professions, then they are also accountable for carrying out these responsibilities, as stated in the contract. Although some consultants have management responsibilities as a head of directorate, they are not accountable in a court of law for the professional work of other professions, even if they do have managerial accountability for this work, which is rarely the case.

Consider for example, a community psychiatric nurse treating a mother for post-natal depression, and the mother commits suicide. Is the consultant accountable? Would the consultant's accountability be any different if he had known of the referral to the team, but had not done a psychiatric assessment, or if he had done an assessment and was prescribing anti-depressants at the time?

The first issue is one of culpability, not accountability — of how to apportion blame in a mishap. Who is to blame is not the same as who is accountable. Certainly the consultant would be called to account by a court of law for his actions, or lack of them, as would every other person involved. The court would consider whether each proferssional practitioner had exercised a 'reasonable duty of care' — that he had carried out his professional responsibilities. There is nothing in national requirements which states that consultant medical practitioners are in any way accountable for the actions or inactions of other professions, only that they should make sure that the people they delegate work to are 'appropriately qualified'. The above statement by the psychiatrists' professional association refers only to medical care, and to ensuring that this is coordinated, and has no legal status.

Many consultants' employment contracts include responsibilities for directing and managing the work of junior doctors. Their professional responsibilities include formulating procedures for their staff, and if they were found not to have exercised these reponsibilities, and this contributed to a mishap, then they may be found culpable.

Let us turn to the issue of whether the consultant in the example did a psychiatric assessment. If referrals are to be made directly to the team, consultants and GPs require that adequate arrangements are made to detect and treat organic pathologies. There is a general issue here of how any member of the team who is not involved or does not know the case has the opportunity to draw attention to matters which members working on the case may have overlooked, or are not trained to detect. One of the advantages of teamwork is to pool the expertise of a variety of specialists, and an important feature of the team organization is the mechanism within the team to make this possible.

The referral process within the team must ensure that allocation and routine reviews provide opportunities for medical members to undertake assessments if they suspect medical problems. It must also ensure that any team member has easy access to specialist medical opinion in the team. The requirement is that discussions of cases not known to medical members, and the information available, are such that medical members can satisfy themselves that there is little likelihood of medical problems. If there is doubt, medical members must be able to 'opt in' to do a specialist medical assessment. If they decide that one is not necessary, GPs need to be informed of the decision and reminded that the medical care of the client is still their responsibility.

The real issue is ensuring that there is adequate case coordination. In the past consultant medical practitioners automatically carried care coordination responsibilities both for the medical care of all clients with a service, and other aspects of their care. This included responsibilities for directing other professions. Case coordination and accountability were clear, and consultants had the authority to match their responsibilities. More recently other professions have acquired autonomy, and medical direction of their work no longer happens, or is necessary. However, with the increasing complexity of services in the community, care coordination is more necessary than ever.

Employers and managers of teams have to ensure that there are clear arrangements for coordinating care and for monitoring the quality of team members' work. This is necessary to minimize the chance of mishap and legal actions, as well as to ensure a high quality service. One option is to revert to consultant medical practitioners having responsibilities for directing the details of others work, as well as for coordinating care. This is not practical in most community teams. The other option is to have a clear case coordination role that different members of the team can assume and arrangements for assigning this role, as discussed earlier.

The chapter now uses the concepts outlined above to show how to understand, resolve and prevent some common role problems in teams. A general point about formal responsibilities and work relationships is that they are specified to avoid common problems, not because 'some people want to bureaucratize everything'. Not all responsibilities can be or need to be specified in detail, only those where it is likely that problems will happen. Things will get clarified when a problem happens, but it is easier to do so before rather than during a dispute.

COMMON ROLE PROBLEMS IN TEAMS – SOLUTIONS AND PREVENTION

The following problems are common in teams, and clarifying responsibilities and working relationships beforehand can prevent them from occurring.

No care coordination, or confused or disputed coordination

A team member may find that a client or carer does not know who her care manager is. The client may not need one (see Chapter 4), but she will if she is receiving or may need to receive other health or social services. If the others involved, or likely to be involved are within the team, then the team member can use the team's method of care coordination. This is usually a case coordination role, and the team needs to define the responsibilities of the role, who can take on the role and in what circumstances he can do so (see above).

More frequently, people outside the team are also serving the client. Who should coordinate them? The team member should check first with social services, or with any of the other people serving the client, whether there is a care manager assigned. If not, the next step is to contact whoever offers care management in the area for clients with similar needs. It may be that there is an agreement that members of the team can provide care management, in which case the team member may be able to assume this role, making sure that others know that he has done so. Failing all this, and if the client does need care management, then the team should consider offering this service – not least because the team member's work is less effective if it is not coordinated with others.

Skills dilution or deskilling

One reason why some teams do not offer care management is that it leaves members less time for other direct-provision professional work. This is true even if the model of care management agreed in the area allows care management to be combined with direct provision. By taking on care management responsibilities, or even case coordination within a team, team members have less time to use their other skills. Some refer to this as 'skill dilution', although this term is used more often to describe what happens with too much 'role-blurring'. This is when teams play down the differences between professions and there is an ethos that most types of work can be done equally well by any member of the team. Skill dilution comes from not using skills which one has acquired through training – usually profession-specific skills.

Certainly professional demarcation and professional stereotypes make it difficult for teams to respond flexibly to client needs. The professional background of team members is only important for clarifying whether they have the skills and knowledge to meet the client's needs. Team members can benefit from learning new skills from other team members, which also benefits clients. All team members need to be able, willing and helped to move away from the security of their profession-specific skills. However, there is a point where the profession-specific core of their working week becomes so small that they lose the skills and knowledge that called for them to be in a multi-disciplinary team in the first place.

Skill dilution is not necessarily a problem if a team member is acquiring other more valuable skills which are of use to priority clients, in which case skill dilution is not a good description. Beyond a certain point, skill dilution becomes deskilling. This can happen in super-egalitarian 'democratic teams', but this ethos should be apparent to anyone joining the team. More usually, deskilling happens because management has not structured the team in the right way for the needs of clients whom the team is trying to serve, or because there is a sudden change in clientele.

Contested role overlap

Role overlap is where two or more members have skills and knowledge in common. It is not a problem in itself, but to be expected, and allows the team to be flexible. What can cause problems are situations such as the following:

- two or more team members do the same work and duplicate each other;
- no one does the work – each assumes that, because others can do it, they are doing it;
- difficulties deciding who does the work, if any could do it equally well;
- one profession questions whether others have the skills and knowledge to do the work.

The first two problems arise because of poor case coordination or care management. All teams need arrangements for each team member to check quickly whether another team member is involved, and if so, who is to be case coordinator, if there is no care manager (see Chapter 9).

Resolving the second two problems depends on team members comparing skills and knowledge, discovering those in common, and discussing degrees of expertise. Doing this need not be as fraught or difficult as some teams think it is, or make it. It is true that in a multidisciplinary setting members tend to be unsure about what they have to offer and defensive about their skills and knowledge. For some, community working is new and unfamiliar and it is easier to retreat into routine professional work.

It would be unusual if a person did not find it difficult to state what skills and knowledge he or she has which is distinctive. This can be a threatening experience when one is not surrounded by colleagues from the same profession who take the competence of the profession for granted. In fact, if done the right way, comparing skills, knowledge and training can be reassuring, and a useful team-building exercise. One method I have found successful, and which teams can do in an hour and a half, is for each profession to meet and complete the exercise in Box 6.2 on a flip-chart. Where there is only one person from a profession in the team, it is better if that person meets with others from the same profession beforehand to help work through the exercise. Then the team can meet for each person to present their flip-chart and to answer questions. It helps to have a list of common client needs and to discuss what each profession might be able to offer.

Box 6.2 Role clarification for each profession

Each profession in the team lists:	As we see it:	As we think others see it:

Core profession-specific skills,
   knowledge and responsibilities
Skills, knowledge and responsibilities
   common to others
Case coordination skills,
   knowledge and responsibilities
Management or supervision
   skills and responsibilities

Professions in the team can draw on this exercise to write a paragraph, describing what the profession has to offer, and profession-specific skills. These paragraphs can be used in the team operational policy and in publicity material, together with statements about each member's particular skills, knowledge and experience and a statement about what all in the team can offer.

Using this method, team members can take turns to ask questions about the length and type of training, about experience, and about the type and complexity of client needs that each can help with. This knowledge is essential to be able to call on others in the team to help a client, and to resolve the third 'role overlap' problem: it helps to match skills to client needs at allocation or other times. If all have the necessary skills and level of competence then other criteria come into play to decide the match (see Chapter 5).

An exercise like this makes it less likely that the fourth problem will arise when a team member is working with a client – that one team member will question another's level of expertise. However, teams must have clear arrangements for one member to raise concerns about the quality of another's work, especially if a client could be at risk, and because practitioners in teams are usually less closely supervised by managers than in other settings. This issue is discussed later under 'Role overload' and in Chapter 7.

Reduced role autonomy

Practitioners used to working independently find that they have less autonomy in a team, but there are compensations. However, some team members raise 'lack of autonomy' as a problem because they feel that they are not able to use sufficient discretion in their casework, or to do other work. One example is the pressure on psychologists in teams to do more direct casework, when they feel that their skills are used to better effect in other types of role, such as consultancy. Another is a team agreeing a policy which prevents a member from taking certain referrals, or carrying out certain treatments, or puts limits on the number of treatments.

Teams have to recognize that practitioners in different professions are used to and need different degrees of discretion. Some need more autonomy to use their skills to the best effect, and are trained and have the experience to make decisions about the way they practice. The concepts of case and practice autonomy help clarify some of these differences (Øvretveit 1985), and show that a team operational policy needs to allow for these differences.

> *Case autonomy:* The right to carry out assessments and treatments of individual cases without regular review, or being overruled by higher authority, unless negligence or policy breaches are suspected.

Some members of the team may carry case autonomy, which means that their *professional* casework decisions cannot be reviewed or overruled by team meetings, unless special arrangements are agreed. However, the team can check that they properly undertook case coordination work and implemented team decisions with which they agreed at the time. Problems may arise where members with case autonomy disagree with and refuse to implement team casework decisions.

In addition to case autonomy, some members of a team, such as psychologists and psychiatrists, have 'practice autonomy'. This refers to discretion about what type of work to do and about the balance of time spent on different activities, rather than discretion over casework decisions. Team members used to 'practice autonomy' are more resistant to team operational policies which influence workload management decisions (Chapter 5). Teams often have to recognize differences in members' autonomy, which can conflict with the egalitarian ethos of some teams.

Another form of professional autonomy is practitioner client choice: the right of a practitioner to refuse to take on a client whom he believes he is unable to help. It is not clear whether some members of some teams have this form of autonomy, as well as case autonomy.

Role overload

The first of four problems which team members raise on the subject of 'overload' is too much of the wrong kind of work. This may be due to the same things that cause deskilling, such as there being no one else in the team or area to do the work. Or it may be due to the team member or the team serving the wrong clients or needs. This happens when the team or member does not have priorities or does not follow them. Role clarification helps team members be clearer about what their priorities are in the team, which include making their skills and knowledge available if others in the team do not have these. They cannot do this if they are tied up in work which others can do. Priorities and keeping to them are discussed at the end of Chapter 5.

Too much work is a common problem for team members. Again, clarifying and keeping to priorities is one answer – agreed, it is difficult to do this and to meet exhortations for a 'quality service' with no waiting list, and restless fund-holding GPs. Publicity and clear eligibility criteria are important. Too much work is an opportunity and invitation to look for finance to expand the team. More serious is too much work when others in the team do not appear to have the same problem. Again, this may be due to poor structuring of the team – the wrong amount of the right skills, resulting in one profession always being overloaded. It may also be due to unfair sharing of caseload or managers outside the team or other commitments taking up a team member's time. As discussed in Chapter 5, these issues of work management have to be addressed by clarifying how much time members have available for teamwork, and by making information available on the amount and type of work which they are doing.

The third problem is a member having too many different roles. More usually this is because a team member has roles in other teams and services, and perhaps one or more management roles, as do some consultant psychiatrists. If too much of the work is too different this can be very stressful, even if the total amount does not seem much. It can also cause role conflict. There are limits to how many teams a person can usefully take a part in, and agreeing associate status or other part-member roles is one solution.

The fourth role overload problem is where a team member finds that the level of work and responsibility is too high for him. For example, the team allocates him clients with needs which he finds too complex to understand or to meet, or which become too complex or difficult for him to deal with. Most team members feel 'out of their depth' at times, but they can often continue to be of help if they discuss the case with other team members, or if a more experienced team member or professional adviser supervises them in their work. Teams must make it easy for members to support each other and encourage team members to take on challenging work: this is one way of developing team members. Ensuring that responsibilities are clear, especially in supervision, is a necessary part of these support arrangements. In addition, there must be ways of transferring cases without loss of face, or a feeling that it reflects badly on the team member − it could be a personality clash with a client.

Another possibility is more serious: where one or more team members feel that another is not able to cope adequately with a particular client, and they refuse to discuss the issue when it is raised informally. For the answer to this and to other team role problems we need further to consider issues of accountability, as well as management and team leadership which are discussed in the next chapter.

Non-formal roles and teamwork

The chapter emphasized aspects of formal role and the need to clarify and negotiate these to avoid problems and to ensure effective teamwork. This was for two reasons. First, because doing so has proved to be critical in developing teamwork and to establishing teams which survive and remain effective over frequent changes of membership. Second, because most discussions of team roles elsewhere emphasize informal roles, and may even ignore formal roles in teams. However, before finishing we note how non-formal roles of team members affect teamwork.

The role mix in a team of race, sex, age, social status and roles of parent, school governor etc., that team members bring to the team is important to team effectiveness, and to getting people in the team who understand the life experiences of clients served by the team. Conflict in the team is more likely with certain mixes than others, but a team with little diversity leads to too many unexamined assumptions and the danger that the team does not understand or respond to certain client group needs. Some parents I worked with in Wales regularly remarked that all the members of one team were English and could not be expected to appreciate or properly understand some of their relative's concerns or 'how we work things out here'.

Turning to the subject of 'role styles', the following notes research by Belbin (1981) on management teams and invites readers to consider whether or how the ideas might apply in a community team. Belbin concludes from his research that for a team to be effective it has to have the right mix of personality styles to ensure that certain functions are performed in the team. He describes eight roles and notes that some people naturally assume one or more roles in different circumstances:

1 Company worker: turns ideas into practical actions, good organizer and planner, dutiful and sometimes inflexible.
2 Chairperson: manages time and clarifies objectives, draws out and helps combine contributions.
3 Shaper: sets team objectives and imposes pattern on discussion in a more precise way than chairperson.
4 Strategist: relates immediate issues to wider concerns, points out inconsistencies and puts forward new ideas.
5 Resource investigator: develops links with others outside of the team.
6 Monitor/evaluator: evaluates ideas and checks progress.
7 Team worker: concerned with team relationships and the emotional climate in the team, supports others and resolves conflict.
8 Completer-finisher: checks detail and discourages dilution of team energy on too many projects.

Community teams need to have ways of ensuring that these functions are performed. It is possible to analyse teams for their gaps and weakness in such things as encouraging ideas, time management, maintaining social support and other functions. If a team is aware of such gaps and weaknesses it can try to compensate in different ways. We consider these issues further when looking at leadership and team facilitation in the next chapter.

CONCLUSION

For clients to get the help they need, team members have to know what help others in the team can offer, and to be able to explain what they can do to help clients. Team members have to spend time clarifying their own and others' roles. A well-structured team will have the right mix of skills in the right amounts for the needs of priority clients served by the team. Teams then need to work out who does what on a day-to-day basis, and members have to be reasonably flexible to make it possible for the team to respond to changing demands.

The concepts of formal requirements, responsibilities and accountability help team members clarify the scope they have to take on different work, and who in the team has the skills and knowledge to meet a client's needs. Where a client is served by more than one team member, teams have to agree and define a case coordination role and have arrangements for deciding who will carry this role. Some teams may also have a care manager role with responsibilities for coordinating other services outside of the team. Much confusion and conflict occurs when these roles are not defined, or are incompatible, or where a coordinator assumes that they are accountable for others' work when they are not.

Teams also have to recognize differences in levels of skill and experience in order to give clients with complex needs the expert help which they require. Ignoring these differences makes it more difficult for teams to arrange more than informal support, or proper supervision which is of benefit to team members and clients. To make use of the strengths of team members these differences have to be recognized: doing so need not be as divisive or difficult as some teams fear.

Chapter 7
TEAM LEADERSHIP

Show me a democracy without a leader and I will show you a dictatorship. Show me a leaderless group and I will show you who really holds the power.

Team leadership makes the whole greater than the sum of the parts.

INTRODUCTION

More team problems are caused by inadequate team leadership than by any other single factor. Problems rarely come about because the leader is inadequate for the work – it is more likely that his or her formal leadership role is not clear, or not right for the type of team and situation. It is fashionable to emphasize leadership style and abilities rather than the formal position. And in teams with different professions and where people often have different employers, it does seem at times that leadership depends more on style and persuasion. However, there are limits to personal power, and for a team to work the formal leadership role must be defined and agreed by management and appropriate to the type of team.

This chapter uses the term 'team leader' in a general sense to describe any leadership role in a multidisciplinary team, both formal and informal. In this sense a person who only chairs a team meeting is a team leader, but so is a manager managing a multiprofessional staff team. There are many leadership roles between these two extremes. The chapter describes these roles, shows the problems that arise when people are not clear about the types of role, and shows how to establish the type of role which is needed.

The chapter uses three concepts to help clarify a team leadership role which exists, and which is needed: the concepts of responsibility, accountability and authority. The most common problems stem from team leaders being given or assuming responsibilities for which they have no authority, or for which they are not held accountable. Even the most limited leader position needs the agreement of profession or line managers. The chapters shows what these managers have to do to help team leaders and teams to work, and why clarifying the type of leadership role helps them to be clear about their own management accountability and responsibilities for team supervision. It describes the three options for managing practitioners in teams.

This is not to suggest that establishing a formal team leader role is all there is to team leadership. Just as important are the skills of leadership a person uses having taken up the role. Other team members also use leadership skills when they chair meetings, run therapy groups, or organize a project. The chapter considers some of the skills and the theories that are particularly relevant to leading and facilitating multidisciplinary teams, and shows the part of leadership in decision-making and conflict management which are discussed further in the next chapter.

WHY TEAMS NEED FORMAL LEADERSHIP POSITIONS

Just as nature abhors a vacuum, human groups cannot cope without a leader. If you want to create sustained anxiety and bring out pathological processes then form a group without a leader, and have a rule that does not allow one. People react in different ways, but soon there is conflict and competition for leadership. Some therapy groups run on this basis, but after a short time the people 'running the group' intervene to help people examine what they felt and how they behaved. It is curious that some professionals and managers who know about these techniques set up teams without leaders, or argue against any sort of leadership.

There are many reasons why people do not want a team to have a leader, or why they try to sabotage leaders. Managers do not want to loose control of their staff. Team members are afraid of loosing their autonomy. It is a fallacy for teams to think that leadership will undermine democratic processes which they have developed: quite the reverse. The enemy of democracy is not leadership, but rather those who argue against leadership of any type in order to create a space within which they use undemocratic means to pursue their ends. In fact accountable leadership is the guardian of democratic processes. I believe it is managerial negligence to set up a team without a leader, and managerial incompetence not to define the role properly. Box 7.1 lists the common problems that result.

Box 7.1 Problems which can occur when the leadership role is not clear

- Profession or line managers may over-control their staff, making it difficult for them to contribute to the team.
- Managers may under-control their staff because they assume that the team or team leader is doing the necessary management work.

- Managers are unsure of their accountability for their staff in the team, and the accountability of the team leader.
- Staff do not know whom to go to for a decision.
- Some team members are tempted to exploit the lack of clarity to get their own way – for example, by telling the team that their manager will not allow them to do something, when no one knows whether this is true.
- The team leader's authority to uphold a team policy is not clear. He or she may not be able to find out or act if a team member does not follow the policy. This undermines the credibility of the policy and devalues the work which everyone put into creating it.
- Channels and responsibility for complaints are unclear: should a person go to the team leader or to a team member's manager, or to someone else?

Some reasons why teams need a leader are seen in teams that do not have a leader: they do not last long or do not get work done. Leadership is necessary to ensure that people work to a common purpose, and to deal with things that make this difficult. It is needed to ensure that there are team rules, and that the rules are followed, or changed when they are not working. The type of team leader a particular team needs is another question, to which we now turn.

FORMAL AND INFORMAL LEADERSHIP

Team leadership is helping different disciplines in a team to act towards a common purpose. Most team members and sometimes outsiders exercise informal team leadership at different times. Formal team leaders have organizational authority to help them. Informal leaders do not – their power to influence people comes from a variety of sources, such as expertise, status, charisma and trust. People occupying formal leadership positions also draw on these sources of power in doing their leadership work. For example, they may be more experienced than most members of the team, or have high status. However, their ability to lead does not rely on personal characteristics and power alone – they are given authority to lead by others, often team members' managers.

There are many different types of formal leadership position. If a team does not have a leader, it will elect one, if only to chair meetings. The leader's authority comes from those who elected him or her, and team members know this – they know that their elected leader is accountable to them, and that they can stop their elected leader from doing things that they do not like. Teams discover some of the limits to the elected chairperson role when they find that one or more managers remove staff from the team, or stop them from following a policy decided by the team. Another limitation is that managers may not take much notice of team chairpersons who 'represent the team'.

Team coordinator positions differ from elected team chairperson positions. In the way I define the term below, coordinators are appointed by management, are accountable to them, and are delegated authority by them to coordinate the team. It is common that management will invite a team to nominate a person from the team and then appoint the nominee as a team coordinator. Whether they also pay the coordinator more is another issue. Note that both these formal chairperson and coordinator roles are different from informal leadership roles, where the person does not have explicit accountability or authority. Note also that teams use different titles for leader positions: a team may call its leader a 'team coordinator' when that person is what I would define as a team chairperson. I used the term 'team chairperson' to describe a leader role which is created by and accountable to the team. People in the position have no authority other than that which the team allows them.

The strongest team leadership role is that of the multidisciplinary team manager. Here the team leader is the manager of different disciplines working in the team. An example is a 'locality manager' who manages community nurses, administration staff, and sometimes therapists covering a 'patch'. Staff in the team do not have any other managers, but may have more senior advisers.

Box 7.2 Leadership problems: what do teams or managers do?

There are two common circumstances:
- where management has not agreed and defined the role, and the team realizes it needs stronger leadership;
- where managers decide that the type of leadership role in a team needs to be changed.

In both it is necessary to:

- clarify what type of leadership role exists now;
- clarify the alternatives and the type of role that is needed;
- seek agreement from the relevant managers and consult the team;
- formally authorize the role and appoint someone to the position.

It is the responsibility of managers to decide and define the team leader role. The following shows how to do so and leads us into a discussion of how team leader positions affect profession managers' roles, and of supervision and accountability in teams.

CLARIFYING THE LEADERSHIP ROLE

To define a role more clearly; and to discuss and agree what type of role is needed, we need three concepts: formal responsibility, accountability and authority. The last.chapter discussed the responsibility and accountability of team members; here we summarize these concepts and add authority.

Formal responsibilities are the work expected of a person. They are the tasks which are delegated by higher management from time to time, as well as ongoing duties. Team chairpersons have responsibilities delegated by the team meeting. The responsibilities of this role are different from the responsibilities of a team coordinator, which, in turn are different from those of a team manager. Formal accountability is the position or body to whom one is answerable for meeting defined responsibilities, and for observing set rules and regulations. Accountability implies that those to whom a person is accountable have authority to call them to account. If they do not have authority, then the person is not accountable to them.

Authority is powers over people, finance and resources which are delegated by higher management and employers. Authority is delegated to a position in order that the person in the position can do the work and meet the responsibilities of the position. It is often assumed that there is only one type of authority – to decide or direct, or not to decide or direct. In fact there are degrees of authority and the right type needs to be specified for the work to be done. Even having the 'weak' authority of the right to be consulted is important – it is a socially -agreed right which must be observed, otherwise the final decision does not count. Team leaders often do not have the authority they need to meet their responsibilities, usually because people are ambivalent about the team. Frequently they are not called to account for their performance in leading the team. Box 7.3 uses these concepts to distinguish and define three different team leader roles.

Box 7.3 Three types of team leader role

Team chairperson (elected)
Responsible for: chairing team meetings. Some chairpersons are given other responsibilities by the team meeting (for example, to follow up items which other team members do not, to receive items for the team agenda, or to 'represent' the team). Frequently their responsibilities multiply up to the limits of the chairperson's goodwill and time.
Accountable to: a specific group of people, usually the team meeting. Often there is a time limit to how long one person has the position, and an election or a rotating chairperson.
Authorized to: deal with members in socially acceptable ways to ensure the best use of time in the team meetings (for example, to keep talkative

members quiet, ensure all who need to have their say, and to decide the order of meeting business).

Chairpersons are not authorized to take action outside the team meeting unless directed to do so by the meeting. The group limits their authority in subtle ways, for example by joking about 'our dictator'. Usually *unpaid*.
Examples: elected chairpersons in Buckingham mental health teams before 1992; chairpersons of some primary health care teams in Powys.

Team coordinator (appointed)
There are many types of coordinator role within this category, but generally:
Responsible for: chairing team meetings, upholding and reviewing the team policy, and for some staff management tasks. (The responsibilities of one role are listed in Box 7.4).
Accountable to: a manager or group for carrying out the above responsibilities.
Authorized to: take defined actions to uphold the policy, including to seek information about a team member's actions to check if he is following policy, to ask the member to change his behaviour if it is against policy, if he does not, to report to his manager and ask for her help, but not authority to overrule case decisions for which the coordinator is not accountable.
In addition, the coordinator has authority to carry out whatever staff management tasks are delegated (e.g. taking part in appointments, reviewing work, etc. (see Box 7.4)).
Paid to: carry out these responsibilities instead of casework, or in addition to a reduced caseload.
Examples: team coordinators in services for a learning difficulty in many Welsh counties, and in many mental health teams.

Team manager (fully accountable)
Responsible for: their own work and for delegating work to and managing team members.
Accountable to: their manager for their performance, and for the performance of their staff team in carrying out these responsibilities.
Authorized to: refuse to have staff appointed to them who are not acceptable to them, assign and review work, decide team policy, decide training, and initiate disciplinary action.
Examples: some managers of primary community services (for example, some 'locality' or 'patch' managers); managers of 'core' teams of nurses and occupational therapists in mental health and learning disability. Core team managers may coordinate or contract in therapists and other staff ('associates') to the team under agreement with their managers elsewhere.

Deciding the best type of role for a particular team

Some problems are caused by having the wrong leadership role for the type of team (for example, trying to impose a coordinator role on a large network, which should continue as a network). Some are caused by trying to have one leadership role for all members (for example, a chairperson role when some team members do not have effective management elsewhere). In some areas, managers require all teams to have exactly the same type of leadership when the teams are very different. Problems may also arise when a team changes but the leadership role is not redefined.

A team chairperson role is appropriate to a network type of team (for example, most primary health care teams). Here each network participant is a member of another service, and managed by profession or line managers. The network needs a chairperson to run meetings, and sometimes to carry forward business outside meetings and to be a point of contact. The chairperson role is also necessary in teams where managers have not defined a leader role. To get work done the team has to elect a chairperson, but what that person can do is limited not by any personal capabilities but by his or her lack of authority. If closer multidisciplinary working is wanted, then a stronger team leader role (not a stronger person) is needed, with authority from outside the team.

Appointed team coordinator roles are the most common leadership role, and are appropriate for many types of multidisciplinary and multi-agency team. Box 7.4 gives an example of the responsibilities of one team coordinator position.

Box 7.4 The responsibilities of one team coordinator role

- Drafting or redrafting the team operational policy.
- Monitoring team members' adherence to the team policy which is authorized by higher management.
- Leading reviews of policy.
- Chairing team meetings and taking action about absences.
- Ensuring that cases accepted by the team are allocated a case coordinator when necessary.
- Ensuring that case coordinators do their case coordination work.
- Ensuring case reviews take place.
- Arranging cover for absences.
- Carrying out other personnel management work as agreed.
- Arranging building maintenance.
- Ensuring effective secretarial services, records and communications.
- Dealing with complaints and seeking feedback from users.
- Collecting statistics and preparing a report for the management review of the team.
- 'Representing' the team where appropriate.
- Receiving and investigating complaints.

Team manager roles are appropriate for services where all the relevant staff have the same employer, and a fully integrated multidisciplinary service is called for. A 'mixed' leadership is appropriate for some teams, where the leader manages some staff and coordinates others. Here the leader coordinates associate staff who are either part-time or employed by other agencies (described in Chapter 4).

Teams wanting to clarify or strengthen the leadership can use the concepts to define what the role is now, and what it needs to be, and to discuss this with higher management. Managers wanting to clarify or strengthen the leadership role will need to find out if any one manager is responsible for team performance, as well as other managers' views. Many teams have an established leadership, and their views and wishes will need to be considered. Seeking agreement is helped by using the concepts to define and discuss the role, and by reference to the team policy. Box 7.5 shows four questions which help in working out what type of leadership role is needed.

Box 7.5 Four questions to help clarify a team leader role

1 How did the person leading the team get the job?
   If the person was elected by the team, and nothing else, then he has a chairperson role. If he was appointed, what was he appointed to do, and who appointed him?

2 What authority does the team leader need to enforce the team policy?
   What parts of the team policy are overruled or could be overruled by profession managers?
   The policy becomes discredited if it is ignored by some team members or their managers, or only followed when it suits them. This affects morale and can put the team at risk. Sometimes managers' actions conflict with team policy because they do not know what the policy is, or because they did not agree the policy. A team policy will not last long if there is no team leader with authority to uphold it. Managers must agree the team leader's authority if they want the policy to work.

3 How are complaints made and dealt with by the team?
   What does the team leader do if he gets a complaint about a team member? Does he raise it with the team member? What if the team member does not give a satisfactory reply, or says that it is none of the team leader's business, or that she has professional autonomy to act in the case as she sees fit? Does the team leader pass the matter on to the team member's manager? If the team leader has authority to enquire but has to pass the matter on at some point then he is not a team manager (see below).

4 Does or should the team leader have any management responsibilities for staff in the team?

The question of what a team leader does if there is a complaint about a team member takes us deeper into the issues of accountability, the roles of profession and line managers, and team members' autonomy. We need to look more closely at accountability, and also to consider the role and relationships of team members' managers or advisers outside the team. What are they accountable for? Does their role change with a team leader on the scene?

PROFESSION AND LINE MANAGERS' ROLE

This section and the next discuss management arrangements and accountability for practitioners in teams. Profession managers are heads of single-profession services (for example, a specialist social work team or an occupational therapy team). Line managers are general managers (for example, of social workers occupational therapists and others). Profession and line managers' role has to change if practitioners are properly to take part in multidisciplinary teams. Often managers 'over-control' their staff in the team and make it impossible for them to be full members. There may be good reasons for managers to act in this way, but if teamwork is to develop then team leaders need to have some control over team members, if only to keep order in meetings. The profession manager's role is the inverse of the team leader – the stronger his or her role the weaker the team leader's role, and vice versa.

Another reason for considering the managers' role in a chapter on team leaders is that team leaders' accountability and supervisory responsibilities are often unclear. For example, a team leader may be unsure how to handle a complaint about a staff member. Or a team member may come to the leader for help with a complex case or feel 'unsupported'. Does the team leader always pass this on to a manager?

We consider three options for managing staff in teams. Each has clear management and accountability and also allows practitioners to take part in and benefit from a multidisciplinary team. Our starting point is the management work which needs to be done to manage practitioners. This depends on the practitioners' experience and level of responsibility, and varies between professions. It involves the following work:

- ensuring that basic standards of practice are met, and minimizing employer liability for possible negligence claims (protection);
- work management guidance or direction (for example, setting priorities and policies to help decide what cases to take and when to close them) (workload control);
- staff support and development (enhancement).

These responsibilities are further detailed in seven tasks in Box 7.6 and in Øvretveit (1992b).

This is the management work to be done. Who does it and how it is done are another matter. Traditionally employers established management structures for each profession. UK health services replaced this in 1986 with general management, but most general managers set up profession management structures at lower levels. These structures can be quite complex: it is not always the case that every practitioner has a single manager; they often have one or more senior 'supervisors' as well. This can cause problems, but if the practitioner also works in a multidisciplinary team with a team leader then the situation is ripe for confusion.

Many problems in teams are caused by not changing profession management structures to enable teamwork. One reason why these structures are not changed is that managers do not recognize that there are other ways to ensure that this management work is done. Another is that no one is given the responsibility to secure agreement among all the professions involved as to what new arrangements will be used. Sometimes the structures are not changed because profession managers fear loosing their jobs. Sometimes team members feel that they have more autonomy under profession managers or without any clear management. The following describes the three alternative arrangements.

MANAGEMENT OF PRACTITIONERS IN TEAMS – THREE OPTIONS

Management by a team manager – with or without the help of a 'professional adviser'

The first is for people from different professions to be managed by a team manager. This is simple and there is no confusion about accountability and who manages the team member. Where team managers do not have the expertise properly to manage someone from another profession, then they need a more experienced person from that profession to help them. This 'professional adviser' is accountable to the team manager and may be authorized by that person to carry out some aspects of the team members' management.

Management by a profession manager – with a contract for 'service agreement' with a team leader in non-network teams

The second option is for the team member to be managed by a profession or line manager, usually separate from the team. Again there is no confusion about accountability and who manages the team member. However, if there is no change to the management structure, this limits the amount of team working which is possible.

One solution is to have a team leader who buys in staff from the profession or line manager. The team leader has a budget and contracts staff from different managers to work in the team. Alternatively, the team leader may reach a 'service agreement' with profession managers if the financial systems are not sufficiently sophisticated for contracting. Such a service agreement is similar in some respects to the joint management arrangement described below (Box 7.6), but the management responsibilities are easier to understand with a contract.

This 'contracting' solution allows team working, but also retains clear management. However, it is not possible in some trusts and in many inter-agency teams. For example, in many mental health services social workers are employed by a local authority social services department, and there are problems in contracting them to a health service team. In services for people with a learning difficulty in many Welsh districts, health service staff work in a predominantly social services team, and there are similar problems about contracting them to the team.

Does this mean that a team leader cannot be involved in managing staff employed by another agency? Team members may spend most, if not all of their time in the team and their managers may be remote in many senses. Does it also means that these staff cannot benefit from the support and supervision available in teams?

Joint management – between a team coordinator and a professional superior

The third option is an alternative to the contracting arrangement. It is a joint management arrangement, where a team coordinator shares management with another profession or line manager, whom I call a 'professional superior' to distinguish her role from adviser or manager – it is in-between these two. The professional superior or her employing agency agrees that the team leader is in the best position to undertake certain management functions.

For this option to work, the responsibilities, authority and accountability of each need to be carefully defined to avoid problems. Box 7.5 gives a checklist of the areas where each party's responsibilities and authority need to be specified to ensure that key areas of management are covered. It is also useful for deciding arrangements for volunteers.

Box 7.6 Detailing joint management

What authority do the team leader and the professional superior need to meet their responsibilities for the seven key areas of management below? Choose from three types of authority:

A: Right to propose or be consulted
B: Right to veto (must be joint decision)
C: Right to decide.
• What should each be accountable for?

	Team leader's authority	Professional superior's authority
1 Drafting job description		
2 Interviewing and appointing		
3 Assigning		
(a) casework		
(b) other work		
4 Reviewing		
(a) what happened		
(b) details of individual cases		
(c) other work		
5 Performance appraisal		
6 Training		
7 Disciplinary action		

This third 'joint management' option is complex and costly to set up, especially if different arrangements are needed for different professions, or for practitioners in the same profession with different levels of responsibility. For these and other reasons the second option above of profession managers contracting to team leaders is becoming more popular. Even then, joint management or service agreements for some team members may be necessary where contracting is not appropriate.

It can be difficult to reach agreement among the people who manage staff in teams about what the team leader's role should be. Managers are concerned about letting go of some aspects of staff control. They may be unsure about their accountability for what their staff do in the team. Their agency may not allow them to hand over authority for certain personnel functions to a team leader employed by someone else. Sometimes they feel that their own jobs are threatened and that increasing control over their staff may protect them.

Not defining the leader role does allow people flexibility in a changing situation, but a point is reached where an unclear role causes too many problems. Common problems are over-control of staff in teams by their managers, or the opposite – inadequate monitoring or accountability for staff in the team. Team members sometimes experience the latter as a lack of support and supervision because managers assume that 'staff will get it from the team'.

These three options help to redefine management arrangements to allow staff to work in multidisciplinary teams and to have clear management. The reasons for being clear about these matters are explained further when we look at accountability in more detail and the subject of supervision.

ACCOUNTABILITY AND SUPERVISION

Differences in interpretation of the terms 'accountability', 'supervision' and 'autonomy' are one reason why it is difficult to work out new management arrangements for practitioners in teams. These issues often evoke strong feelings: practitioners fear loosing their autonomy, or feel unsupported, and managers may be anxious about their accountability for someone with whom they have little contact, or about loosing their job.

Practitioners from different professions have different degrees of autonomy when they first qualify. Some professions recognize that more experienced practitioners with higher-level responsibilities should have more autonomy (see Chapter 6). These differences go with different types of management in each profession, where accountability means different things and managerial review and supervision are done in different ways. We saw above how new arrangements could be established in teams to ensure accountability and which recognized these differences. Here we consider the *process* by which managers meet their responsibilities (for example, *how* they monitor staff).

One function of a management structure is to ensure that poor practice will be recognized and put right before a practitioner makes a mistake. Every employer has to ensure this minimum requirement is met, and delegates this task to managers. One way in which managers carry out this task is by monitoring and reviewing practitioners' work, in whatever way they need to and is customary in the profession. Different professions use different methods. For example, some community nurse managers review practitioners' each and every case. In doing so they monitor standards, but they also regulate workload and give guidance about priorities, as well as trying to develop nurses' practice skills. Some call this 'supervision'.

Supervision

Generally, supervision is giving a higher or different view of a person's work in order to help him or her do the work better and to develop his or her capabilities. A variety of aims and needs are met through supervision activities:

- minimizing employer liability and ensuring that minimum standards are met;
- enabling the practitioner to give a better service to clients;
- practitioner learning and development;
- emotional support and reducing practitioner stress.

Arrangements can be made for these things to be done in teams, sometimes more effectively than by managers. Traditionally, managers use different methods to do these things. Each method may be called 'supervision':

- *Routine managerial review:* a profession manager examines each and every case, and can direct action.
- *Manager decides review:* a profession manager asks a practitioner to bring selected cases for review. A date is often set for the review of complex cases when they are allocated.
- *Practitioner requests manager to review:* a profession manager makes clear to a

practitioner that the practitioner can and should request a review with the manager if necessary.

- *Practitioner requests advice from peer:* a practitioner asks a colleague for advice, or the chance to talk through a case to get a different perspective. The practitioner remains responsible and accountable for his or her casework.
- *Collective peer review:* case presentation or audit to colleagues for learning and quality improvement.

If the accountability of a manager for a practitioner's work is not clear then this can discourage the practitioner from seeking support – this is the 'accountability/support dilemma'. Practitioner and manager do not know whether the latter has to direct the former if he or she takes a different view about treatment, or whether the manager is not accountable and can take a different view about treatment, or whether the manager is not accountable and can take a different view without directing the practitioner (that is to say, the manager is not a full manager).

To summarize: at a minimum, agencies with staff in teams have to ensure that there are arrangements to minimize their liability and avoid mishaps. On the more positive side, for their staff to do their best and to uphold quality standards, agencies have to make adequate arrangements for support and supervision. In teams it is often assumed that conventional line management is the only way to ensure this, but, as we have seen, this puts limits on the amount of teamwork which is possible. It also does not make use of the potential of teams for learning and development, and for allowing clients to benefit from a multidisciplinary perspective.

The key question we are concerned with here is what new arrangements are needed in teams to ensure that essential management work is done and which also strengthen team working. One way of answering this question for a particular team is to clarify first, which of the three management options are to be used. Then arrangements for support and supervision can be made which supplement the management arrangements. Here we need to recognize whether the team meeting and the team decision-making process fulfil many of these management functions such as work management (see Chapter 5).

New arrangements for teams

Employers and their managers can establish or agree to arrangements in teams which they feel fulfil some or all of their responsibilities. For example, agreeing to the team leader monitoring some aspects of the practitioners' work, or agreeing a team case review process. Some other team arrangements include:

- easy-to-use team complaints and comments systems;
- monitoring of practice by the team leader;
- appropriate procedures for team members to raise concerns about other members' practice without destroying trust and 'personalizing' the issue;

- 'co-supervision' or 'shadow supervision' for each case;
- case presentations;
- case reports to team.

Box 7.7 is a checklist for judging whether supervision and management arrangements are adequate in a team.

Box 7.7 Checklist – supervision of team members

How would poor practice be recognized before a complaint or mishap?
Who is responsible for taking action?
What does that person do to check that the changes were adequate to ensure safe practice?
What does he or she do if nothing changes?
What are the responsibilities of team members for:

- making it easy for others to raise problems with their casework?
- giving help without undermining the practitioner's responsibility for their case?
- recognizing problems with another team member's work?
- ensuring that action is taken?

Is there the maximum potential for support and learning in the team, without the possibility of confusing accountability?

LEADERSHIP AND TEAM FACILITATION

Of a good team leader they will say, 'the team decided, we did it ourselves'.

In this section we move from structure, to process through time. We look at how team leaders can use certain skills and methods to facilitate teamwork. The next chapter continues this discussion by looking at specific methods for dealing with conflict and decision-making.

Team facilitation is whatever makes it easier for people from different professions to work together. It means understanding the structural and personal aspects of a team which affect how people relate to each other. This book argues that getting the structure right is important to facilitating teamwork, and tends to be neglected. For example, getting the right mix of professions for the work to be done by the team. If the wrong structure is in place then methods to facilitate teamwork will be of limited use. For example, group sessions to share feelings may needlessly personalize issues and take attention away from other causes of the problem which continue after the group session. Team leaders need to be able to understand the structural causes of problems and how to solve them. But they also need to know about and use other methods to facilitate teamwork.

Team leaders use many skills to make it easier for people to work together, often without being aware that they are using these skills. Literature and courses on leadership can be a great help, but team leaders do need to be selective about choosing approaches which are relevant to multidisciplinary teams. There are a number of systematic approaches to team facilitation and development, and many methods for intervention. Methods such as role clarification, problem-solving and many others can be used on their own, or in combination with other methods, as shown in Box 7.8.

Box 7.8 A team development process

Team leaders can use different team facilitation methods in a structured team development process, with or without outside facilitators. The following is an example of a programme, in four phases, which could be worked through.

Phase 1: Diagnosing team 'health' and identifying problems
Methods: Inviting team members to raise problems in a meeting, or in a short structured questionnaire.

Phase 2: Planning intervention
This phase involves understanding how different problems may be connected, deciding the problem(s) to focus on, and finding out what methods could be used to intervene.
Methods: Grouping problems and organizing them in a hierarchy, drawing a diagram of links between problems; clarifying root causes; judging problem importance and 'solvability' to decide which to tackle with some prospect of success.

Phase 3: Intervention
To solve chosen team problems(s) or to readjust balance or deficiencies in the team.
Methods: Some methods involve working with individual members to change their behaviour, or influencing managers; others involve the team as a whole (for example, working on power in the team).

Phase 4: Review
To judge if the intervention has had the intended effect.
Methods: Individual and team judgements can be improved by collecting data or measuring changes. It helps to think about how the success or failure of an intervention could be measured before taking action. For example, recording members attendance at meetings and apologies if there are problems about attendance.

Keep it simple, involve all members of the team in an appropriate way, and be selective – these are three considerations in deciding the methods to use. The means should reflect the ends. Leaders should choose methods which balance the need for full involvement with the time available. There is no need to use a sophisticated method when a simple one will do the job more quickly and cost-effectively. Why do a detailed questionnaire if it is easier and just as effective to take 30 minutes in a team meeting to ask team members to list some of the problems? How necessary is the extra detail which more time-consuming methods might gather?

One last approach we will consider is how team leaders can ensure that certain essential activities take place in the team. We noted at the end of the last chapter the balance of different role styles that Belbin (1981) argues are necessary in management teams. Other leadership studies find that successful groups have a 'task-orientation', they carry out 'maintenance' functions, and they continually develop and change in ways that improve effectiveness. Most studies agree that the following activities need to take place:

> *Initiating:* To keep the group's attention on objectives, to start the group and keep it moving in the right direction.
> *Regulating:* Keeping the group to timetable, limiting activities not related to overall objectives, summarizing.
> *Informing:* Ensuring that the right information is gathered and brought to the group, that views are expressed.
> *Supporting:* developing and sustaining a climate of openness and trust that values each person's contribution.
> *Evaluating:* Judging group decisions or processes, testing agreement.

One implication of this research is that team leaders do not necessarily have to do all these things themselves. If one or more activities are lacking in the team then team leaders can fill the gap, or encourage others to do so. For example, if there is little 'supporting' going on in the team, then there are many ways for the team leader to readjust the balance, perhaps by sharing his or her own feelings about a task or inviting others to do so. Teamwork can be strengthened by supplying lacking functions. Some high-performance teams are structured not just for the mix of expertise, but also for the mix of personalities.

Team leaders should also choose a facilitation approach which is appropriate to the stage of development of the team. They need to be aware of theories about the stages teams go through as they form and mature (De Board 1978; Bion 1968). If carried out in the right way, a team development programme will accelerate this 'natural process'. The next chapter considers conflict in teams and what team leaders can do to ensure that conflict is creative.

CONCLUSION

Multidisciplinary teams are working groups with a collective purpose other than examining their members' feelings and behaviour towards each other, although this can be of help in some teams. To pursue their collective purpose, teams need leaders. The need for leadership is evident when their is no leader, and the need for a clearly defined role apparent when people have different ideas about what the leader's role is. The questions are: what type of leader, and how to get the right type.

Team leadership decides the type of team and teamwork more than any other single team feature. The personality and skill of the leader are important, but so is the often neglected formal role of the leader. Leading a team is never easy, and all leaders call upon all their personal skills to get things done. These skills are not enough to lead most types of multidisciplinary team. In teams other than networks, leadership is impossible without having defined authority and an operational policy.

The type of leadership role affects members' autonomy and profession managers' role and position. Old management structures must change if teams are to work. Team members and profession managers are ambivalent about teams. There are advantages to them in not defining the role. Clarifying the role also means clarifying exactly how different agencies' staff are to take part in the team. No wonder the role is often left vague or up to the team to define, especially when it is not clear whose job it is in higher management to secure agreement about the role.

Having a team leader does not mean that practitioners lose their autonomy, or that profession managers or agencies lose control of staff: it depends on the type of role and on the team operational policy. A team leader cannot act without a team operational policy – it is the leader's main working tool and source of authority. Without agreement by profession managers to the policy, and their wish to have a team leader to uphold it in everyday practice, then there are limits to the teamwork and leadership which are possible.

Part of the problem is that, traditionally, different professions have different management arrangements. To make the most of the potential for support and supervision in teams, we need to be clear about who manages each practitioner, what their responsibilities are, and what they are accountable for in relation to the team member. Then we need to consider if any of these responsibilities can or should be delegated to the team leader. Finally, we need to examine how the team can help uphold standards of members' work and provide support and other types of 'supervision', and how this compliments or can replace managers' responsibilities.

Chapter 8
DECISIONS AND CONFLICT IN TEAMS

Richard was in a gloomy mood as he came back from visiting a client who had just been discharged. The situation was not good – the parents were at their wits' ends and their son's 'outbreaks' were threatening the marriage. Their son was still in a bad way, even with the drugs, and could not answer many questions. But before Richard could get on with phone calls and other visits, there was the team meeting.

In fact, for some reason, four of the team were not there. Jean tried to get in first, insisting that the team discussed the issue she raised two weeks ago – she was obviously angry. Then there were the new referrals, the usual discussions about what the GP really meant, and people 'taking' the cases each thought was a priority – the rest went on the waiting list. Time was passing – the team secretary had to remind people that a decision had to be made today about who would run the client group after the volunteer left. People began to go half-way through 'client updates' because none of their cases would be discussed today, and because the meeting was running over time. Mark used his 'client update' to launch into his speech about the lack of day services, to which those remaining could only nod. Jean did not. She asked if the next meeting would find time to discuss 'her issue' – how little time anyone was spending with the ethnic community and their GPs to the north of town. The atmosphere was of pent-up hostility as Richard left, pleased to be outside, and off to the relative sanity and peace of the acute psychiatric admissions ward.

INTRODUCTION

A multidisciplinary team without differences is a contradiction in terms. The point of a team is to bring together the different skills that a client needs, and to combine them in a way which is not possible outside a team. If a team does not organize to combine different perspective and efforts, then there is no point in going to the expense of having a team. To make the most of these differences, a team must have agreed decision-making procedures.

All too often differences degenerate into disputes, and then divisive conflict. In many teams the arrangements, or lack of them, for raising and resolving issues are guaranteed to cause problems among the most mild-mannered and good-willed people. Not to expect differences and conflict in a multidisciplinary team makes conflict more likely, and more destructive when it finally breaks out. Not recognizing differences in a team and not thinking about how to make the most of them is to miss an opportunity to use the diversity of skills and knowledge for the client's benefit, and for team members' development. The real benefit from teams comes not just from coordinating separate professions' activities, but from combining them in new and creative ways, and producing a sum which is greater than the parts.

Most of us have been in client assessment meetings where different professions have worked together with the client and carers in a creative way. People did not just agree who would do what at different times, but invented solutions to problems and altered what each would do to complement each other. We have been there when this has happened, but how did it happen? Was it a lucky mix of personalities? This chapter proposes that we can enhance this creative process with the right decision-making procedures, and with skilled leadership. Decisions are *made*, not taken.

The chapter describes two types of team decision: decisions about one client, and policy decisions about the team's services to all clients and about how the team works. All teams need procedures for making decisions about a client served by the team, and we consider the different client-care decisions to be made and the different methods for making these decisions. Some teams also make general policy decisions. They make 'management' decisions about how the team will work as a collective, for example agreeing team policies about which clients to serve, or when to hold regular meetings. The chapter shows that teams need different decision-making procedures for 'management' issues which affect how team members work with all of their clients.

The chapter shows that problems reaching or carrying out collective decisions are rarely due to 'personality clashes' alone. They often occur because personal responsibilities prevent the agreement or reaching of collective decisions. Although it is often more interesting to talk about personalities and personality differences, this does not help get to grips with the underlying issues fuelling personal conflicts. The chapter argues that team members and their managers must make clear what their responsibilities are, in order that a team can develop workable decision-making procedures.

A common problem for team members is whether something is a team issue, and to be decided by the team, or whether they can make the decision on their own. The chapter shows how to resolve this problem by clarifying types of decision, and working out a decision-making method which is compatible with each member's agency and professional responsibilities. We see that members' responsibilities can limit the amount of multidisciplinary decision-making or teamwork which is possible. This allows us to clarify exactly what type of team is possible, and what changes would be needed to allow closer teamwork, if this is desired.

For issues that are clearly 'team issues', what is the best way to get and combine views to reach creative solutions which are agreeable to all? The chapter shows methods for recognizing, raising and resolving differences of view. It emphasizes the need to clarify and agree procedures before conflict arises – doing so after differences have polarized and hardened and a team has developed a 'conflict culture' is much more difficult, and sometimes not possible. We see that such procedures not only prevent destructive conflict, but also build a culture of trust and respect which also supports positive relationships with clients and their involvement in decision-making – the subject of the next chapter.

First we consider differences in teams and why some teams deny or accentuate the differences. We consider team members' responsibilities, and different types of decision and decision-making method. Then we show how team members can use these ideas to work out how they and their team make decisions, and how to improve team decision-making.

DIFFERENCES, CONFLICT AND CREATIVE CARE

People in most work groups differ in age, sex, race, beliefs and education. Members of multidisciplinary teams differ in these ways, but there are other more important differences which are central to the purpose of the team – people have different professional backgrounds and training. Years of professional education shape how they understand a client's needs and give them ways to meet the client's needs. As well as knowledge and skills, this education shapes attitudes and values. Professional socialization and culture are powerful and instil an ethic and world view. Professions both attract people predisposed to a given world-view, and accentuate this way of seeing things. In addition to these professional differences, people in multidisciplinary teams often have different employers, with different policies. They also have different experience, pay, conditions of work, status and power.

Why do some teams minimize or deny the differences which are central to their purpose? In my view, there are four main explanations. The first is that people are fearful that differences will destroy the team. This may be a realistic fear in teams with a history of conflict and fragmentation. It is also understandable in newly formed teams where people feel, often unconsciously, that the differences could jeopardize a fragile unity.

Another explanation is professional competition and jealousy. Practitioners in teams have some skills and knowledge in common. Each professional association emphasizes that these skills and knowledge are either unique to the profession, or that they are most developed in the profession – that members of the profession have the most expertise in overlapping work areas. Practitioners in teams fear that these national battles could erupt in the team, and that competition for valued work could undermine the cooperation and give-and-take that a team has fostered. In some cases there is unconscious collusion to deny the differences in skill and competence which are obvious in order to defend against unacceptable feelings of envy.

There is also the explanation that people wish to defend their hard-won autonomy. Members fear losing the independence that they had as individuals and as a professional group in separate profession services. They fear that, if differences in skill, expertise and experience emerge and become more important in the team, then this may lead to one or more professions becoming more dominant and to others losing autonomy. There is not the same 'protection' in a multidisciplinary team as there is in a single-profession service.

A fourth explanation for minimizing differences is that it helps support more equal relationships with clients. I have less evidence for this explanation, and will say more in the next chapter. My point here is that, if there are power differences and conflict in the team, then power differences and conflict will also be found in team members' relations with their clients – a 'mirroring' occurs. It may be that members' conflict with clients 'overflows' into the team where it is easier to express, or the other way round. It is notable that teams which try to minimize power differences in their relations with clients, also emphasize equality in the team and discourage status symbols and power displays or power-based conflict. This is most marked in some teams for people with learning difficulties, where members have common values and share a belief in 'normalization' (Brown and Smith 1992). Some of these teams are still able to value professional differences in skill and knowledge while also minimizing power differences, but it is a difficult balancing act.

It is fear of the consequences for team unity that leads many teams to deny or minimize real differences that should be recognized to organize the best care. How can the team ensure the best match to clients needs if there is no recognition of differences of skill, experience and knowledge? Clients with complex needs have a right to the most experienced and expert team member. If they were allocated to a less skilled team member, that member would have difficulty coping, and the clients might suffer. If differences in skill and experience were recognized, team member and clients could have the benefit of supervision.

Not all teams minimize differences. At the other extreme differences in a team can become accentuated and result in conflict, open warfare and team breakdown. Some of this book draws on experience working with such teams, notably child and adolescent mental health teams. People usually reach for the easy explanation: it is a conflict of personalities. I have never found this to be so: personalities only intensify structural conflict which, over time, produce an intolerable and impossible situation for anyone. I already noted some of the

Box 8.1 *Team culture and procedures make differences creative or destructive*

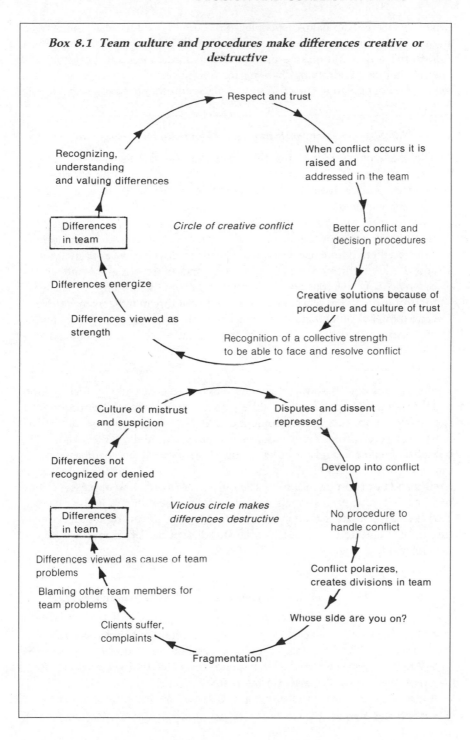

explosive elements in teams – people from different professional 'tribes', with an overlay of different employers, conflicting policies and service competition. Add to this a decision-making process which is guaranteed to bring out and intensify conflict, with no mechanisms for resolution, and it is no wonder that the team is not effective. Indeed, it sometimes seems that a team is set up to fail.

Box 8.2 Stronger teamwork through recognizing and using differences

The challenge is to use the differences to the client's and the team member's benefit, and as a source of strength. To realize the benefits, a multidisciplinary team must encourage team members to give their different views about a client's or client group's needs, about the best interventions, and about other matters. A team must develop ways of recognizing areas of agreement and common ground, and of isolating exactly where differences lie. A team needs to develop ways of living in and working through conflicts of view and of creatively combining differences. Teams that do so successfully become stronger – it is easier for people to air differences because they do not threaten the team. People can experience differences and conflict as a source of strength, energy and creativity, rather than a cause of fragmentation, bitterness and poor morale.

Some teams find these ways of using differences creatively by luck, instinct and the right mix of personalities. If they do not then agree explicit procedures, the 'magic' disappears when people move on. All teams can use differences more creatively with better decision-making methods and a skilled leader. The potential of teams should not be left to luck – clients and team members deserve more. We can no longer afford the waste that comes from teams locked in conflict and poor communications. The right decision-making process is critical to using different professionals' expertise to the best effect, and to energy, morale and work satisfaction in teams. It is therefore surprising that it is one of the most neglected and least understood aspects of team design and development.

Box 8.3 Decision-making in your team: is there a procedure? How good is it?

- Are there issues which the team should discuss, but which are never raised, or which the team should decide but never does?
- Are there issues which the team spends too much time on, or which do not need to be discussed in the team?
- What is guaranteed to cause conflict, or will never be resolved in the team but should be?

List some things which the team discussed successfully, and made a fair and good decision about.
- Was the decision carried out, and did everyone follow what was decided?
- Consider if any of the ideas discussed below suggest better ways for ensuring that:
    issues that are team issues are raised and prioritized for discussion and decisions;
    issues that need to be are properly examined collectively, and that differences are expressed and valued;
    decisions are reached within a reasonable time;
    that all follow decisions which are reached through agreed decision-making processes.

We now look at ways to improve team decision-making. First we distinguish between different types of decision, and discuss how these relate to team member's responsibilities, and then look at ways of making decisions.

TYPES OF DECISIONS AND DECISION-MAKING METHODS

This section shows how making a decision is connected with a person's responsibilities. A person's responsibilities are their work, and doing work is making decisions. To do our work we need to know the limits to the discretion we can exercise, and the freedom to make decisions within these limits. We need freedom to judge which influences to take into account, and how to include them in the decision we make. If someone else or a team is able to direct us in fine detail, we do not have this freedom and do not exercise responsibility. It is important to be clear about individuals' responsibilities, and what we mean by 'collective responsibility' or 'team responsibility'.

Types of decision – decisions about what?

For the purpose of improving team decision-making we divide decisions into the four types, summarized in Box 8.4. These correspond to different responsibilities and different types of work. The first type are decisions made by a professional about how to carry out a profession-specific assessment or treatment for a client, and which methods to use (Chapter 6 described these profession-specific responsibilities). Few teams need to or should make decisions about such things because profession-specific issues, by definition, fall entirely within the competence of that profession. For a team to do so could prevent the practitioner from meeting her responsibilities, and put her at risk of disciplinary or professional action.

However, a care manager, for example, might not be able to finance treatment or care beyond a certain point. Or a team might need to agree maximum lengths of time for any single treatment in order to control team resources. The care manager and the team are responsible for making the most of their resources. These are examples of decisions which are not just profession-specific, and which will always and rightly be controversial. There will be disputes about what is a profession-specific responsibility, and what is a team issue, and whether particular responsibilities should be changed if they conflict with the type of teamwork which is desired. We will return to this issue shortly.

The second type is a care-management decision about one client, such as the one just mentioned. These include decisions about which service to call on for an assessment, a treatment or a care service, and how much of this service the client will get. We will see that some teams make care management decisions by the 'consensus' method, while in others one team member makes the final decision – for example, a care manager. These care management decisions can be difficult, for example where a care manager's resource limits means there are no funds for the services required – the care manager's responsibilities and those of the professional conflict. If all of the required services are within the team, then a care management decision also commits team resources, and is a team issue. These types of conflict are to be expected.

The third type is a policy or 'management' decision. Decisions of this type affect all members of the team and govern how they will act. Examples are decisions about which clients members of the team will serve, and about general policies governing how team members will serve clients, such as how records will be kept. Some teams do not make decisions of this type because team members are entirely governed by their agency or professional policies. Even collective agreements about team meeting times depend on members' prior agency or professional responsibilities – the team agreements are not binding decisions.

The fourth type is about long-term team objectives, priorities, plans, and proposals for other community services. Some teams are called upon by higher management to make proposals about these subjects, but teams do not decide these things themselves, even if they do reach agreement about what to propose. Some teams do decide these issues in the sense that they reach agreement and act collectively to carry out their decisions – they do so in the absence of management decisions elsewhere. Management should make these decisions because it is its responsibility to plan and run the overall service, and to ensure that the team links with other services and meets purchaser contracts. However, managers are better able to do this if teams agree and put forward worked-through proposals.

Box 8.4 Four types of decision

Type 1: *Profession-specific* decisions about one client (e.g., which method to use for profession-specific assessments or treatments, and when to change a treatment).

Type 2: *Care management* or care coordination decisions for one client (e.g., whom to involve, when and for how long).

Type 3: *Policy and 'management' decisions* about how all clients will be served, and about how care management or coordination will be done.

Type 4: *Planning* decisions about client group needs, team objectives and plan.

Type 4 decisions set the context for and should influence type 3 decisions, which in turn influence type 2 and type 1 decisions. Each type of decision relates to team members' and managers' responsibilities – the authority to make a final decision must be compatible with their responsibilities.

Decisions and responsibilities

A person's right to make a decision should relate to his or her responsibilities. People must be able to decide and act to carry out tasks which they are employed or directed to do, or which are required by their professional code. Otherwise they risk losing their job or their professional registration. This is not to say that they should not or could not be influenced by others' views or a 'team view'; rather, that they must be able to make the final decision about what they do, where they have clearly defined responsibilities and can show that these apply.

Chapter 6 described the areas where professional and agency responsibilities are clear. For these areas it is possible to clarify and agree that practitioners make a given decision because any other method of decision-making would conflict with their responsibilities. To improve teamwork it is possible to agree ways in which a team can influence these decisions – whom practitioners should consult, if anyone, and what they should consider in making their decision. We discuss these decision-making methods shortly.

Most team decision-making problems arise for two reasons. First practitioners' agency and professional responsibilities make it difficult or impossible for the team to influence their decisions and how they act. For example, their workload and other responsibilities prevent them even coming to meetings, let alone acting on meeting views. Confronting the issue as one of responsibilities makes it easier to resolve. One might change the responsibilities to make teamwork possible, or recognize that the practitioner cannot be a member of the team in a full sense, or change the type of team.

The second reason for many team decision-making problems is that many issues arise where responsibilities are not clear, or overlap, or are matters of interpretation. Team members may make the decision themselves, when the decision should be made by, or influenced by the team. The team should be involved because there is a collective team responsibility or because what the individual member does affects others in the team. At the other extreme, team members may take too many issues to the team to decide, taking up team time unnecessarily.

There are two approaches to tackling decision problems that arise from unclear or overlapping responsibilities. The first approach is to clarify and work out responsibilities with team members, the team and managers, using the techniques described in Chapter 6, and then to work out decision-making procedures for different types of decision using the types of procedure described below. The second is to agree decision-making procedures that do not obviously conflict with team members' responsibilities which are clear.

In some situations, changing how decisions are made is a better way to clarify or even change responsibilities. The following illustrates and develops these points about the link between responsibilities and decision-making authority in describing different ways of making decisions.

Decision-making methods – who makes the decision and how?

The following describes the five most common methods of decision-making in teams. Readers are invited to think about how a team which they know makes decisions about a client's care (for example, whether to do an assessment), or about a team policy issue (for example, whether to change the venue of a regular team meeting), as well as to think about how team members work out whether something is a team issue or whether it is something which they should decide on their own (for example, whether to accept a referral, or when to take time off for a training course).

The first of the five methods is professional-only: the practitioner makes the decision alone, without reference to the team meeting or a team policy. He or she is guided by professional or agency policy. The justification for this method is that, if the practitioner is to be held accountable for agency or professional responsibilities, he or she needs the authority to make decisions which arise from these responsibilities. There are some decisions which the team cannot or does not need to influence, for example about how to adjust a profession-specific treatment such as a drug prescription.

There are also some decisions which the team member must make, but where the input of the team is required, for example about finishing profession-specific casework. The method used in this case is referred to as *professional after consultation.*

Some decisions are made frequently by team members, but under the guidance or influence of the team or in light of policy formulated by the team. This decision-making method we will call *professional following team policy*. One example is the disclosure of client information outside the team. The policy may be general and allow the practitioner wide discretion, for example 'team members may accept referrals from other sources, if appropriate'. Or the policy may be a prescriptive: 'no team member will take a referral outside the team meeting, or from sources not approved by management'.

Where decisions have to be made which affect all team members, for example on matters of team policy or the application of policy in a particular situation, one of two methods of decision-making may be used: the *majority vote*, where the view of the majority is binding on all members, or the unanimous vote, where all must agree and the opposition of one team member is enough to prevent a decision being made.

Note that not making a decision is a unanimous decision to continue as at present. Another method is for a third party to decide, for example, an independent group, or managers or a management group, when an issue clearly falls within a manager's responsibilities.

Teams usually need more decision methods than just 'majority' or 'unanimous' – majority for some issues, unanimous for some, and an 'opt-out' variation for other issues. The 'unamimous' method means that anyone with a vote can stop a decision from being made. This method should be reserved for decisions where a majority vote could not bind one or more members to follow it – where they are likely to exert a veto anyway by ignoring a policy.

A method of decision-making has to reflect or change the reality of the power of individual team members – teams with no power do not gain it by majority voting, unless all agree to use this method. The reality may be that some individuals can and may have to 'opt out' of majority decisions; on some issues they have higher (statutory or professional registration) responsibilities which prevent them from carrying out the majority view. Opting out is recognized in the method of 'qualified majority voting'. This is majority voting for everything which does not conflict with the responsibilities of a team member which are over and above their team responsibilities.

Teams should recognize explicitly which subjects they cannot decide for team members, and exactly what the 'higher responsibilities' are which prevent a member from being bound by a majority vote on that subject. All team members have a duty to point out any such subjects to the team, and to make clear what their 'higher responsibilities' are. Otherwise the team decision-making method becomes discredited: a team will agree something by majority vote but then some people will not follow the decision because they find (or knew all along) that their other responsibilities prevent them from doing so.

Many 'democratic' teams try to operate by informal consensus, and avoid forcing a vote. Certainly voting is time-consuming and often unnecessary, but doing so can save time in some situations. It can also encourage people to clarify their views, or whether their responsibilities prevent them from following the majority decision, or whether the procedure is unfair. Sometimes 'democratic' teams do not recognize that not reaching decisions can threaten the continued existence of the team, or reduce its effectiveness. The risk of informal consensus is that, instead of allowing greater commitment, it may allow people quietly to ignore the decision, which can undermine the team. As the former Israeli Foreign Minister, Abba Eban, put it: 'consensus is something agreed in public but ignored in private'.

We can understand how a particular decision is made by putting together the concepts of method and type of decision. Think of a specific decision – whether a practitioner should accept a case, or what method of assessment to use. Where would you place it on the matrix in Box 8.5?

Box 8.5 Understanding team decision-making

Who makes which decisions and how?

Type of decision	Decision method				
	Profession only	Profession after consultation	Profession following policy	Majority vote	Unanimous
1 Profession-specific casework					
2 Care management one client					
3 Team policy priority and resource allocation					
4 Team plan					

UNDERSTANDING AND IMPROVING TEAM DECISION-MAKING

Better decision-making in teams usually means better ways of doing three things: first, clarifying what team members should decide, and what the team should decide or influence through team policy; second, being able to draw on and combine different views about the care of one client; third, being able to raise and work through policy and management issues about how the team operates.

Client care decisions

The first step towards improving decision-making is to understand how decisions are made at present. The best way to start is to look at how decisions are made about one client. To do so, teams can first use the client pathway model described in Chapter 5 to clarify which of the five types of pathway the team uses. Then a team can work through an exercise for considering each of the ten stages of the pathway. Box 8.6 suggests that a team thinks about two or three important decisions about a client which are made in each stage (D1, D2, D3). Then team members consider how decisions are made in each stage, using the concepts of type of decision and decision methods described above. Box 8.6 shows these stages, and the different ways in which decisions could be made in each stage. The exercise finishes with members comparing and explaining their understanding of who makes which decisions in each stage.

Box 8.6 Clarifying how decisions are made about one client – a team exercise

Stage 1	Stage 2	Stage 3	Stage 4	Stage 5	Stage 6	Stage 7	Stage 8	Stage 9	Stage 10
Referral sources	Reception	Acceptance for assessment	Allocation for assessment	Assessment	Acceptance for longer-term care	Allocation for longer-term care	Intervention and/or monitoring	Review	Closure

1 For one client coming to and 'going through' a team, list *three important decisions* in each stage:
   D1:
   D2:
   D3:
2 For each decision, note what *type of decision* it is, from the following types:
   • A profession-specific decision
   • A care management decision
   • Could be either of above, or both
3 For each of the three decisions in each stage, describe how a decision is usually made using the following *decision-making methods*:
   1 Professional only
   2 Professional after consultation
   3 Professional following team policy
   4 Majority vote
   5 Unanimous (one may veto)

Often teams find that different members have different understandings of how decisions are made. These concepts help break down and examine decision-making and make it easier to discuss and be specific about the improvement which the team can make. Improvements become obvious by just working through the exercise as a group. The exercise helps to agree procedures for making casework decisions which are compatible with professionals' responsibilities, but which also make more use of different professions' perspectives.

There are some casework decisions which are not just about the care and treatment one client will get, but which clients the team is to serve – for example, a decision about whether to accept a client for assessment. This takes us to the next step for improving team decision-making: clarifying how policy and management decisions are to be made.

Team policy and management decisions

By working through the exercise in (Box 8.6), teams recognize how many decisions are made by team members and exactly what influence the team has over certain stages, such as acceptance and closure. We saw in Chapter 5 how critical these stages are for resource management. The exercise makes it clear whether the team is a network of professional services or a collective service team, or somewhere in between (described in Chapter 5).

If all members and their managers are clear that the team is for case coordination only in a professional network, then there is no need to agree how decisions about workload are to be made – they are made by professional services and individuals. There may be some other collective policy decisions to be made, such as when and where to meet, and the team can use one of the methods described for making these decisions.

However, for some team clarifying how the key workload management decisions are made about acceptance and closure raises the question of whether the team should have more influence over team members' workload decisions. By separating team policy and resource management issues from individual case decisions in the way described above, teams can clarify whether and how the team should influence these decisions. Teams which do have a collective service responsibility can then go through the pathway stages and look at how the third type of policy decisions are made at present (Box 8.7).

Box 8.7 *Team workload and priority decisions*

Stage 1	Stage 2	Stage 3	Stage 4	Stage 5	Stage 6	Stage 7	Stage 8	Stage 9	Stage 10
Referral sources	Reception	Acceptance for assessment	Allocation for assessment	Assessment	Acceptance for longer-term care	Allocation for longer-term care	Intervention and/or monitoring	Review	Closure

List *two decisions* in each stage which commit team resources and affect members' workload:
Use the decision methods below to *describe how decisions are made* about acceptance and closure and other workload and priority decisions:
1 Professional on their own
2 Professional after consultation
3 Professional following team policy
4 Majority vote
5 Unanimous (one may veto)

Chapter 5 considered decision choices or 'options' in each stage – for example, the sources from which the team takes referrals, how it takes referrals, what alternatives there are to acceptance for assessment, and how quickly a client is assessed. Where these issues are not clear, teams can agree which decision-making method to use to work out a policy. Again, the method has to balance individuals' responsibilities with making the most of a multidisciplinary perspective. To get more team resource management it is often necessary to change team members' responsibilities, and those of their managers.

It is by explicitly recognizing such issues that team members and managers can clarify exactly what type of team the team is, and what type it needs to become. If too many people have to opt out of too many team decisions, then there is no formal team, and perhaps not even a network. Sometimes the solution is to redefine the team by redefining who is a member or membership roles (Chapter 6). Teams sometimes fail to confront such issues, for example, when some members frequently miss meetings and 'did not know' a decision was made, or refuse to be bound by it.

Just as the team has a responsibility to keep team members informed, so team members have a responsiblity to take part: those who do not, for whatever reason, are not fulfilling their responsibilities as a member of the team. Worse, they may be effectively preventing the team from making a decision about subjects which require a unanimous vote. This can only go on for so long before a team has to change its decision method, or change its membership, or re-form for other purposes.

Combining for creative decisions

The above ideas help teams formulate procedures which prevent unnecessary conflict, and allow trust, respect and cooperation to develop. However, procedures can also maximize creative cooperation. Creativity and innovation depend on individuals' talents, attitudes and the right 'chemistry'. But the right conditions will bring out and strengthen the creative potential of any group.

In some teams, professions and services come together to pick up and cross-refer clients. At meetings team members quickly exchange information about clients, or occasionally discuss one client in more depth if many in the team are working with that same client. Each profession or service decides whether to be involved and, of so, they then do their work as if the client were referred to them and as if they were not in the team: the team meeting simply makes it quicker to exchange information than telephoning or writing. The cooperation is 'scheduling cooperation', typically informing each other of dates, as for example in some network teams with what Chapter 5 described as 'postbox allocation'. There is little if any team decision-making, and cooperation is limited. However this is entirely appropriate for separate services, and the coordination meetings and 'scheduling cooperation' are an excellent way to obtain and combine services for a particular client.

In some such network meetings with a stable membership, and where practitioners have a common client group, practitioners may hold longer discussions about individual clients. Members are prepared to alter their work with a client to take into account others' contributions, and to do tasks for others to avoid double visiting. In the discussions practitioners are concerned less with their professions' or services' policies, and more with what is called for in the situation. There is more brainstorming, about what the client really needs. Decisions about treatments become more multidisciplinary, with each member fitting into an overall plan produced collectively, and less a scheduling of separate services.

Such teams develop ways of working where the total is more than the sum of the parts – where collective discussion and decision-making produces solutions which would not have occurred to practitioners working separately. Because people have contributed to this process they are more committed to carrying out the agreed plan than if they were called in after the plan was developed. A creative process is better not only for client care decisions but also for team policy and service decisions, where such decisions need to be made. A decision-making procedure can work through policy and workload management issues in creative ways, or in ways which limit the possibilities of new solutions emerging.

Many practitioners want more 'teamwork', and mean by this more collective decision-making, but are afraid of losing their autonomy and 'professional identity'. They are uncertain about where to draw the line between what decisions should be made by the team and what decisions they should make. We saw, above, ways to clarify the limits which pre-existing responsibilities place on the amount of cooperation and team decision-making which is possible. To move to more creative multidisciplinary approaches these limits have to be recognized and altered. We also need to recognize that team decision-making can waste time, dilute individual responsibility, and delay action. The same group processes which can result in creative solutions can also produce paralysis if the procedure is too long, or without time limits, or badly led.

Box 8.8 Conflict resolution

Conflict is a solution, albeit an unsatisfactory one, to differences between two parties. A conflict re-solution is working together to find an outcome which advances both parties' interests, rather than an outcome which satisfies one party at the expense of the other. Conflict resolution, so that the parties can collaborate to find a common solution, can only happen when the relationship between both parties changes.

It is difficult for one party in a conflict to start to change the relationship to find a common solution, especially if the conflict is at an advanced stage – the other party suspects everything that they do. In advanced conflict a 'mediator' such as a team leader is necessary to initiate conflict resolution. Better still is to have within a team a procedure for recognizing and working through and using differences. In the absence of this, here are some tips if you are caught in a conflict which you wish to resolve:

- Recognize and control your feelings about the conflict or difference (immediate anger, fear about losing something).
- Remind yourself that your disagreement or conflict is with an idea or a person's behaviour, not with the person as a person.
- When the time is right or by making a time, devote yourself to really understanding the person's feelings or view by asking questions and hearing what the person says. There can be no resolution to the conflict unless you take this first step (this in itself changes the relationship).
- Show the person that you have understood his or her feelings and views, and check that you have by explaining your understanding.
- Ask whether they wish to do the same for you. If they feel that they have been heard and understood then they will.
- Now, start to work on possible win–win outcomes, and find areas of agreement.

Note: conflict resolution is not bargaining, and is only successful when both parties' interests are advanced, or their wants are satisifed.

SUMMARY: FORMAL PROCEDURES FOR TEAM DECISIONS

Teams need formal decision-making procedures to prevent unnecessary conflict, and to ensure that differences are aired and worked through in a creative and fair way. They need such procedures to make decisions about each client, and to make decisions about how all clients will be dealt with by team members, and about how team members will act. The formal procedure should describe each part of the process for reaching a decision: what a team member should do to raise an item for discussion or decision, and what the team should do to consider and make the right decision.

Most teams need procedures for:

- a team member to find out if an item is a 'team issue' (for example, by discussion with a team leader or by reference to team general guidance);
- formally raising and placing such 'team issues' on the team agenda;
- prioritizing team issues for discussion and/or decision which are currently on the agenda;
- starting discussion and ensuring that all who need to or wish to contribute their view are given the opportunity to do so;
- closing discussion and exploration to move to a decision;
- agreeing which decision method to use (see methods discussed above);
- involving those who cannot be present if a decision is put to a vote;
- ensuring that those bound by the decision carry out the decision;
- ensuring that the procedure is revised and agreed as necessary.

Formulating and agreeing a formal decision-making process itself calls for a decision process to discuss and decide what process to use for which types of decision. Often the process to be used in the future is agreed by unanimous vote, or by higher authorities' decision. It is better to agree decision methods before conflict breaks out because it is much more difficult to agree a fair process for reaching a decision once parties have become polarized. Indeed, not having a process makes it more likely that destructive conflict will occur.

The team leader's role in decision-making

Team leaders play an important part in decision-making. Much depends on their formal role in the team – which of the types of team leader role, described in Chapter 7, they perform. In fully managed teams the team manager makes most decisions, although he or she frequently consults with the team or may even appear to be directed by team consensus. At the other extreme, team chairpersons have no decision-making authority beyond that which the team assigns to them.

In between there are a variety of team leader roles, often titled 'coordinator'. These types of leader are responsible for ensuring that there is an explicit and agreed decision-making procedure for team issues, which may mean proposing one if the team does not have one. Then their job is to ensure that everyone knows what the procedure is, and that it is followed, or change when it is not working. They do not make decisions for the team, but they make the team use its procedures to make decisions.

Part of upholding the procedure is encouraging people to use it when it should be used. Team leaders have to be able to give guidance about whether a matter is a team issue, or something which does not need team discussion or decision. Sometimes people do not use the procedure because it takes too long, or because they know they will not get the decision they want. It is quite possible that the procedure is unfair, or ineffective or too time-consuming. Gossip and rumours may circulate, and secret sub-groups may form because there is no other way of discussing matters. Team leaders also need authority to find out if agreed decisions are being followed and, if not, are responsible for raising the matter with the appropriate person or manager. Team leaders also need to make sure that team time is not taken up with issues which are clearly the responsibility of individual members' or their managers'.

Team leaders need to have or acquire the skills and knowledge to manage the procedure. This means:

- before meetings, helping people clarify the views which they wish to present to the meeting, and advising them about how best to present their views;
- making sure that people know the procedure and possible outcomes;
- in the meeting, ensuring that they or the team prioritize issues for discussion and decision, and setting time limits;

- ensuring that all who need to give their views are given room to do so;
- checking with people whether they feel that they have been heard (differences escalate to conflict if people feel that they are not heard – they will tend not to listen to other's views);
- containing the anxiety of the group when it is raised by strong differences of opinion, by calling for breaks if necessary, or by assuring the group of the strength of the decision process and reminding it of the issues that it has confronted and resolved in the past;
- summarizing and clarifying the essential points of disagreement;
- remaining neutral and ensuring that nothing they do as team leader could indicate their views; if they cannot remain neutral they must say so and give their views;
- keeping time, and judging the advantage of further discussion in terms of individuals' need to be heard, and the likelihood of further discussion leading to a better decision or stronger commitment to the decision.

All team leaders can develop their skills in managing decision-making and in revising procedure by referring to the many books and videos on chairing and running effective meetings. Training officers regularly organize groups and sessions on the subject.

CONCLUSION

Differences and conflict are normal in any work group. Where people from different professions and employed by different agencies work together, there are bound to be differences. These differences can lead to serious conflict which makes it difficult for people to work together, or may threaten the existence of the group. The answer is not to deny the differences, or explain them away as 'personality conflict', but rather to find ways of allowing differences to be aired where they need to be, and of reaching resolutions which are agreeable to all. There are many decisions that are best made by individuals, with or without reference to the team. Frequently teams are less effective because members are not clear what should be a team decision, and what should be up to the individual to decide.

To an outsider the chaotic procedures for some team meetings and the decision-making appear guaranteed to cause frustration, create conflict and prevent collective decisions. This chapter showed how teams can ensure that differences can be expressed and resolution achieved to reach better decisions. It shows how neglect of decision-making procedures makes it difficult for teams to work effectively and make the best use of the variety of skills and abilities of people in the team.

Frequently teams have mysterious ways of discussing issues or making decisions, which newcomers (and old-timers) find difficult to understand.

Sometimes differences are unresolved, or there is open warfare over issues ranging from whether certain staff can take referrals direct from GPs to what type of coffee to buy. Poor decision-making procedures waste time, cause conflict and resentment, and can lead to team breakdown.

Teams can organize themselves to ensure that issues which are properly team issues are discussed, that differences are aired when they need to be, and that decisions are made within a reasonable time and are then followed through. Decision-making procedures can bring out the worst and the best in people, and can create conflict or harness group creativity.

This chapter did not consider one aspect of decision-making – the part clients and carers play in making decisions and in creating new choices about services. This subject is of such importance that much of the next chapter is devoted to it.

Box 8.9 Summary using differences creatively to make decisions

- Differences are a feature of teams: differences in members' skill, knowledge, experience, status, pay, and power.
- Different views about a client and about services to a client group are central to the purposes of multidisciplinary teams.
- Differences in teams are often denied by their members, or intensify into conflict, dissent or personal disputes.
- Formal decision-making procedures and a skilled team leader are essential to ensuring that differences in view are harnessed and combined in a creative way to benefit clients.
- Agreeing and refining a procedure is necessary when teams first start, and before unnecessary conflict happens.
- Management should guide how a team develops its procedure, and ensure that it is compatible with members' responsibilities.
- Teams use the procedure to make decisions about one client, about how all clients will be served, about how team members will act, and about details of priorities and plans.
- If the team collectively serves a population, decisions about who services which clients, and about what other work members do, should be influenced by team policy.
- Decisions about team policy and criteria to guide acceptance and closure decisions should be based on an understanding of client needs, and of the team's resources and responses.

Chapter 9
COMMUNICATIONS AND CO-SERVICE

Well, we don't know anything about it . . . you say you were told to contact us because it was passed on to us . . . when? . . . six weeks ago . . . Well, we don't know anything about it . . .

Err . . . we seem to have lost your file. We're always having problems with this. Could you say again why you came?

Didn't the . . . worker say I was coming? What . . . you've never contacted the . . . service . . . Well why am I here? Oh, here comes the social worker now . . . maybe he knows . . . What? He was here this morning and said he'd come back with me because I had the information!

I was not there at the meeting and nobody told me. You left a message? I never got it and there was nothing in the file. Well, I've given it to the police now because they said it was cleared at the meeting . . . Oh, I thought the client was at the meeting.

Well we didn't know what agoraphobia was, someone said it could be to do with allopathic medicine? . . . Oh, agraphobia! . . . No, I didn't say communications corrupt, just that there was a communications cock-up, it's no one's fault.

Can anyone explain to me why transport showed up with £9,000 of conversion equipment, just as the funeral hearse was leaving? Didn't anyone tell them!

INTRODUCTION

There are three themes to this chapter: good communications are essential to service quality; communications are relationships; and that changes in communications must parallel desired changes in relationships – how team members relate to clients, to each other, and to managers.

Coordination and service quality depend on communications. Without effective communications, a client has to wait unnecessarily, keep repeating the same story, suffer practitioners calling at the wrong times for the wrong things, or arriving at the same time for the same thing, or just not arriving. More seriously, poor communications can result in mislaid or delayed referrals, confusion about responsibilities and unnecessary suffering or death. Of all the quality problems they are the most costly, yet are the least expensive to solve (Øvretveit 1992a). One of the quickest and most cost-effective ways of improving coordination and service quality is to improve communications.

This chapter shows that it is through communications that people do or do not relate to each other. Problems in communications produce or are produced by problems in relationships. We see that sometimes we can improve a relationship by improving communications. The chapter argues that practitioners can be helped to change their relationship with clients through changes to communication systems. It also shows how to improve relations between professions in teams through better record systems.

If it is not a problem of personalities, it is a problem of communication. The 'easy guide to diagnosing team problems' has these two 'explanations' at the top of the list. We will see that some 'communications problems' are not always overcome by better systems, or by more meetings and discussion. For example, different professions' and agencies' confidentiality and disclosure policies hamper good communications and cannot be changed so easily. Some of the reasons why people do not communicate, lie beyond not having the time, or systems which are easy to use. Trying to develop common policies, and improving these systems, reveals more deep-rooted problems. We discover what 'information is power' means in teams.

This chapter starts by defining communication as what a 'receiver' understands, and by distinguishing three types: one-way, two-way and dialogue. It argues that increasing client choice and involvement in decision-making means changing the way professions and agencies communicate with clients. It considers the limits to client participation and 'co-service' for different clients at different times, where this way of working may not be in their or other people's best interests.

Turning to practical steps for teams, the chapter shows how client confidentiality is essential for the right relationship with clients and how client access to case records also increase client trust. It argues that involving clients in checking records and in assessment and planning increases the clients' trust, choice and decision-making. Certain types of record system enable team members to make the difficult changes to their traditional ways of working which are necessary for new types of relationship with clients. The chapter considers how team members' relations with clients are paralleled in their relations with other team members, and at how to improve communications within teams.

INFORMATION, MEANING AND DIALOGUE

Communication happens when one person receives information sent by another person. I put it this way around to emphasize the part played by the receiver rather than the sender – we are meaning-creating animals, and we often make meaning where there is none, or no sender communicating. We think we communicate when we send a message by speech or in writing, but if the receiver does not receive the information, then we do not communicate. This can be due to practical problems, like a written message not getting through, or due to the receiver mishearing or misreading the information, for example a client mishearing the time of a visit, or misreading when to take a medicine. At issue is whose responsibility it is to ensure that the receiver gets the information. If we send information to another service, it is reasonable to expect that this service has ways of receiving and handling the information. Clients and carers are different, and our responsibility goes further to ensure that they have received the information.

More complicated communication problems are when the information gets through, but the receiver does not understand its significance, or misunderstands what the sender intended. For example, a social worker gets a message that the client is suffering from diabetes, but does not understand that this means that the client cannot have meals with sugar at the day centre, or that the nurse assumed that the social worker would inform the day centre.

Again, how far is it the responsibility of the sender to ensure that the receiver not only receives but also understands what the sender intends him to, and how far is it the responsibility of the receiver to make sure that he understood? Is it the social worker's responsibility to know about common medical ailments in older people, or to learn if she does not? Or is it a doctor's or nurse's responsibility to ensure that she spells out the significance if harm could follow if the information is not understood in the way she assumes it will be? If the client had a severe reaction and died as a consequence, what would the court decide?

Another common communication problem is too much information. People wanting to communicate recognize that some things may be misunderstood, and give all the information they can. This is appropriate up to a point, but beyond this point the receiver can be lost in the detail. Often too much information is sent or recorded because the sender does not know what the receiver needs to know, or what is significant.

All these problems arise because the sender does not think about the receiver – how he receives the information, how he interprets it, and what he needs to and wants to know. Good communication means understanding the receiver.

The simple part of improving communications is to arrange ways to send, receive, record and retrieve basic factual information quickly, easily and accurately. Here I mean the sort of information which is specific and not open to interpretation. For this a team needs a basic communications and records system such as the one discussed later, to send, receive and store verbal and written information.

The more difficult part of improving communications is how to improve exchanging and understanding meanings. This involves 'reaching out' to the receiver and exchanging perceptions. Sending and receiving information in this type of communication is for exploring and creating meaning and significance – it is more about dialogue and a meeting of minds than about transmitting or exchanging facts.

We can summarize some of these points by describing three types of communication:

Types of communication

One-way: where one or more people receive information from a sender, which may or may not be the information the sender intended (the receiver may interpret the sender's body language). Example: a team member receives referral information over the telephone or in a letter.

Two-way: where two people or groups send each other information, often in succession or in exchange. Example: a care manager sends a team member information about a client, and receives an update in return.

Dialogue: where two people or groups work together to create a new shared meaning and understanding. Example: a client and a team member discuss possible causes of a problem and together discover something new about the client's situation.

There has to be two-way communication for dialogue, but many two-way exchanges are not dialogue.

Box 9.1 Analysing and diagnosing communications problems

For example: not knowing the client's GP, or that the client was discharged from hospital, or that someone else in the team was working with the client.

To analyse communications we need to clarify:

- what is to be communicated (facts or more complex meanings);
- who is to receive the information;
- why that person needs to receive it and for what purpose we are sending it;
- how to send it to ensure that the receiver gets it in time, and understands what we wished to communicate, or is able to use it for his or her purposes.

To locate and diagnose a communications problem we need to clarify:

- between whom the communication is, or should be;
- what should have been sent and received, and for what purpose;
- what was sent and received, if anything;
- where and when the information stopped;
- why the right information was not received, by the time it was needed.

COMMUNICATIONS AND RELATIONS WITH CLIENTS – CHOICE, POWER AND PROFESSIONAL PRACTICE

The concept of communication as the receiver's understanding is important to improving the quality of service to clients. Teams and practitioners need to make sure that clients and carers get and understand the right information at each phase of the pathway discussed in Chapter 5.

Teams can usually improve the information they give about the service, and about what to expect. People who need the service may not know about it – this is often so when teams do not give information in a way which is accessible to ethnic groups or referrers. If people do know about the service, they may have the wrong expectations. If their expectations are too high, then they will be dissatisfied and consider the quality of the service to be poor. Creating the right expectations is critical for service quality, and there are many opportunities to do this and to check and negotiate expectations at each stage of the client pathway. It is the responsibility of teams to ensure that clients, carers and referrers get and understand the information the team wishes to give.

Just as important to service quality is the team member as receiver: her understanding of what the client wants her to know, as well as any messages the client may be sending through body language or other behaviour. Service quality involves meeting the client's wants and needs. Teams cannot begin to do this without properly understanding what the client wants, and also assessing what he needs, in part by being sensitive to non-verbal ways in which he may be communicating his needs. Team members have a responsibility to help clients to communicate their wants, and to become more aware of their needs. This usually calls for dialogue communication, rather than just two-way exchange.

Teams need to create the conditions for the type of communication which is necessary for a quality service. At its simplest this means being able to talk to clients without distractions and in private if necessary. Many also argue that the communications needed for a quality service mean changes in traditional professional attitudes towards clients, and in relationships with them. It is to these changes that we now turn.

Choice, involvement and participation

For clients and carers to be involved in decision-making, they need to be able to obtain and understand information. This is central to the community care reforms and to service charters. People cannot choose or give consent if they do not know that they have a right to choose, or what the choices are. They cannot make an informed choice if they do not understand the information they are given, or do not get the information they need to understand the advantages and disadvantages of each option. They cannot be involved in decision-making. To increase choice we not only have to develop alternatives, but also change the way we communicate and relate to clients to enable them to choose and make decisions about services.

Further, we need to be able to work with clients and carers to create new choices, choices which would not occur to us alone, and which are more satisfactory ways to meet their needs, within the constraints. Client choice, involvement and participation are not just a matter of handing out a menu and explaining it, but about 'cooking' with clients and carers. To work in this way calls for new skills and methods of working which are not well developed in many professions. It calls for radical changes at all levels, and an understanding of the limits to clients choice and decision-making and of what type of involvement is possible (Box 9.2).

Box 9.2 Types of client and carer involvement in decisions about services

Population						
Client group in locality						
Group of clients using a service						
One client carer						
	No client/carer involvement	Informed/told	Consulted	Equal say/ true veto/ negotiate	Client-directed	Client or their representative do it themselves e.g. Self-managed

Type of involvement — how is a decision made, about what?
What power do clients and carers really have (type), about what (scope), and what redress or sanctions if services do not involve them in the agreed way?

'Delivering a service package' is an entirely appropriate way to describe how some services are provided. The 'package' is left on the doorstep for the client to unravel. The client's involvement is to place an order, sometimes to sign for it if he or she is in when it is delivered – the 'producers' do the rest, 'assembling' the 'package' from the items 'in stock'. To emphasize a different approach, and the one which I believe is called for by most clients and carers, I use the term 'co-service'. This is where the persons in need work with others to meet their own needs – they take the fullest part they can in co-producing the service by co-assessing, co-planning and co-providing.

The idea of 'co-service' recognizes that giving and receiving service to other people is not like consuming or using a product. The product and production metaphors are now limiting our ability to think about better ways of helping other people, and of cooperating with others to do so. This chapter shows some practical steps towards co-service, and some of the barriers. Changes to the way practitioners communicate with clients both bring about and depend on changes in their relations with clients. It means a change in the power balance in the relationship.

Paternalism and partnership

What exactly are the changes in communications and relationships which have to occur to increase client choice and involvement in decision-making? For practitioners in teams, increasing client involvement does not just mean giving and receiving information with more care. It means enabling and creating dialogue, and changing professional practice and power relations. These changes are difficult, and held back by legitimate arguments that, for some clients, the changes are not appropriate. Before looking at practical ways to improve communications we consider some of the arguments for and against greater client involvement in decision-making.

Most professionals 'involve clients' in different decisions about care and treatment, and much is said about increasing client involvement and practising 'client participation'. Within the traditional framework of service provision, the professional and the state service holds the power and makes or strongly influences decisions about care and treatment. The client is 'allowed' to take part in decisions in a process which is 'owned' by professionals.

There are many good and bad reasons for the 'traditional' type of relationship between clients and professionals in health and social services. However, consider for a moment the service from the point of view of the person-to-become-client and his or her carer, rather than from the perspective of the service and of professionals.

Most people coming to health and social services have suffered from some time before they or their carers decide to seek help. For some (and for more than professionals like to admit) the result of their brief contact with statutory services is temporary relief, and not cure, and a lifetime's fear of recurring illness – often a realistic fear. There are people who are not able to cope without continuous expert support. Many have to cope with the after-effects of a social, physical or mental breakdown, long after professionals have come and gone.

Perhaps to talk of 'client involvement' or 'participation' is to get things the wrong way round. We forget that most people choose to involve services in their lives. They choose to involve professionals in helping them to find some solution, relief or cure for their suffering and distress. By taking the client's perspective we can see services' and professionals' work in a new way. We can explore new methods and aims for services where the client is enabled to direct the process, a service partnership, or 'co-service'.

To take the extreme, is it absurd to consider 'mad' people directing their own 'treatment'? Frequently a client-centred approach takes us into immediate collision with professionals. The ferocity of professionals' objections sometimes suggests a concern to protect their estabished position and privileges. This can blind us to their valid criticisms of an overly simplistic client-centred approach, criticism which can contribute to developing a balanced approach and one which recognizes that different clients have different needs at different times.

The first objection is that some people do not choose, but *have to* receive a service, because they are at risk of harm to themselves or to others. Professionals explain that some of the people they work with are not choosing to involve the service in their lives, but are receiving it against their will. In the extreme a person may be detained against his or her will under the Mental Health Act.

Certainly there are situations where the state and the law require that professionals make the decisions. However, where the interests of others override a client's interests, little change can take place until the client chooses to take part in the process. In the extreme, few criminals change as a result of punishment, but can be helped to reform if they choose to change themselves.

A second objection is that many people do not actively choose, but are referred to services by other professionals or carers. Many are 'going along with things' because other people want them to, or because they feel they have no alternative. In these situations the process is owned by professionals and 'involving the client' is difficult and time-consuming. However, professionals also note that their help is less effective if the person does not have a part to play. In some cases 'support' masks a recognition that the client will be continually rereferred. This is good for team statistics, but not for clients, morale or the team's reputation.

A third objection is that clients and carers who do choose a service are often at the limits of their coping abilities, and desperate for relief from internal and external pressures. They cannot or do not want to take decisions and exercise responsibility. For professionals to try to get them to 'participate' is itself to impose a professional process owned by them, which is not wanted. It simply exchanges an insenstiive 'authoritarian' approach for an insensitive 'progress-ive' approach. This objection is related to the objection that to enforce decisions and responsibility on people who cannot cope is to promote an anti-welfare political ideology of individual responsibility and self-reliance.

There is truth in all these objections. But if we accept them without question and defer to the professionals who work in the service every day, and who are the 'experts', we act in the same way as clients: the professionals know best. We, like some clients, give up responsibility and accept professional direction. The danger is that a professional and a client collude to perpetuate this artificial and dependent situation longer than is necessary. If we are considering the service from the point of view of the client, who chooses to involve it in his or her life, we can consider how long it is necessary, if at all.

Pursuing a 'client-centred' approach means confronting some of the most difficult and long-debated philosophical questions, as well as political issues about the role of the state. In what way are people responsible for their social problems, illnesses or disabilities? Can they be held responsible for their actions? Should they take responsibility for their future while ill or disabled? They may act irresponsibly and take decisions which harm themselves or others, even if they are aware of the consequences of their decisions.

This is not the place to address these issues, but it is the place to declare some of the assumptions underlying the approach to client participation which is outlined in this chapter. In some situations it is necessary to take responsiblity for people, and to take decisions on their behalf. The point of doing so is to take the pressure off them to enable a healing or development process to take place which would not otherwise occur, and through which they can regain control over their lives. Enabling people to take decisions and exercise responsibility and choice strengthens them for the future, supports a 'healing process', and is integral to many 'treatments'. Professions and teams need to develop new methods to enable people to do this, and to recognize and reward them when they take decisions which promote their well-being.

Box 9.3 Participation and responsiblity

The role of the professional and the design of the service should be such as to enable clients to regain control over their own thoughts, feelings and ultimately their lives: to strengthen their decision-making powers and responsiblity whenever these are manifest. Once the stage is reached where clients are making decisions, the professional's role then turns to working with them to understand the consequences of their decisions, and how their decisions cause harm to themselves or others.

The issue is the balance between taking responsibility and decisions for people, and enabling them to make their own informed decisions. Different degrees of 'participation' and 'involvement' in different decisions are appropriate at different times, but clients should also have a choice. The underlying principle is of co-service; that clients play an active part in 'producing the service'. Clients and professionals are engaged in a joint journey to understand and explain the problems, and to work out together what to do.

What are the arguments for taking this approach? Is there any evidence that a co-service or partnership approach is more effective or cost-effective than traditional methods? Surely there will always be some people who can never care for themselves, and cope with life as it is lived by the majority?

In mental health services clients' ability to make decisions and exercise responsiblity is often viewed as an indication of the effectiveness of a treatment and of their recovery. But enabling them to make decisions and live with the consequences may in itself be therapeutic. It may also be an essential part of treatment for clients who have lost confidence and feel worthless. Help to make a decision, to carry it through, and to be recognized and rewarded as being competent may be the best help or therapy for some clients.

There is some evidence that participation and involvement are clinically effective, as measured by certain indicators (Galano 1977). There is also some evidence that, although it appears to take more time, in the long run co-service approaches do not cost more (Øvretveit 1986c). The service quality is higher, in terms of outcome and satisfaction, and there are fewer readmissions.

However, even if this approach were shown to be less effective and less cost-effective, there would be an argument for pursuing it. There is a moral argument for striving to enable people to make their own decisions and to take control of their lives. Once they are viewed as incapable they appear to have fewer rights and to be of less value. One result is that staff who work with such clients feel of less value. The approach is also necessary for staff self-esteem.

IMPROVING COMMUNICATIONS WITH CLIENTS – PRACTICAL CHANGES

There are three practical changes which teams can make to improve communications and client participation in decision-making: ensure appropriate confidentiality, provide access to records, and involve clients in creating records.

Confidentiality

Trust is essential for understanding and effective communication, and professions have long recognized the importance of trust to professional practice. For clients to feel able to discuss and explain what can be the most personal and intimate secrets they have to trust the professional. Confidentiality is an important precondition for trust (confidence in the professional's fidelity). It is difficult enough to discuss personal details, without the added anxiety that what you say may be passed on to others. Breaking confidence is a betrayal of trust, and one of the most hurtful and damaging things that one person can do to another.

There are good reasons for professional confidentiality, but also consequences which are to the advantage of professionals, and which sometimes prevent teamwork. Professions need to assure confidentiality to create and maintain a market for their services. Clients put themselves in a vulnerable position when they enter into a relationship with professionals. Professionals have to assure confidentiality to get clients to come, and to get them to trust enough to give the information the professional needs and to trust in what the professional proposes. The very fact that the client has sought help should itself be confidential. All this makes it easier for professionals to get work and to do their work. It also makes it possible for the professionals to exclude others.

Absolute confidentiality protects professionals from evaluation, and enables them to escape accountability and from justifying their actions to anyone, apart from the client, who already trusts them (see Box 9.4). Absolute confidentiality maintains a particular type of autonomy. It also creates a dependency in the relationship: the client discloses intimate secrets and thereby comes under the power of the professional. Although the professional has sworn not to break confidence, the client is dependent on the professional's decision not to do so – the professional gains power where she or he had none. The professional–client relationship is one of mutual dependence. An understanding of how trust is established and maintained in the relationship, and of how the power of both parties is regulated, is necessary to increasing client involvement in decision-making.

Box 9.4 Confidentiality and medical audit
(from interim guidelines of conference of Medical Royal Colleges)

It is possible that medical audit data will be considered part of the medical record . . . discoverable in law in relation to litigation conducted on behalf of patients' interests and also may be used by employing authorities for disciplinary purposes . . . the only exception to discovery in relation to litigation would be that the disclosure of records was not in the public interest . . . No record of an audit meeting should contain any information that could allow identification of patients or clinicians . . . All records of audit meetings, written or computerised, must be anonymised.

Source: British Medical Journal, Vol. 303, p.1525, 14 December 1991

Although 'absolute confidentiality' is preferred by some professions, confidentiality is never absolute. Even for solo private practitioners, confidentiality is continually redefined as conditions change. There are occasions when the professional may break confidentiality if he or she judges that the client's interest is best served by doing so, or where other interests are greater than those of the client, for example the life and safety of a young child. There are conflicts of interest involved in deciding whether and to whom it is justified to disclose an HIV-positive diagnosis.

These conditions are recognized exceptions to the principle of 'absolute confidentiality' in professional codes, although they can involve agonizing decisions and situations of 'client betrayal' for a greater good. Some of the Acts of Parliament and guidance listed in Box 9.6 describe recognized exceptions.

Absolute confidentiality is a myth, but one which professionals can use to their advantage, even when it is to a client's disadvantage. Absolute confidentiality make it impossible properly to involve others in assessment, care or treatment. It restricts professionals' ability to call upon other team members, and team members' ability to help a client without having the information they need. Sometimes professionals in teams use confidentiality to protect their autonomy and work which they value.

The important point is to recognize different types of confidentiality, to agree what type is appropriate, and to explain to clients what type of confidentiality the practitioner and team can assure (Box 9.5).

Box 9.5 Types of confidentiality

As we move down the list, the client has less control over the information he or she gives, and the decision to disclose passes to the practitioner.

Absolute: 'confessional' confidentiality: nothing written down and no disclosure in any circumstances.

Client consent – specific: disclosure only if the client agrees to what is disclosed and to whom.

Client consent – general: client gives consent for the practitioner to decide what information to pass on, and to whom, on the understanding that this is done only in the client's interest.

Unless harm is probable: disclosure justifiable if there is a strong argument that harm would come to client or others if the information given by or about the client is not disclosed.

Client can require confidentiality: the client is given the option to be able to ask for and get confidentiality for certain information before giving that information.

Necessary disclosure a condition of getting a service: the service is only provided on the understanding that the practitioner will disclose information if it is necessary to do so to help the client or to prevent harm.

Which type is best for meeting the client's needs and wishes? Who decides?

Teams need to clarify what type of confidentiality they observe for different situations, and make this clear to clients and to other services. Acts of Parliament and guidance (Box 9.6) require certain types in certain situations.

Box 9.6 Acts of Parliament and guidance governing client access and disclosure

The relevant Acts and guidance are:

- Data Protection Act 1984: Confidentiality of computer records.
- Client Access to Social Services Files, DHSS Guidance (LAC(83)14).
- Access to Personal Files Act 1987: effective from 1 April 1989 (subject access to information (the subject is a person who can be identified by the information)).
- Access to Medical Reports Act 1988.
- Access to Health Records Act 1990: effective 1 November 1991. (except Northern Ireland: Guidance in NHS Management Executive document HSG (91)6).

The *general principles* promoted by these Acts are:

- No right of retrospective access (for example, clients do not have right of access to social services records compiled before 1 April 1987, or to health service records compiled before 1 November 1991).
- Balancing the rights of the data subject to access information about them, with the rights of others to privacy.
- Grounds for preventing access are likely harm to the client or to others.
- Specified situations where the interests of the community or others override the client's rights to privacy.
- In other situations, it is usual to require the client's or data subject's permission before disclosure of information about him or her.

The paradox is that client access policies and Acts of Parliament may reduce the open working practised by some professionals and teams.

We consider disclosure and access within a team after considering the next two practical improvements to communications and client involvement: client access to records, and client involvement in creating records.

Access to records

A second condition for trust and better communications is clients being able to see information about them in case records, so long as this does not break assurances of confidentiality given to other people ('third parties'). This condition for trust is less enthusiastically promoted by professionals than the first condition of confidentiality. In part this is because there are occasions when a client reading the professional's assessment or plan, or other statements, can be harmful to her or lead her to harm others. My view is that there is never justification for withholding access indefinitely, but that it is always a question of timing, and of weighing the benefit against possible harm – if the client wants access she is ready for it and more harm usually comes from denying it (Øvretveit 1986c, 1991a).

Jointly creating assessments and planning records

A more active approach than informing clients about their rights, and allowing access to their record if they ask for it, is to share the record with them. There are many benefits for both clients and teams in getting clients to check the accuracy of records and to take part in creating certain records. This third practical way to improve communications also involves clients in decision-making by taking part in writing an assessment and care plan. A team record system for this was developed and tested for community mental health teams, and is now used in a number of teams (Øvretveit 1991a). The general principles apply to all types of team and enable the team to meet access and confidentiality requirements, as well as to improve record standards and prepare for computerization.

TEAM COMMUNICATIONS

The causes of poor communications between team members are various: no message system, people based at different sites, part-time membership, no list of contact telephone numbers and times, unclear responsibilities, no team record system, no up-to-date index of clients served by team members, different confidentiality policies, and so on. The quality of communications within a team is a good index of its level of organization and of the health of relationships between members. The quickest way to get a sense of the degree of development of a team is to telephone and ask to speak to one of its members – ideally someone who is not likely to be in the office at the time, or is a part-time member.

Many problems that are, at first sight, 'communication problems' are problems with the design and structure of the team, such as there not being a single team base, or there being too many part-time members. Other problems can be overcome by simple measures, such as installing an answerphone, or a client index that is easy to use, or regular meeting times. Curiously, some teams overlook or find it difficult to arrange the simplest of message and communication systems. There are other issues at stake: people do not want or do not see the need to communicate, and it is not because they do not have the time. In looking at these reasons we find concerns about professional identity and autonomy, as well as issues of professional power, competition and lack of respect.

Here we consider two barriers to team communications. Overcoming these two barriers does more to improve teamwork than any number of development activities. Teams agreeing confidentiality, access, and disclosure policies, and team record systems, make remarkable discoveries about each other's professional, agency and personal values. They produce a system that saves time and improves service quality in a cost-effective way. In the process of doing so the team builds relationships and understanding which makes everyday teamwork more enjoyable.

Confidentiality, disclosure and access in teamwork

Just as important to professional work as client confidentiality is free and easy exchange of client information between professionals serving a client. It is true that each professional and agency could work separately, and make their own assessments and plans. However, clients are beginning to object to repeating the same story, and cannot afford the time to do so, even if agencies can afford to pay their workers to record and store the same information.

In fact modern professional practice has for some time been interprofessional practice, and information has flowed freely between professionals and agencies, some say too freely. The idea of the lone professional practitioner and client and absolute confidentiality is no longer accurate, even if it ever was, but professions do invoke this idea when it suits them. There is no contradiction between client confidentiality and the free flow of client information, if the flow is between professionals serving the client. To best meet the client's needs it is in the client's and professional's interests that there is this free flow. Problems only arise if client information is disclosed outside the 'client's team' or is accessible by people not serving the client, and who are not bound by confidentiality rules — this can happen with voluntary workers.

Confidentiality, disclosure and access

In practice the confidentiality principle which many teams apply is that team members tell clients that they are able to give a better service if they discuss their situation and treatments in team meetings. Sometimes clients are given the opportunity to object to this, but in some teams services are only provided on the understanding that other team members will discuss treatment, or will have access to clients' records if they are actively involved. Clients are thus assured that the information is confidential to the team, and team members make information available to the team on this understanding.

Confidentiality in most modern health and social services settings is in fact 'team confidentiality': the client's identity, or information about them, will not be disclosed to or available to anyone outside the team, without the client's permission. This is possible to assure so long as team members all agree to be bound by this policy. Problems arise when different members of the team are governed by different confidentiality policies, or when the sanctions for breaking confidentiality are weak or non-existent for different members of the

Box 9.7 Access, confidentiality, and disclosure of recorded information

Recording, confidentiality and disclosure

Case worker gathers verbal and written information in case file

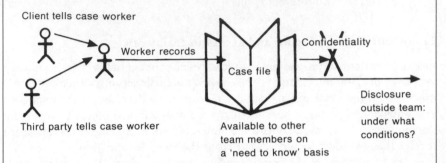

Client tells case worker

Worker records

Confidentiality

Case file

Third party tells case worker

Available to other team members on a 'need to know' basis

Disclosure outside team: under what conditions?

Client or data subject access

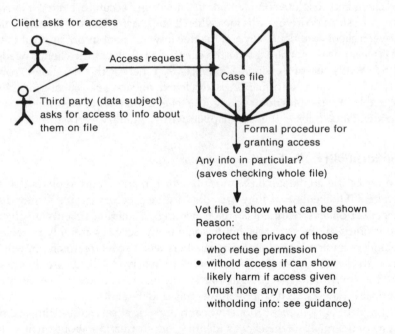

Client asks for access

Access request

Case file

Third party (data subject) asks for access to info about them on file

Formal procedure for granting access

Any info in particular? (saves checking whole file)

Vet file to show what can be shown
Reason:
• protect the privacy of those who refuse permission
• withold access if can show likely harm if access given (must note any reasons for witholding info: see guidance)

Note: formal client access to records is different from 'live access' for client participation team. This can happen when agencies have different policies, or volunteer members of the team do not sign enforceable confidentiality agreements.

The issues here are disclosure of information about a client by a member of the team to someone outside the team, and whether each team member is governed by the same rules. There are two types of situation: verbal and written. In the first, one team member working with the client shares with another (or with the team at a meeting) information about the client, which is then subsequently disclosed verbally outside the team. People are usually aware of the issues and careful about confidentiality in this type of situation – it is easier for them to control.

The 'written situation' is where a team member has access to a client record, and makes his or her own record, which is then accessed by or passed to someone outside the team. A recent example was a clerk supplying client names, addresses and treatment to finance departments for invoicing. The young girl's uncle working in the finance department discovered that his niece had an abortion. In the written situation it is more difficult to control paper flows and access to manual or computer records. Also the longer the 'chain' from the original verbal discussion, the higher the probability of inaccuracies.

These and other situations have led to professional concern about confidentiality which are often entirely justified, and to professionals exercising greater control over 'their' records. It is possible to develop a team policy which meets these legitimate concerns and statutory requirements. Examples are available in Øvretveit (1986c, 1991a). However, professions and agencies may not agree a common policy for other reasons. Control of information, and of access to it, is power. The confidentiality principle is used at times to assert or exercise power, or prevent it from being challenged. This is apparent where one profession wishes to assert or avoid losing power with regard to other professions, and in relations with managers.

In teams where one or more professions (or agencies) are concerned about their power and autonomy, agreement about a common access and disclosure policy may not be possible. Without such a policy the team's effectiveness is limited, which may be an underlying reason why a profession or agency will not discuss or reach agreement on one. There are few more effective ways of undermining teamwork than by controlling information. It is easy to give a list of reasons why information cannot be supplied: files have to be stored at a distant site, one record file per client is not possible, and so on. Some professionals espouse a pro-teamwork philosophy, but undermine cooperation by preventing other professions accessing their records, and by not supplying information to other professions.

Finally, it is of note that there are parallels between the type of communications and working relationships which professionals have with clients, and their working relationships and communications with each other. It is a striking observation that teams which practice co-service and partnership, also work hard at creating and maintaining open and participatory relationships within the team. Where there is little respect between professions in a team, or simply little contact or indifference, there is often also an attitude to clients which does not fully value or appreciate the clients' situation. A change in the quality of communications both depends on and brings about a change in the quality of relationships, both inside the team and between the team and clients.

Record systems

A common team record system is just as important to team communications as are confidentiality, access, and disclosure policies – it's also a way of applying such policies.

The types of case record system which a team uses reflect the degree of fragmentation in the team. Three systems are commonly in use:

> *Separately held professional records:* each team member holds his or her own record files and provides summaries or reports to other team members working on the case, on request.
> *Single case file, separate records:* each member's record files are held in one place (e.g. in the team office), or the separate records are held in one file, under the name of the client. Team members have the right of access to other team members' records on the client with whom they are working, or may be working.
> *Single case file, common record forms and supplementary reports:* The third arrangement is where team case coordinators (or care managers) have a client file, and make records on the client which cover basic information, assessment and plans. There is an agreed type of file and agreed team record forms for the areas to be covered by case coordinators, who may be from any profession. The case file starts with these record forms, and holds other supplementary reports from other team members or specialists in a reference section.

Moving from separate professional and agency systems to shared records, and then shared files, brings about closer cooperation between team members and makes it easier to meet confidentiality and client access requirements.

There are strong arguments for a one-client-one-file system, but more questions about agreeing common record forms. In research to develop a common case record system in community mental health teams we found it surprisingly easy to agree the items and format for the following forms, to be used by all members of the team: referral form, basic information, contacts sheet, detail record form, first assessment and planning form, reassessment and review form, closure form, and care coordination record. What was more surprising was that, over the nine-month period of testing, no team members found the need to write any other profession-specific records (Øvretveit 1991a).

The question of whether a team record system should be used, and the format of the system, is ultimately one of whether a common approach to assessment and planning can and should be agreed, and about how profession-specific assessments and decisions should be incorporated into the record. It involves clarifying the profession-specific competencies and shared areas of competence and responsibilities discussed in Chapter 6. It involves examining differences and similarities of view about clients' needs, the causes of common client problems and the types of help or treatment different members provide.

Developing and agreeing a common access policy and record system forces professions and agencies to confront the most central issues in cooperation. It forces them to recognize and work through differences which they otherwise avoid, and allows them to realize the benefits of teamwork. Frequently practitioners try to cooperate more closely with other practitioners, but the record systems stay the same and work against cooperation. The record systems and forms which team members use have evolved to support the work which they do. If they change the way they work then their record systems will also need to change. Record systems must reflect and support the team's preferred work process, otherwise the system will not be used. The secret to designing a common record system is first to clarify a team's preferred work process – the best way for the team to receive, process and finish work – using the client pathway model in Chapter 5, and then decide on a record system.

Box 9.8 A team record system and recording standards

Records and client access

Client access to records means that team members have to be more careful about what they record. However, improvements to recording are made not only to prepare for possible access requests, but also to raise the quality of the service given by the team through:

- saving time recording and accessing information;
- better communications between team members and others;
- involving clients more closely in the assessment and treatment process.

Participation is an end in itself, and improves outcome in most cases.

Recording principles

In general, too much detail is more harmful than too little.

Record standards

A good case record is relevant, concise, accurate, timely, accessible, jargon-free, 'behavioural' not 'attributive', with an assessment which links to a plan with time-targeted objectives and actions.

Purpose and relevance

- The main purpose of gathering and holding information about a client is to provide the best possible service to the client.

- Only as much information as is needed for this purpose should be sought and written down. Team members should be able to explain and justify why they need to discover and to write down any piece of information.
- Choose to write detail only for a specific purpose.

Descriptive not abstract
- Use descriptive or behavioural statements, rather than general or abstract ones which may not be understood.

Distinguish on record between:
- your observations (behavioural);
- reported facts or opinions (state whether verified);
- personal feelings (when should they be recorded and why?);
- your concerns/intuitions/hunches (for which there is no clear evidence as yet);
- your professional assessments/judgements based on evidence or reasoning, or experience of similar situations.

External team communications

Teams and their members communicate with other services, management, purchasers, client and carer groups and others. Some of this communication is about a particular issue or item, such as a new service. Some is dialogue about one issue, such as planning, financing, and starting a carers' group which becomes self-supporting. But most communications are about one client or about aspects of many clients, such as how many clients the team served in one month. This communication is regular and predictable, and to give service the team must have easy-to-use systems for sending out and receiving information. Ideally, the team should have a system for recording something once, and using the record to supply information others want, rather than recording the same thing many times for different purposes.

Communications with other services are mainly about what services the team provides, guidance for referrals, how to contact the team, and about individual clients. Disclosure of client information is guided by the team's confidentiality policy, which others need to know about to keep information flowing freely and with the necessary precautions. A common problem is when a team member does not pass on to another service information about a change in a client's or carer's status that the other service needs or wants (for example, letting a GP know that the team doctor has changed a drug prescription). A second problem is when others do not inform the team about a change in a client's status (for example, the client dies in hospital or is discharged). Often both problems arise when people are too busy to do their own work, let alone worry about keeping others informed. But if serving the client is their work, then it is also their work to ensure others get the information they need to help the client. If the systems are too difficult and time-consuming to use then management has failed in its work.

As is often the case, the communication problem arises because it is not clear whether it is the responsibility of one service to tell another, or of another service to ask for certain information on a regular basis. Where a service needs to inform another to meet its responsibilities it takes more trouble to provide the information (for example, early warning about discharge when a hospital needs a team to make arrangements before the client can leave). What is important is that to meet the client's needs, others must have certain information. A service has not met its responsibility to a client until it has given others the information they need to help the client, and until it has let others know what information it needs to help the client. To do both a service must have effective systems to make sure that the necessary information is easy to give and to get.

Communications between a team and management are about single items, or the team regularly providing routine information for financial and management purposes. The routine information is of two types, the first concerning clients, and the second concerning team members' activities and use of time. Again the information flows reflect and sustain the underlying structure of relationships: an integrated team collects information about its members and their clients and routinely sends this 'aggregated' information in an agreed format to management (see Chapter 10). At the other extreme each member 'sends' or records for her profession or agency manager information about her work or clients. In between, each member does both, and complains about the paperwork. Arguments about to whom management information is to be supplied and how, are often arguments about how the team will be managed and about what type of team it will be. And again we see how changing communications changes relationships, and that to change relationships we have to change communications.

The minimum financial information is a client's postcode and a code for the service the client is getting from the team or team member. This is to ensure that the right purchaser pays the right amount for the service the team provides. This information is also the basis for other management information about cost and quantity of service. Quality of service is more difficult, but at a minimum has to cover waiting times and items required in patient and carer charters (Øvretveit 1992a).

The most important design principle for an information system is that a team member only records items once (for example, a client diagnosis, or time spent on a visit. The system must be able to abstract from the basic client information the information that the team and managers need to do their management work. This is easy to do if each case record is on computer, because a computer system simply collects the weekly and monthly information needed from each client's case record. The danger is that the people designing such systems add more and more items to the case record format so that the usefulness of the system for casework declines and each team member ends up having to learn and use categories designed for other services. Result: the team reverts to manual files, or never uses the system, unless someone knows how to use it for word-processing reports.

CONCLUSION

Communication happens when someone makes meaning out of an action or sign given by someone else. Communication depends on yet also creates a relationship: it may be one-way, two-way or a dialogue where two create new meaning and a new relationship. The latter is important for creating new choice for services which meet clients' needs better. It is central to co-service where a team member not only makes it possible for clients to make informed choices about their future, but creates new choices with them. This is the opposite of 'delivering a service package'.

To help clients we need to be able to communicate with them, and the better our communication the more we are able to help. We need to make sure that the people we can help know what help we can provide, that they can get to us easily or that others can send them to us easily, that we can understand what they want and need, and that they understand what we will do. To do this we need to give and get information, and to establish and develop the right relationship with clients so that we can understand each other, and work out between us what to do.

However, the quality of service to a client and carer depends on more than ensuring that information was sent and received. It depends on more than the practitioner making himself understood, and understanding the client and carer. The quality of service depends on client and carer making or being involved in decisions about their care or treatment. Communication in this instance is for the purpose of jointly creating a decision — it is dialogue. And for this the practitioner has to establish a relationship with the client and carer which is closer than one of exchanging information, but which does make information exchange easier.

The trusting relationship necessary for dialogue and co-service depends on confidentiality and can be developed by client access to records and their involvement in assessment and planning, and even in writing the records if appropriate. This helps team members change traditional ways of practising, which can discourage clients from exercising more choice and autonomy when they are able to.

Absolute professional confidentiality prevents teamwork and is usually against the client's interest. Legitimate agency and professional concerns about confidentiality which are in the client's interest can be met by a team confidentiality, access and disclosure policy. Other services need to know about such a policy, and about what information the team needs about clients and how to provide it on a routine basis.

A team record system helps to apply the policy, and to increase cooperation and efficiency in a team. Such a system can also form the basis for a financial and management information system, which aggregates items of client information so that team members waste less time on paperwork. Developing and agreeing a team record system is a good way to work through some of the practice issues which must be resolved to achieve effective teamwork and to develop team organization.

Box 9.9 Improving communications: checking the basics

	Do we have it? (How good is it? (1–5))	Do we need it? (or to improve it?)	How do we get it? (or make it better)
1 Shared client index (each profession/ practitioner registers its involvement with a client)			
2 Contact points and times for each team member			
3 Message system			
4 System for requesting information from another service, and for sending information to it			
5 Access to each profession's case files			
6 A common case file for each client			
7 Common forms for: • referral • basic information • assessment • planning • reviews • closure			
8 Common language			
9 More understanding of each others skills			

Complete the following:
The most common team communications problems in our service/team are . . . not informing . . . about . . . by telephone, writing, speaking to, or . . . (other).

Chapter 10

COORDINATING COMMUNITY HEALTH AND SOCIAL CARE

INTRODUCTION

This chapter summarizes practical points for forming, building and improving community teams and care management. It draws on the previous chapters of the book to show how to review and improve cooperation between agencies and professions at the practitioner level. It starts by raising the prior issues of who has or will assume responsibility for improving cooperation between the variety of agencies at different levels, which were discussed in Chapter 2.

The chapter assumes that the difficulties in improving cooperation are both practical and conceptual. It assumes that only some people recognize the need to make improvements and want to work at doing so – most give lip-service or are indifferent or opposed to changes. The knowledge that clients get a better service and staff find work less frustrating is not always a sufficient incentive for improving cooperation and for putting in a lot of effort for little recognition. Few have ideas about what the options are, their costs or the steps to get there.

The chapter assumes that those giving lip-service may become more motivated if they can be persuaded to contribute to discussions about options, ways to improve cooperation, and the costs and benefits. As a result, they begin to see what the changes would mean for them in practice, and that some changes would be in their interests, saving time and money and giving a better service to clients. By being specific about improvements in cooperation, people become less fearful and suspicious, are able to evaluate changes and see that they could gain more than they might lose, and can contribute in a meaningful way to planning new ways of working. Such discussions themselves make future cooperation easier and more likely.

We assume that some managers are designing new teams or care management systems from scratch, while others are aiming to improve the cooperation which currently occurs and to resolve team problems. Both will find the chronological sequence of the chapter of help – current problems often arise because of missed steps in setting up teams or care management systems. For example, management not setting a policy framework for a new team and then finding that the team is serving the wrong clients. Or not first taking stock of the coordination arrangements which a team has developed in an area over the years.

The chapter starts with a planning or review stage. This assumes that someone has taken the initiative to improve coordination, either because he or she has a responsibility to do so, or because the problems have become so acute. The chapter shows how understanding needs is the key to assessing current cooperation and to deciding improvements. It shows how to use the descriptions of types of team and care management system from earlier chapters to clarify how things are organized now and what the options are for the future.

It then considers ways to improve cooperation in networks, concentrating on primary care networks which are the most common of this type of team. It then turns to setting up and improving more closely integrated 'collective service teams'. It describes annual management reviews of formal information needed for such reviews as well as team service quality. It closes with summaries of common pitfalls and problems.

PLANNING AND REVIEWING TEAMS AND CARE MANAGEMENT

We know that clients, carers, and sometimes practitioners, suffer because of poor cooperation, and that they are often the first to perceive and raise the problems. To whom do they go to get a solution? Who 'owns' problems of cooperation? Whose job is it at higher levels to ensure that there is effective cooperation?

We saw in Chapter 2 that there has to be a degree of high-level cooperation in order to address the issues in the first place. Typically one agency may have more responsibility than others for developing cooperation between practitioners and services, or one may perceive or suffer the consequences of poor local cooperation more acutely – for example, an NHS hospital trust unable to discharge clients because of poor cooperation between community agencies. Because of split responsibilities, getting such reviews started is difficult because no one really 'owns' problems of cooperation, or has a clear responsibility to ensure that it happens. Long-standing client group joint planning teams may no longer exist. Alternatively there may be duplication – more than one cross-agency planning group looking at the issue, and each group unsure what the other is proposing or working on.

Chapter 3 described models for collaboration at higher levels and Chapter 9 discussed ways to involve clients and carers at different levels. Where cross-agency groups do not exist, and even where they do, changes and improvements are often driven by middle managers from health and social services working on issues of cooperation within a locality. The following assumes that a team, a locality group, a purchasing group, or some other cross-agency group forms to review local cooperation or to plan a new team. We are concerned here with contributing to and carrying out community care plans.

The starting point for planning or reviewing cooperation is understanding the needs of localities and client groups, and the services currently provided by different professions and agencies. Chapter 2 shows how purchasers and providers could become better informed about needs and services and pool their understandings. It proposed drawing boundaries around different localities and client groups, and ways for gathering knowledge about needs within client groups, and about services in a locality.

With this always incomplete, but shared, picture of needs, managers or practitioners in teams can take stock of how much of which types of service are provided, and how services are organized. If practitioners are already grouped together in teams, the membership and structure will be close to one of the types of team described in Chapter 4. The first step in understanding current service organization is to clarify whether a team is a network team, or an integrated collective service team, or somewhere in between. Chapter 5 underlined the difference by describing the collective work responsibilities of the collective service team, and the separate priorities and responsibilities of professions and services in a network. The second step is to clarify what types of care management system are operating or planned, and how they run separately to multidisciplinary teams, or are part of such teams (Chapters 4, 5 and 6).

With this broad understanding of current service organization, the review group can begin to clarify the options for the future. Chapter 4 argued that people too readily assume that a team is a solution without looking at the other options, or describing what type of team to develop. The key issues are:

- whether to improve cooperation in a network, or to create a formal team (Chapter 4), or, if a formal team already exists,
- how to improve teamwork (Chapter 5 onwards), and,
- how these options fit in with or establish care management (Chapters 2, 4 and 6).

We now consider improvements to networks, and then to formal teams.

IMPROVING COOPERATION IN NETWORKS

Barriers to cooperation

The following describes the main impediments to cooperation in networks and the possible ways of overcoming them. It also considers the incentives to cooperation and how people might change their arrangements to make it easier to work together when it is in their and their clients' interests to do so. It concentrates on primary health care teams as these are the most common type of network team, and in order to give specific examples.

No time
One of the most frequent barriers to cooperation and communications is not having time, because of pressure of work or emergencies. There are two issues: first, not having time to establish and maintain systems to make cooperation and communications quick, easy and automatic (for example, to set up regular meetings, agree contact points and times, devise referral forms); and second, not having time to use the systems properly (for example, lateness or missing meetings, not keeping common client indexes up to date).

It is indicative of the fragility of cooperation in some networks, and of the underlying profession structure, that when practitioners are under pressure they spend less time informing, negotiating and consulting with others. Just when many of the benefits of teamwork could emerge, practitioners retreat into their professions. Cooperation and communications are not absolutely essential because the current structure is profession-based. But, even with the current profession-based structure, cooperation and communication save time in the long run.

A number of solutions are available: first, for all to understand how cooperation makes work easier, and is necessary for an effective end result for the patient; second, to invest time in setting up and maintaining effective systems; third, to hold others accountable for not using the arrangements properly; fourth, to make more effective use of the time which is available by having well-organized meetings.

Part-time working
Some practitioners and staff work part-time in networks and primary care teams, either because they are employed part-time, or because they also work in other areas. The more people have in common, then the more they are likely to associate. The fact that some members of a group are part-time will mean they are less involved, although they may well be more committed to the group. The practical problems part-time membership gives rise to are greater difficulty than normal in scheduling meetings because there is less flexibility in the time in which the part-timer is working. The more part-time receptionists there are, the greater the problems of communications and of ensuring each is up to date with changes.

There are no real solutions, but some of the problems of part-time membership can be minimized. A general rule of thumb is that it is difficult for people working less than two days a week to be full members of a team, and this should be recognized by giving them 'associate member' status (Chapter 4), and by ensuring that they are kept informed. The total time these members have available for the population and the times when part-timers are working for the team should be made clear to all concerned, as well as where they can be contacted. An effective message system and a policy on callback is also important, as it is for all members of the team. The more part-timers the more there is a need for regular formal 'updating' meetings and communications.

Large numbers

Just as there is a minimum number of practitioners and degree of contact necessary to form a team, so there is a maximum number. Too many members (over, say, 15) makes contact difficult and arranging meetings and collective decision-making impossible. The difficulties of knowing whom to contact, and contacting them, and of arranging meetings increases exponentially as numbers increase (Box 10.1). Paradoxically, the wish to maximize involvement and communications leads to an undermining of teamwork. Solutions are formally to define the boundaries and full membership of each network group, and to recognize associate membership and liaison links.

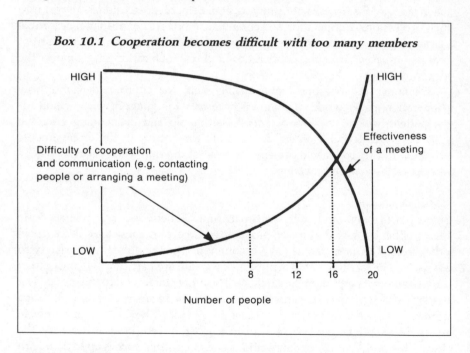

Box 10.1 Cooperation becomes difficult with too many members

Different patient populations

A third factor which works against closer cooperation in primary health care is where practitioners have different patient populations. If all the members had the same patient population then they would have an incentive towards more frequent contact and better coordination. To the extent that members have different populations, there is less to draw them together.

General practices are based on registration by people with the practice and GP of their choice. GP lists tend to be geographical, but there are areas where some people choose a different, neighbouring practice. District nurse (DN) populations have been defined by geographical boundaries. Thus GPs in one practice will relate to DNs which cover their area, but also to DNs which cover other areas. The problem this gives rise to is that GPs have less contact with DNs from neighbouring areas, who themselves complain of the difficulties they have in contacting GPs. Some large practices have a further geographical subdivision of district nurse patches. This situation is further compounded by the fact that health visitors (HVs) may also have different client populations. The biggest single change which could be made to improve cooperation would be to align all practitioner patient populations. However, it would be difficult to zone GP populations because this would restrict patient choice to the GP or GPs within the area, which conflicts with increasing choice and competition.

Changing DN and HV populations from a geographical basis to a GP list basis – what GPs call 'true attachment' – would also be difficult: nurses argue that there are advantages in having one HV and one DN who are known to people and themselves know the area. If they aligned to GP lists, then in the practice boundary areas there would be HVs and DNs from different practices all visiting the same area, which would be less efficient. In addition, if a client changed her doctor, in principle it would mean that she would then have a different HV and DN. There are also those GP practices which extend into other district health authorities, and are served by the other health authority community nurses – aligning populations would mean nurses serving other health authority populations (and vice versa).

If closer cooperation is to be achieved then practitioner populations must be aligned. If GP zoning is out of the question, the only solution is to align nurses. The advantages of having populations in common are, on balance, greater than the disadvantages of 'multiple coverage' at the boundaries, and the problems of changing nurses as well as GPs for the few clients who do change their GP. There is also no reason why one community nursing service cannot serve a 'non-host' purchaser's area where it would provide a better, more integrated primary health care service. It is in GPs' interests to seek such arrangements because they are then able to offer patients in other areas a more attractive team service, a valuable competitive advantage.

Different bases and base design
A fourth barrier to cooperation is where practitioners have different bases. This makes it less likely that frequent informal contact will occur. There are also different points for leaving messages, and files and other records are held at different sites. Although there is provision under the cost-rent scheme for GPs to arrange accommodation for health authority nurses, some GPs are suspicious that the government might not honour agreements. One solution is for health authorities to enter into a formal long-term contract with GPs wishing to offer

nursing space and assure continued finance if there are changes to cost-rent schemes in the future.

It is rare that there is not the building space available for extra accommodation. If an FHSA and health authority wish to improve cooperation in primary health care it is necessary for them to examine ways to finance accommodation for nurses at GP surgeries, or offer GPs and nurses suitable accommodation elsewhere. Having the same base is not enough – it is also important to design the building in a way in which contact is easy and with formal and informal meeting areas.

Unclear roles

Although common populations and a common base help cooperation, they do not ensure that it happens. A further barrier is not knowing whether or how other team members can help patients. To cooperate, network members need to know what other members can do for patients, when and how to refer and have quick and easy ways to do so, and to be able to recognize and negotiate in areas of overlap (Chapter 6).

Unclear case coordination

A sixth barrier to cooperation is not knowing whether other members are involved, and not being able to find out quickly and easily. Without this knowledge it is not possible to agree different tasks with the other practitioners who are involved, which can lead to duplication and unnecessary visits, as well as conflicting advice and treatments.

The most common way of finding out if others are involved is to ask the client, but this is too late to prevent an unnecessary visit and extra work. Other methods include all agreeing to record their involvement in an index of current cases for all involved, which can be easily checked. All methods depend on each practitioner taking the time and trouble to notify others of their involvement, and of their finishing work with a client. To ensure that this is done, formal policies usually need to be agreed.

Simply knowing that others are involved, however, does not guarantee that all will coordinate their work. There needs to be active collaboration with others to ensure that clients' needs are effectively and efficiently met. Some teams have an explicit policy covering what needs to be done if a number of practitioners are involved. It is usually necessary to agree that one person will take a lead role as 'case coordinator' or care manager. In primary health care the case coordinator is often the GP, but does not have to be, especially if the responsibilities and authority of the role are defined, and the procedure for deciding who is to undertake the role is also agreed.

Different policies

A further obstacle to cooperation is where different practitioners have different and conflicting policies (for example, about access to records). In group practices each GP may have a different policy about different administrative and clinical issues, which may be confusing and time-consuming for practice staff and nurses. For their part, nurses and social workers may have different policies which they cannot ignore to fit in with other members of the team.

Effective teamwork requires common policies regarding a variety of aspects of working. When the number of people in the team rises to over five or six it is usually necessary to make explicit the different policies and procedure and agree common approaches. Sometimes a full operational policy, which is sanctioned by different employing and contracting authorities is necessary in a network (see below).

Different management and accountability
The previous issue of different policies relates to the final barrier to cooperation, which is that community nurses and practice staff are accountable to different employers and purchasers and subject to direction by them. Although GPs are independent contractors, they cannot ignore certain rules and directives of the FHSA, which at times may be in conflict with those of nurses, social workers and others. The practice staff are accountable to the GP or group practice as their employer and can be directed by them. The other nurses are accountable to locality managers and to their employer, which can decide to use their time and skills in a variety of ways.

Different accountability is a reality which cannot be ignored and may assert itself – for example, when a nurse is withdrawn from the team to cover for short-staffing elsewhere, or prevented from undertaking 'teamwork' because of other priorities. GPs preferred solution is for nurses to be employed by them or the FHSA. For their part nurses vigorously oppose such an arrangement for a number of reasons. GP fund-holder contracts for community nursing do allow clarification of policy conflicts.

Removing the barriers in networks-conclusion

To create and develop networks it is necessary to recognize the forces which act on people to pull them away from the group, and to eliminate or minimize these forces. The forces which bind people together also need to be maximized. The basic human need to associate with others is one such force but it is relatively weak in a multidisciplinary group, especially when people have separate employers and are members of other uniprofessional groups. The main uniting force is what people have in common, either patients or programmes, such as clinics or setting up a self-help group. It is not sufficient to remove the impediments: the positive forces pulling people 'inwards' need to be recognized and strengthened, as do communications and other links between people in the group.

DEVELOPING TEAMWORK IN FORMAL TEAMS

If a decision is made to develop a network into a more closely-knit formal team, or to set one up from scratch, then there are five essentials to ensuring and improving cooperation in such teams:

- a manager or management group responsible for team performance (Box 10.2);
- team accountability reviews, led by this manager or group, to take up team problems, and to ensure that the team fits in with other services and is meeting client needs and purchaser requirements;
- a defined team leader position;
- a team operational policy;
- a team base.

The following considers the first four and notes where more details can be found in this book and elsewhere.

Box 10.2 Team problems caused by lack of cross-agency management coordination

Formal teams sometimes find themselves having to define their own organization and 'managing upwards'. Formal teams need to understand which problems are caused by management not doing their work, and which problems arise internally and can be solved by the team. Problems can often be traced to:

- a planning group not making a sufficiently comprehensive initial assessment either of the needs of the client group, or of the existing services and resources;
- a community care plan not considering why a multidisciplinary team rather than any other arrangement was required, or what type of team should be created;
- a planning group not outlining the initial aims and purpose of the team, its role in relation to specialist and general services, how it relates to care management, and its management arrangements;
- a planning group not having a reliable indication of the resources which each agency would commit to serve the needs of the particular client group – the extra resources required for the plan are not accurately costed;
- many members of the planning group not committing themselves or their agencies to implementing the plan because they were not sufficiently senior and did not have the authority to do so, and because of rapid political and financial changes in their agencies;
- members of the planning group not developing and agreeing an over-arching service philosophy and aims for the client group, but

aggregating a number of existing services and proposed extra services to fill gaps;
- no clear timetable and structure for implementing the plans, reviewing progress and for making overall adjustments – execution of different aspects of the plan by different agencies poorly coordinated;
- managers in each agency responsible for providing services to a range of client groups apart from the group served by the multidisciplinary community team;
- most team members' managers were not involved in the structure for managing the team, and knowing little about the work of the team, or about how they should manage team members.

Starting policy framework and objectives for a team

If the intention is to set up a formal team rather than a network, then the most important requirement is for higher management to agree a starting framework for the team and specify the initial operational policy guidelines, objectives, organization and team leader role. This is necessary to define the place and purpose of the team within the overall service, and to arrange for staff management. However, it is not appropriate that team objectives and organization are too closely defined at the outset. Higher management should require the team to make a detailed report on local needs and resources, and to propose the details of organization which the team believes to be most suitable for its work.

The operational policy document is the central working tool of management and practitioners for this ongoing review process. The mistake which is often made is not having a formal review point where the team and higher management agree and specify the details. This is often because there is no structure and process for *team* accountability, as opposed to individual members' accountability – no clear management level and responsibility above the level of the team.

Accountability structure and process

There must be one individual or a group at a management level above the team, who is responsible for managing the team, and who is in turn accountable to senior management for the team's performance. The process of team accountability ensures that senior management received formal reports from the team on progress and problems in order that those in authority can deal with difficulties which cannot be solved within the team. This process also serves to redefine the place and purpose of the team within the wider service. The structure and process of team accountability are especially important when teams are first established. Box 10.3 shows the two-phase process which is necessary.

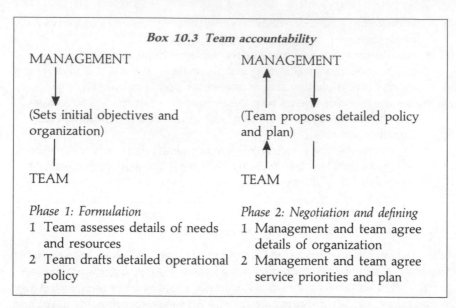

Box 10.3 Team accountability

MANAGEMENT

(Sets initial objectives and organization)

TEAM

Phase 1: Formulation
1 Team assesses details of needs and resources
2 Team drafts detailed operational policy

MANAGEMENT

(Team proposes detailed policy and plan)

TEAM

Phase 2: Negotiation and defining
1 Management and team agree details of organization
2 Management and team agree service priorities and plan

In the first phase managers, often from different services, form the team that was planned. Assuming that they have agreed the professional membership and structure (Chapter 4), team member selection should aim for a balanced mix of membership from social groups that correspond to clients to be served, and a mix of role styles (Chapter 6). Once the team is working it begins to form a detailed view of needs and resources and clarifies the details of its operational policy (formulation phase). The team must have some initial guidelines and framework to work to, and basic features of organization should be set – for example, the 'team leader' role if there is to be one (Chapter 7), and case coordination arrangements (Chapter 6). The second phase (negotiation and defining phase) starts with the team proposing its detailed policy and putting forward its report of client needs and of local resources to a higher management body, at the first formal accountability review.

Box 10.4 Common symptoms and problems in formal teams

Look out for:
- Team meeting problems: poor chairing, frequent absences, avoiding issues, too many issues which do not need team discussion, no decision-making processes known to all;
- 'emergency work' driving out longer-term more effective work, or too much long-term work;
- difficulty allocating new cases because members brought their old caseloads to the team and never reviewed these caseloads in the light of the team's priorities, or because of problems in closing cases;
- no team influence over closure decisions;

- team members taking referrals or work separately from the team: under what conditions?
- lack of common awareness of agreed priorities and of ways of implementing priorities;
- no forum for in-depth case discussions of selected cases;
- separate professional information and record systems, or difficulties getting information from others;
- Insufficient administration support, and inadequate team base (no good coffee/meeting area);
- Leadership with no authority.

Purposes of accountability reviews

The accountability review serves three important purposes. First, it ensures that management receives a detailed formal report from the team about the help which the team needs from higher management. Without this report, senior managers are not able to do the work of securing resources, and of negotiating among themselves and with management in other agencies over a variety of matters. This is work which team members do not have the authority to undertake.

Second, it ensures that senior managers are able to review team organization and to check that staff management arrangements are adequate (see discussion of accountability and quality in Chapter 7). For example, it makes it possible for the team to raise problems about over-control of members by professional superiors at a level where negotiations with professional superiors can be carried out.

Third, the first accountability review makes it possible for senior managers of the team to define team objectives, priorities and organization more precisely, and to set the targets for the team to work to for the next review. It ensures that organizational problems are identified and not ignored, and that the team does not start services which do not fit in with purchasers' priorities or community care plans or providers' business plans. We now turn to the third of the five essentials noted above – a clearly defined leadership position.

Team leader position

One of the quickest ways to establish teamwork, and to ensure that teamwork continues to be successful, is to start with a clearly defined team leader role. I do not know of any teams which have close teamwork and which have survived changes of membership without a clear team leader position. One of the biggest mistakes is to believe that inter-professional and inter-agency conflict, rivalries and protectionism can be avoided by not defining a team leader role. By not agreeing the role managers cause more conflict and bad feeling in the long run in the mistaken idea that they do not have time, and that to leave things ambiguous gives them more room to manoeuvre in the future. It is better to face up to differences and to agree the role before problems arise, than to try to establish a team leader after problems and conflicts have produced a climate of recrimination and mistrust.

Chapters 7 and 8 showed that even so-called 'democratic' teams have leaders for different functions, and recognize that to get things done leaders need agreed authority, at least within the team. The only issue is what type of team leader a team has, and this depends on the type of team, the work which the leader would have to do, to whom he or she is accountable, and the agreed and sanctioned authority he or she has in relation to team members. Chapter 7 described the three main options for members' management: one team manager; a leader contracting in team members from other services; and joint management. It described the three leadership positions of elected chairperson, appointed coordinator and team full manager.

Team operational policy

One of the main tasks of a team leader during the 'formulation phase' (Box 10.3) is to work on the details of the operational policy to propose to team management. The operational policy is the team leader's main working tool and the fourth essential for formal teams. If a policy is agreed by higher management and the professions involved, it authorizes the team leader to call for changes to team members' behaviour if they do not follow agreed ways of working, or to call for changes in policy if the policy cannot be followed.

Broad initial guidelines and terms of reference set by senior management make the task of drafting a first policy easier, and prevent the team wasting its time doing work which is not viewed by management as high priority. If there are no guidelines, then the work of drafting a policy is even more important because it serves as the only explicit statement to help all clarify the broad parameters of working. Sometimes teams are set up with no objectives, no parameters, and no defined organization, and drafting a policy is a way in which team members can begin to resolve issues neglected by higher management. An early draft policy is important because the process of discussing and agreeing basic aspects of working helps create a cohesive group, and clarifies different assumptions and expectations. It provides a way for team members to develop a consensus about ways of working and priorities.

If an operational policy is formulated, then particular problems, cases, or tasks can be dealt with according to a policy which all have previously agreed. For example, if an individual member feels that a decision was unfair or poor, the matter is more easily raised and dealt with as a possible problem with the team policy, than as a personal matter. A policy also serves as a statement to others outside the team as to what team members agree to be their aims and methods of working. It can be used as a basis for negotiations with higher management about what the team should and should not be doing. It can also be used to publicize the team's service.

Finally, a policy is necessary to ensure that there is a clear and agreed process for the responsible handling of cases within the team. This is especially important if the team is not organized with a medical consultant who is clinically and managerially responsible for team members' work (Chapter 6). Teams are able to work in different ways as long as there are clearly defined arrangements for case transfer and communications, and that there are proper precautions to avoid mishaps. If such arrangements are specified in the policy, then the employing authority can agree and sanction the procedure. A good starting point for a team first establishing a policy is to write down their arrangements under certain headings, before discussing and agreeing improvements. The client pathway models in Chapter 5 help to discuss the key parts of the policy. Box 10.5 is a list of headings used by teams detailing or reviewing their policy.

Box 10.5 Example of team operational policy headings

1 Aims, priorities, client group and catchment area
   General purpose of the team, definition of client group which is and is not served by the team, boundaries of catchment area.
2 Team philosophy, objectives and priorities
   General principles informing members work and the services of the team, specific objectives, and current ordering of priorities.
3 Team membership
   Name, profession and role, special skills, time available for 'team work' and contact point.
4 Referrals to and from the team (client pathway(s))
   Criteria for accepting (a) for assessment, (b) for long-term work as a 'team responsibility', and criteria for finishing team involvement, and arrangements for informing referrer of actions.
5 Team meetings
   Conduct, agendas, and decision-making procedures for (a) team casework decisions, (b) team management and policy decisions, and (c) team proposals for service developments.
6 Case allocation, case-coordination and cross-referrals
   How cases are allocated (a) for assessment, (b) for long-term work. Responsibilities of case-coordinator, and how cross-referrals and co-working within the team are arranged.
7 Team leader role
   Responsibilities, accountable for . . . to . . . authority, and method of appointment.
8 Professional superior roles
   Responsibilities, accountability, and authority of each professional superior inside and outside the team.
9 Team systems and procedures
   General heading for such matters as workload statistics and informa-

> tion systems, case records and client access policy, finance and
> budgets, complaints procedure, staff performance appraisal and
> development.
> 10 Team accountability and performance reporting
> Group or individual to whom the team is accountable, and their
> responsibilities in relation to the team. Frequency and nature of team
> reports of workload, achievements, and difficulties.
> *Appendices:* Proposals for service developments, and updated plans.

To be a team is, by definition, to have an operational policy: to work together, people have agreements about who will do what in different situations. The only differences between teams are in terms of whether the policy is explicit and written down, or whether it is implicit and assumed, and in terms of the degree of detail and the areas covered. The advantages of the policy being explicit are: all can be clear about agreed ways of workings; it gives guidance to new, prospective (and long-standing) team members; to explain and publicize the purpose and organization of the team, and to enable the team to monitor and improve its organization.

MONITORING, EVALUATION AND TEAM PERFORMANCE REVIEWS

All types of team – networks, client teams, and formal teams – need to set aside a regular time to take stock and plan. However, formal teams and some network teams need to prepare for and take part in managerial accountability reviews, as we saw above. Mature teams with established organization spend more time in these reviews on performance reporting and negotiating future performance targets with management. If management is confident in the team's ability to get to grips with details of organization, managers can then concentrate in these reviews on team output and outcomes.

Here we are concerned with routine managerial reviews of team performance, at least annually, and sometimes quarterly. Such performance reviews are not scientific evaluations, but allow managers to make judgements about team performance, give the team feedback, and negotiate future performance targets. There are two aspects: monitoring feedback, and evaluation feedback.

Monitoring is comparing what happens with what is specified. The monitoring question concerns whether the operating requirements of the team are being met. To monitor a team, managers gather documents describing what the team should be doing and compare this with the information they can get about what the team is doing. What is specified for a team includes operational policy, and purchaser's and other requirements. Managers may also have specified quality standards above and beyond charter requirements, as well as performance targets, some of which might be outcome targets in addition to cost reduction and output targets.

Managers use a variety of sources of information to compare these specifications with what the team is doing, including feedback from referrers, informal discussions with team members, and the team's formal report and statistics for the performance review. Managers draw together their judgements to give the team feedback in the review about how well the team has met what was specified, noting areas where manager's could not tell whether the team had met requirements. This is accountability-in-practice, and underlines the importance of these specifications for team members. By doing this managers show that they view the team as a collective and that it is members' joint efforts and results that are important.

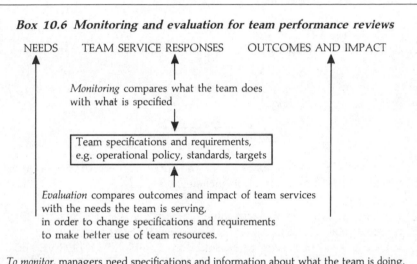

Box 10.6 Monitoring and evaluation for team performance reviews

NEEDS   TEAM SERVICE RESPONSES   OUTCOMES AND IMPACT

Monitoring compares what the team does with what is specified

Team specifications and requirements, e.g. operational policy, standards, targets

Evaluation compares outcomes and impact of team services with the needs the team is serving, in order to change specifications and requirements to make better use of team resources.

To *monitor*, managers need specifications and information about what the team is doing. To *evaluate*, managers need information about needs, outcome and impact of team services, and the relative effectiveness of different services.

Evaluation feedback involves judging the impact of the team's service on the needs and demands of the population. The evaluation question is whether the team's services and specifications are the right ones for meeting the priority needs. This is a more difficult question than the monitoring question of whether requirements are being met, but also a more important one. In evaluating the team's performance, managers use information about the impact and outcomes of the team's services on the population, and compare this with information about needs and demands. They use a variety of sources and methods to get this information to judge the team's impact on needs and to consider with the team what changes to priorities, services and organization the team should make.

The performance review helps focus attention on developing team management information systems. From the team's point of view, systems should be designed to abstract information from each client case file or the client index for regular reports, without team members having to spend time recording and collating other information. From the managers' point of view they need to be able to show purchasers that the team is meeting contract and give prospective purchasers details of costs and quality. In addition, the system must be able to move towards costing and invoicing on a per-client or episode basis, and ultimately for an item of service, such as an assessment. It is easier said than done to develop a system which meets all these requirements and others, but the performance reviews show what is missing, highlight wasteful duplication in recording which all adds costs, and clarify what the team and managers need to work towards. Low-cost management information of the right kind gives a team a competitive advantage. Box 10.7 lists some basic information for contracting.

Box 10.7 Management information for contracts and marketing

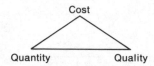

Cost

Quantity   Quality

Information is needed for each of the three corners of the contract triangle. Minimum information includes:

1 *Costs:* staffing, total 'team time', running costs (rent, electricity), consumables.
Decide 'unit' of service to be sold (for example, by time, by item).
Determine unit costs and track this over time.

2 *Quantity:* count 'units' of service provided. For more detailed information and needs-based 'units' of service, decide categories of need or client served by the team (Chapter 2), and collect the following:

	For each category of need/client		
	Current nos	*New nos*	*Closed nos*
Monthly			
Annually			

3 *Quality:* includes basic quality measures which all services gather such as performance on charter standards, purchaser specified measures and team-specific measures based on quality standards developed by the team. Quality measures should include:
  • waiting times (for instance, for first response, assessment, treatment (Chapter 5);
  • complaints and satisfaction data;

- professional quality data;
- outcome measures, and current cost of poor quality measures (discussed in Øvretveit 1992b, 1993c).

Other information: client postcodes for invoicing, summary description of services and priorities and selection criteria.

Clearly managers' monitoring and evaluation can be well informed or overly subjective, and team performance reports may be less than comprehensive. However, the purpose of the performance review is not a scientific evaluation, but aims to move team reviews beyond problem-solving and briefing sessions towards a focus on results and clarifying targets. By focusing on outcomes and the team's impact on needs, the review and the team can then better judge how much time to spend on different process issues – these issues are important in so far as they affect the team's performance.

Box 10.8 Example agenda for performance accountability review

1 *Team's performance report*
   Team summarizes achievements and statistics from the performance report which it submitted to management before the review meeting. Reports on performance against specific targets since last review.

2 *Managers give feedback*
   Summary of monitoring observations – judgement of the extent to which team is meeting requirements and operational policy.
   Summary of evaluation feedback – judgement of the impact of team services on the needs of the population the team is serving.
   Note of information which is not available but needed for above judgements.
   Managers raise key areas for future attention to improve team service.
   Current and future purchaser concerns.

3 *Negotiating future targets*
   Proposals for future targets.
   Proposals as to how to reach targets – changes and problems.
   Proposals as to how to measure and report progress towards targets.

4 *Discussion of particular team problems*

5 *Managers brief team* about service and purchaser changes. Invite questions about service strategy.

6 *Details of next review*
   Timetables for changes, and information to be provided in next team report.

Team service quality

One of the many subjects not discussed in detail in this book is quality. There are two reasons for this omission. First, a number of quality systems have been developed for different types of team, and a full discussion of these systems is outside of the scope of this book. One such system now used for primary care teams in one area is summarized in Appendix 3. Second, although nothing was said about standards, measurement and systems, the whole book is about how to improve the quality of service given by teams. Many quality problems – usually the most costly ones – lie 'between' services and professions, and are due to poor coordination. Many staff say they cannot do their job because they are waiting for information or a service given by others, or that they get the wrong information or services. They are often not able to give the service or information which others require because of 'time and cost considerations'.

I have no doubt that teams which are able to provide a well-coordinated 'package' will give a lower-cost and better service to clients, and will have a significant market advantage. However they will have to prove this to purchasers and give evidence of their systems and measures. Setting standards and measuring quality is not just necessary to satisfy purchasers, but the basis for the team's quality system. In Øvretveit (1992a, 1993c) I argue that the first phase of quality improvement is simply 'getting organized' and that without basic organization there is no team structure to apply or use any more sophisticated quality systems. This book is about getting that basic organiz-ation, and one of the methods it described to help do so is a method for quality improvement: the 'client pathway' framework in Chapter 5. Teams can use the framework to identify where the most common delays and problems are in a typical client's path through the team and use this as a basis for quality problem-solving. This is a much more cost-effective quality method than any number of client satisfaction surveys.

Box 10.9 How to make a team fail

Ten ways to make a formal multidisciplinary team fail:

1 Practitioners in the same profession continuing to meet and work together as a single-profession team, just as they did before they were told that they would each be working in a multidisciplinary team.
2 Each professional or professional group with its own referral procedures and work priorities.
3 Profession managers maintaining close control over practitioners: allocating work, recruiting team members, deciding training, and reviewing cases.
4 Many members only being part-time in the team, with the rest of their time allocated to one or more different areas, or different services.

5 No team base – contact and communication points, records and secretarial support all at different sites.
6 No team leader position with a responsibility for team operations.
7 No team objectives or priorities, but only general statements of intent.
8 No decision-making procedure within the team for treatment decisions, workload management, management issues, or for developing planning proposals.
9 No formal annual review by higher management of team operation and achievements.
10 No plan for wider service of which the team is a part, and no individual or group with a clear responsibilities for creating one. Ensure that the team is drawn into work which purchasers will not pay for and should be provided by other services.

The more of these issues not addressed by management, the more difficult it is for the most willing of team members to cooperate with others.

CONCLUSION

People in need and their carers have no interest in whether they have 'social' or 'health' needs. An elderly person waiting to leave hospital cannot understand why there are delays, or why, when she does get home, no one calls like they said they would. Carers get exasperated telling the same story over again, and do not know why service providers cannot talk to each other. Service providers get frustrated not being able to get help or information from other services. Researchers tell managers about the gap between policy and reality and show poor cooperation between agencies. Managers educate researchers about the financial and practical problems. Everyone blames the government for lack of finance, and the government blames the public for opposing tax increases and providers for inefficiencies.

This book argued for making the most of the opportunities of the present and the experience of the past to improve coordination and that it was in everyone's interests to do so. It is not exhortations and threats of punishment that motivate, but recognition that better coordination makes work more satisfying, and saves time and costs. Motivation alone is not sufficient; we need practical solutions and practical models from which to construct better cooperation. This book aimed to contribute practical ideas for improving cooperation, mostly at practitioner level in teams. Some of the themes and arguments included:

• the need to establish links between agencies, formal and informal, at the levels of strategic purchasing, strategic provision, operational management, and practitioners (Chapters 2, 3 and 10);

- separating, and then linking need assessment and service provision through care planning (Chapter 2);
- linking levels by delegation and accountability, higher levels setting boundaries, resource limits and targets, and lower levels passing up information about needs and resource use (Chapters 2 and 10);
- care management which complements teamwork – using new care management approaches to develop existing team coordinations systems, and learning from teams about how to arrange care management (Chapters 2–6);
- finding the right mix of bureaucratic, market and network association modes of organization and relationships (Chapter 3);
- risking experimentation and evaluating new approaches;
- helping overworked practitioners change their traditional professional practices to work with clients and carers in co-service (Chapter 9);
- clarifying the type of team which is the best organizational vehicle for bringing together the services which clients and carers need, and which is compatible with the way agencies are organized (Chapter 4);
- improving cooperation in network teams by removing barriers (Chapters 4 and 10);
- improving coordination in formal teams by better 'client pathways' (Chapter 5), appropriate team leadership (Chapter 7), clarifying roles (Chapter 6) and agreeing operational policies (Chapter 10);
- confronting workload and priority issues in collective service teams (Chapter 5);
- practitioner management and support in teams – facing up to the three choices for practitioner management (Chapter 7);
- management reviews of teams, and developing team management information systems, where services are to be provided on a team basis (Chapters 9 and 10).

Coordination is even more important with the increasing variety of purchasers and providers. Boundaries need not be barriers. More pressure on resources and 'market competition' can work against coordination, but coordination can save costs and agencies can often better achieve their goals through cooperation than through competition or isolation. Agencies build bridges to meet in the middle from foundations on both sides, and because both sides see the mutual advantage of investing in such structures. Managers will need to recognize areas where there is mutual advantage in cooperation, which means understanding more about the pressures and interests of other agencies. It takes strength to change old patterns of working and to reach out in different ways to clients and colleagues. It takes effort to establish organization that outlasts individuals and gives satisfying environments within which to work. This book aimed to help create the community services which we want to work in, and which we will be proud to use for our families, and when our time comes to seek care and cure.

Appendix 1
MODELS OF CARE MANAGEMENT AND COMMUNITY TEAMS

INTRODUCTION

Care management is a method of organizing care, but should care managers replace community teams? This appendix describes the main models of care management and considers whether care management is compatible with multidisciplinary teams, and some of the implications for team practitioners such as community nurses. It proposes that:

- team members such as community nurses can be care managers, and can work as care managers in existing teams or in specialist care management teams for certain clients;
- there are many different types of care manager role;
- only some clients need a care manager, and those who do do not always need a care manager for all of their contact with a service;
- there is a need for more simple, practical and flexible home care, which can be met by organizing a service of home care assistants, who undertake some nursing and social care tasks (although one of the successes of care management schemes has been such home care services, it does not need care managers to set up these services);
- the need for care management for some clients often highlights service deficiencies which are there for many clients.

As the diversity of services increases there will be more problems of coordination. This will mean setting up or improving multidisciplinary teamwork, as well as care management systems. The experience of teams is that many problems can only be overcome through higher-level agreement. Care managers do not replace the need for teams, or for cooperation between different services at higher management levels.

PURPOSE OF CARE MANAGEMENT

The Griffiths (1988) proposal for care managers (called 'case managers' in the report) was aimed at supporting people at home to prevent unnecessary hospital or residential admission, and to ensure that more account was taken of clients' and carers' wishes. In the Griffiths proposals the *role* of care manager could be undertaken by social workers or nurses, or others. It was implied that care managers would carry out each phase of the *process* of care management: screening for priority clients, organizing a full assessment, planning, and coordinating and monitoring how the client plan is carried out. The case management process is to ensure that:

* resources are targeted to those clients most in need (by screening clients for the care management system, and by defining a budget for these clients);
* a full needs assessment is undertaken, involving all professions and services as necessary;
* the client and carers are fully involved and have a choice of alternative services;
* a flexible, speedy and appropriate service response is arranged;
* there is a clear care plan, with the responsibilities and objectives of each profession, agency and service agreed and defined;
* services are coordinated and the care plan is reviewed and updated;
* the best value for money is obtained in services for the client (by avoiding duplication and double visiting, flexibility in task performance, and through cooperation in pursuing a common set of objectives for the client).

These general principles have been applied in different ways in pilot schemes, and in local proposals for implementing the community care reforms (DoH 1989b). The title of care manager now describes many different roles for organizing care for different client groups. Some care managers are not responsible for all parts of the process of case management – for example, some do not screen clients but take clients from an 'intake team'.

DISTINGUISHING DIFFERENT MODELS

Members of existing teams are concerned about the implications for their work, and for the teams of which they are a part. Will they be care managers for all or some of their clients, or will a separate care management team be set up? Is care management for all or just some types of client? Will care managers buy in or direct other practitioners? Team members can consider the implications of local proposals by finding answers to the following questions:

1 Which clients is the model for?
Most care management systems are established to arrange services for certain elderly people, people with a learning disability, people with physical

disabilities, and people with mental health problems (see discussion below of different schemes).

2 What needs does the model aim to meet?
Clients are usually selected for care management according to certain criteria and needs. Some models aim to meet needs for social care only. Other models aim to meet a wider range of needs. In some systems care management is a role which is transferred after one part of the care process is completed (for example, after the care manager organizes assessment and care planning, another person will coordinate and oversee the execution of the plan).

3 What do care managers do?
In some models care managers themselves provide some, or a large part of the service, for example, themselves undertaking all or some of the assessment, and/or some of the subsequent intervention. In some models care managers are only organizers – they do not themselves provide any services.

4 What team(s) are care managers part of?
Often care managers are grouped together in a care management team. Certain clients are referred to them by primary or generic teams, or by specialists teams (such as mental health or handicap teams). The care manager may then involve a case worker from another team. In some situations practitioners in specialist or generic teams carry out care management (i.e. they provide and purchase), or a care manager may be a member of a number of teams.

5 Who employs care managers?
Care managers are sometimes employed by social services, sometimes by health services, sometimes by a voluntary or other agency. Often social services and health services agree a care management role, agree who will be the employer, and then recruit people to care management positions. Sometimes a non-statutory agency, which does not provide services, employs care managers (e.g. some USA schemes).

6 Do care managers 'have a budget', and, if so, what are the limitations?
'Having a budget' can mean anything between the following two extremes:
(a) *Maximum financial discretion and direct purchasing:* being put in charge of all the finance available for all the services for a client, and having discretion and authority to purchase directly all the services agreed with the client. The limits to discretion are the total sum available, and there is no review or sanction before the case manager spends the money.
(b) *Discretion up to a financial limit from pre-purchased costed services:* knowing the costs of a range of pre-purchased services for which one can apply up to a set limit of cost for each client (for example, two-thirds of the cost of residential care).

Some care managers apply to their team manager for services for their client. Often the services are pre-purchased by a purchasing authority. The team manager is given information about the cost of using these pre-purchased services (similar to non-budget-holding GPs). The team manager authorizes the care manager's use of funds for that client, up to the budget limit for all clients of the team. Sometimes care managers will be given 'indicative budgets' for each client.

Some care managers have more flexibility to purchase services directly, for example by paying local people to provide part-time help, or to buy aids or equipment. Thus systems vary in terms of the level at which services are purchased, the cost information available, and the nature of the budget limits: (a) block purchase by a purchasing authority (and selection by team and care managers from a pre-purchased 'menu'); (b) purchase by a team manager (usually from an authorized list, but not pre-purchased); (c) purchase by care manager.

Budgets for case management are essentially about comprehensive needs-led financing for certain clients and targeting resources. This is different from the traditional financing of different services (such as day care, home help, and transport), where each service separately makes an assessment and decides the priority of each client and what they will get. In case management some finance from each service is gathered together in one budget ('top slicing'), and finance is provided to these other services, following the assessment of the client's needs and care plan. In these 'budget-holding models' of case management finance follows the client, rather than vice versa.

A key issue is thus which services the care manager may 'purchase', with the implication that these services will lose, and then have to gain a portion of their income from the case management system. For example, if care managers are organizing all of the care for some elderly people and they are not community nurses, will community nursing services to these clients be paid for out of the care manager's budget for that client (and 'top-sliced' from the community nursing budget)? Will other community health services be purchased by care managers in this way?

Implications for team members

Team members can begin to clarify the implication of care management by asking the following questions of any proposed models:

1 Is the proposed model for social care only?
2 Will a separate care management team and system be set up, or could practitioners in generic or specialist teams be care managers, for all or part of the time?
3 Will care managers hold budgets, and what type of budget, purchasing authority and limitations will apply?

DIFFERENT CASEWORK ROLES

Clearly there is no single type of care manager role, and some practitioners already carry out some or all the tasks of the care management process. Some of the confusion is because terms are used in different ways. The following lists one set of usages before describing different models of care management.

Case worker: The practitioner working on a case at a particular time. Undertakes mostly profession-specific tasks (for example, medication).

Key worker: The practitioner within a service who carries prime responsibility for that service's care of a client. The client's 'named worker', who may or may not have coordinating authority within the service. (For continuity within the service, and can 'knock on doors' and 'open doors' for the client.)

Case coordinator: The practitioner who coordinates others within the team (and in some teams, outside the team). Usually provides services herself. (May help 'open doors' and may 'keep a foot in the door' for the client.)

Care manager: Practitioner case coordinator with a budget for some or all services to the client, and may herself provide specific services to the client. (Doors open more readily to a visitor offering money.) She may be employed by the same employer who provides services, which she organizes or 'purchases'. Alternatively she may be employed by an agency other than the agency providing services.

MODELS OF CASE MANAGEMENT

Services decide which type of care manager role and system to adopt from a variety of models. The following outlines four models in a way which aims to highlight some of the key differences.

Type A: Case coordination model

A practitioner is allocated case coordinating responsibilities for the client, in addition to her own profession-specific responsibilities. This role was described for community mental handicap nurses in Øvretveit and Davis (1989). They are responsible for:

- calling for assessments from other practitioners and services which they think may be necessary (inside and outside of a multidisciplinary team);
- combining others' assessments (and their own), agreeing others' future contributions, and recording this in a care plan;
- monitoring others' work, and keeping all informed of progress, and calling reviews.

Among the advantages are the development of an existing role (in teams). Among the disadvantages are the following:

- weak authority, especially outside team;
- no budget;
- the case coordinator is also a provider;
- choice is restricted to better organization of existing services;
- and the case coordinator must understand when to call upon other services.

Type B: Budget-holding care management models

Version B1

This is the same as case-coordinator models, but a 'budget' is delegated to the practitioner who is the care manager. The care manager 'buys-in' services from an approved range, or can use the budget to pay for new types of service (for example, to volunteers or neighbours).

Version B2

The team leader (sometimes called 'care manager') 'holds the budget' and does not delegate to practitioners. Practitioners are case coordinators who apply to the team leader to 'buy' certain services.

Among the advantages are the following:

- development of existing team roles;
- greater scope to buy new types of services;
- more authority – other services more responsive if purchased.

The disadvantages are as follows:

- cost of accounting;
- cost of training to use accounting system;
- care manager is also provider;
- the more discretion to choose and purchase different services, the more difficult it is for providers to plan services and there may be lost economies of scale.

Type C: Independent care manager

Care Manager does not herself provide any services. May 'hold a budget' (same as type B), or may not – then essentially an advocate. This model has the advantage that there is no conflict of interest, no bias towards her own service or profession. Among the disadvantages are that the care manager may be over-influenced by what the client wants, not what he needs and that if there is no budget, then there is also little power and the care manager has a mainly 'troubleshooting' role.

Type D: Client-funded care manager

After assessment, funds are decided and allocated to the client/carer for the client/carer to organize and pay for her 'own' services (cf. social security). This gives the user power and choice, but has the disadvantages that the client may be unaware of her service need and buy only what she wants, and that there is only weak accountability to local authority for the use of finance, unless the client shows receipts.

CARE MANAGEMENT AND MULTIDISCIPLINARY TEAMS

How, then, does (or could) care management fit in with multidisciplinary teamwork? The following considers some different types of team and how care managers can work within a team, or separately and in conjunction with a team.

Community mental handicap teams

Some community mental handicap teams in Wales have used a case coordinator model (type A) with success for some time (Øvretveit, in Macdonald 1990). Here a practitioner in the team (nearly always a social worker or a nurse) organizes care and services locally, and manages or accesses local part-time family aids.

Where mental handicap health and social services are integrated, nurses and other staff may be care managers (as in Hillingdon (Spenser and Macdonald 1989)). The question of whether all or some clients need a care manager then arises. In some areas social workers only will be case coordinators of social care, and they may or may not be in community mental handicap teams.

An example of a separate care management team is the Winchester special project. Care managers are from different backgrounds, each with a case-load of about 10, and deal with 'complex cases' only (Beardshaw and Towell 1990).

Community mental health teams (CMHTs)

Care managers have been established in some areas specifically for continuing-care clients in the community. Examples are Bromsgrove and Redditch (a social worker as team leader, two nurses and two psychologists), Hastings (nurse team leader, two other nurses, and one social worker), Lewisham and Southwark (occupational therapist as team leader, one further occupational therapist and four nurses), and Nottingham (two social workers and a nurse as team leaders, eight other social workers, seven other nurses and three occupational therapists) (see RDP 1991). Some systems are for clients being rehabilitated into the community from an institution. In both systems the care management team operates separately to CMHTs. There are some examples where care managers are members of a CMHT (for example, occupational therapists, social worker and psychologist in the Cambridge CMHTs (RDP 1991)), and some where any member of the team can undertake a type A case coordinator role (as in Mold and in Clwyd (Øvretveit 1991a)).

Primary care teams and neighbourhood teams

Care managers for certain elderly clients are sometimes part of primary care teams. One example is Gloucester, where each care manager has a caseload of 30, a limited budget for small aids not normally available from occupational therapists, and acts as advocate/broker with specialist knowledge of benefits and services for elderly. In the Devon Eastover project (Neate 1991) for all client groups, any member of the multidisciplinary neighbourhood team can be a care manager, after an initial assessment.

More often a separate care management team is established which takes referrals from primary health care and generic social service teams. One example for 'vulnerable' people over 75 is the EPIC project in Stirling (Lieberman 1990), which organizes special home care support. A senior social worker leads the project and controls the budget, and the team is made up of seconded health visitor, community psychiatric nurse (CN), occupational therapist and social worker, each of whom assesses and arranges home and other care.

Other examples of separate care management systems for older people are Thanet, and Darlington (multidisciplinary geriatric teams for hospital-discharged elderly), where care managers manage home care assistants who do nursing as well as home-help tasks (Stone 1987). In the Cheshire project (Neate 1991) care managers are social workers with a case load of 20 elderly people who would otherwise qualify for residential or nursing care. The Gateshead project is probably the longest-running, and developed a health 'sub-team' of nurse, and part-time physiotherapist and registrar in community medicine (Challis et al 1990).

Physical disability
An example of a specialist care management team is the Camden project set up by voluntary organizations where social worker care managers act as brokers/advocates (Beardshaw and Towell 1990).

CONCLUSION

There are almost as many types of care management as there are types of multidisciplinary team. The reforms provide an opportunity to build on the strengths of current services and to make improvements. Some teams may be able to improve coordination for complex cases with a care management system within the team. Each service will need to decide which model is best suited for certain clients. In so doing services should collaborate with others to agree what arrangements to establish, otherwise many of the problems which plagued teams will undermine case management. Ideally health department, social services departments, FHSAs, and others should jointly review services for different client groups in different areas. Within these client groups those clients most poorly serviced should be identified.

Care management is, then, one solution if these clients are badly served because of problems of coordination, inappropriate services, or uneven priorities across services which they need. If so, agreement is needed about which model of care management is best for these clients, and whether a separate care management team should be set up. Then consideration should be given to how services for other clients could be improved – sometimes the need for care management highlights problems in services for many other clients.

Appendix 2
AN INTEGRATED PRIMARY CARE TEAM – QUALITY THROUGH TEAMWORK

SUMMARY

Over 12 months the project summarized below established an integrated primary care team providing services to clients and patients in a population of 20,000 in an area to the south-west of Belfast. The project formed a multidisciplinary team and used quality methods to prove and improve the quality of primary care services. The project is part of the overall unit total quality management strategy to develop a competitive advantage from combining, within the unit, the management of hospital and primary care, as well as health and social care. Integration of services and quality methods are used to compete with neighbouring hospitals in the 'health market' which is emerging from the UK government health reforms. The project involved establishing the primary care team and developing the quality system. In a short time significant improvements to service quality were achieved. The approach to teamwork and the quality system is being extended across the unit.

ACHIEVEMENTS

1 Reduction of quality problems and improvements to service quality by bringing together, in one team, a range of community nursing and social services disciplines. The one team provides a range of integrated client-focused services, rather than a set of separate disciplinary services. One example is that clients get a faster and more appropriate response by being referred to one service reception point, where all disciplines agree how to match their skills to the needs of the client. GPs report an average reduction

in waiting for requested service of between 18 and 26 hours, and faster information.

2 Cost savings. By integrating disciplines, more flexible working is taking place and multiple visiting is avoided. Social workers or nurses agree to undertake tasks which others would have done, and avoid unnecessary visits. Cost savings for the second year of the project from this change alone are estimated to be between £15,000 to £18,000, about 5 per cent of the total service budget.

3 Change in attitudes. Previously separate professions with long-established working patterns and cultures, which were defensive about any implied or actual criticism of their services, changed their attitudes to each other and to clients and GPs. Although this is a 'process' change, it ensured that the new quality system was underpinned by a change in staff culture and motivation.

4 Integrated quality system. The project applied a framework appropriate to health services which recognized that quality was defined by and had to be provided for different interest groups. Quality standards were established by and for clients and carers, GPs and other referrers, and for management issues. Conflicts were recognized and resolved through this process. Measures and documentation were developed for each standard and together this formed a balanced quality system. This is the first such comprehensive system in everyday use in primary care in the UK.

5 Continuous improvement. Because of the full involvement of all stake-holders, and the system which was established, action on poor quality is taken and the standards are reviewed.

PROJECT DESCRIPTION

Getting organized

The first few months of the project involved forming the team by bringing together different disciplines in the same base, and agreeing which multidisciplinary sub-groupings would serve each client group. The team manager and the assistant manager had to manage the pace of change so as not to overload staff and administrative systems, as the changes were to be achieved with no extra resources.

Developing quality standards

Two months into the project, the team was introduced to basic principles of quality and agreed to develop a quality system for services to people over 75 years. The framework used is described in Øvretveit (1992a). The unit's quality support team conducted interviews with clients to discover valued features of service, which were then prioritized and defined as standards. It also carried out focus group meetings with carers to define valued quality features, prioritized each and defined the top five as standards. They also met with GPs to clarify what were valued features of service from the GP perspective, and their priorities.

The professionals providing the service carried out a pathway analysis of a typical client being 'processed' through the service. They used this to pick out the main quality problems from a professional point of view, and to define professional outcomes which would show whether the service was high or low-quality. Managers did the same, concentrating on quality issues from a management and population perspective.

Forming a balanced set of standards

The five top-priority valued features from all five groups were brought together by staff and the quality support team and managers, and they formed a balanced full set of standards. Conflicts were recognized and resolved, and the group agreed what measurement methods to establish in order routinely to measure and document performance in relation to the set of standards.

Measuring quality

A variety of methods are used to assess performance on the standards, including quarterly questionnaires, monthly GP ratings, carer questionnaires, carer meetings, case record analyses, and statistical analyses.

Other services

The next phase of the project was to use the same approach to develop a quality system for services to the 0–5 year age range and parents. As a result of developing this system, common standards were discovered across client groups, some of which will be used to save costs in developing systems for the remaining team services.

QUALITY FRAMEWORK FOR PRIMARY CARE

The main reasons for establishing standards and measuring quality performance were to:

- prove the current quality of the service;
- improve quality by taking action where performance needs to be improved;
- judge the effects of any changes on the quality of service.

It is possible to decide quality standards for a service by using standards that have already been worked out for a similar service. We did not do this but developed standards specific to one service, by involving interest groups in a structured sequence. They consider one dimension of quality, decide what quality features are most important to them, and set standards associated with these features.

The 'Wel-Qual' framework distinguishes between three dimensions of the quality of service. It moves from identifying different features of the quality of the service which are critical to each dimension, to specifying the quality standards which derive from these critical features, and on to measuring performance in relation to these standards using different measurement methods (Øvretveit 1992a).

The distinctive features of the approach are as follows:

- multidimensional approach to quality (quality is whether the service meets professionally-assessed need as well as providing what client, carers and referrers want, and whether the service does this at the lowest cost);
- features come from interest groups (users and others themselves define which of the quality features are most important to them);
- involvement (staff and users are involved in the process of developing standards and measures, and in deciding quality improvement actions);
- cost-effectiveness (the aim is to measure a few of the most important things, the way the measures are developed ensures that staff use them, no extra cost on training to use the system);
- links standards to measures to action in a quality cycle (ensures that actions happen and continuous improvement);
- allows the system to develop at a pace the service can cope with, and which is relevant to the local 'market' (allows staff to discover that quality can save them time and trouble);
- as much emphasis on the systems and methods of quality as on attitudes and relationships.

RESULTS TO DATE

Limitations and shortcomings

No baseline or comparative benchmarks. There were few data before the project started which allowed us to evaluate cost effectiveness in the first few months.

Data on changes to outcome and output are beginning to emerge.

Structure/process changes

- Cost reductions estimated of £21,050 in first year.
- Established basic system now in regular use, and there is staff motivation to use the information to make improvements.

Output/outcome results

- Higher client satisfaction, as registered on quarterly questionnaire of items they value.
- Higher carer satisfaction, as registered on quarterly questionnaire of items they value. Possible rise in expectations as a result of being consulted has been managed.
- GP satisfaction higher and shorter waiting times reported.
- Reduced waiting and errors in support and supplies services.

For further details contact:
Brian Dornan
General Manager Community Services
Lisburn Health Centre
Lisburn
Co. Antrim
Northern Ireland

Appendix 3

ENABLING COOPERATION AND COMMUNICATION

Cooperation does not just happen by telling people they are in a 'team'. The more of the following essential conditions are present, the easier it is to cooperate, and the less cooperation will depend on a lucky mix of personalities.

1 Higher-level manager/group *responsible* for improving cooperation/setting up MDT.
2 Align practitioners' client boundaries (i.e. same geographical catchment and/or client group).
3 Define practitioners' time available for 'team' work (e.g. how much time working as part of professional or hospital department, as independent practitioner, as part of team).
4 Common team index of all clients currently served by each team member.
5 Channel referrals (to one point – the base).
6 Common base (in community).
7 Team leader role, with defined and agreed responsibilities, authority and accountability (correlate: profession-manager role redefined to complement team leader role).
8 Explicit policy on:
   (a) procedure for allocation of work within the team once accepted;
   (b) procedure for transfer of cases within the team (internal referral);
   (c) policy on how reviews will be done (updates for team?);
   (d) closure policy and criteria.
9 Defined case-coordinator role for cases involving more than one team member (and procedure for deciding and for changing case coordinator).
10 One client one file (single record file with different records in it, and easy access by team members).
11 And other areas to cover in an operational policy (defining different members roles, and other agreed procedures and policies binding all team members).
12 Regular review of policy – internal, and with higher-level management (e.g. six-monthly or annually).

GLOSSARY

Accountability (formal): The person or body to whom one is answerable for meeting defined responsibilities, and for observing set rules and regulations.

Authority: Powers over people, finance and resources which are delegated by higher management and employers. Authority is delegated to a position in order that the person in the position can do the work and meet the responsibilities of the position.

Care management: This is 'a process of tailoring services to individual needs. Assessment is an integral part of care management, but it is only one of seven core tasks that make up the whole process' (SSI/SOSWSG 1991a).

Care manager role: A role with responsibilities for accessing, coordinating and liaising with all the services a client needs for his or her assessment, treatment and care.

Case autonomy: The right to personally carry-out assessments and treatments of individual cases without regular review, or being overruled by higher authority, unless negligence, or policy breaches are suspected.

Case-coordinator role (team only): A role assigned to a team member, with defined responsibilities for coordinating other team members who are serving the same client. A team case coordinator does not coordinate other services outside of a team. (Sometimes called 'key worker'.)

CLDT: Community team for people with a learning disability.

CMHT: Community mental health team.

DHA: District health authority, responsible for assessing the needs of a district population for acute and some community health care, and for purchasing services from providers to meet the most pressing needs.

FHSA: Family health services authority, assesses needs for a population for mostly medical and dental primary care, and contracts general practitioners to provide care.

Fund-holding general practitioners: General medical practitioners who hold in trust and use a fund for purchasing certain services from other health care providers.

PHCT: Primary health care team, usually including GPs, GP practice staff, nurses, some therapists, and sometimes social workers.

Profession manager: management heads of single-profession services such as a special social work team or an occupational therapy team. Line managers are general managers such as a manager of social workers and occupational therapists and others.

Responsibilities: (formal work role): the work expected of a person by his or her employers – the ongoing duties, and the tasks which are delegated by higher mangement from time to time.

Supervision: each of the following may be called 'supervision':

- *Routine managerial review:* A profession manager examines each and every case, and can direct action.
- *Manager decides review:* A profession manager asks a practitioner to bring selected cases for review. They often set a date to review complex cases when allocating them.
- *Practitioner requests manager to review:* A profession manager makes clear to a practitioner that the practitioner can and should request a review with the manager if necessary.
- *Practitioner requests advice from peer:* A practitioner asks a colleague for 'advice', or chance to 'talk through' a case to get a different perspective. The practitioner remains responsible and accountable for their case-work.
- *Collective peer review:* Case presentation or audit to colleagues for learning and quality improvement.

Team

A small group of people who relate to each other to contribute to a common objective.

Client team: all those serving one client at one time.

Community multidisciplinary team: a small group of people, usually from different professions and agencies, who meet regularly to coordinate their work providing services to one or more clients in a defined area.

Formal multidisciplinary community team: a working group with a defined membership of different professions, governed by an agreed and explicit team policy, which is upheld by a team leader.

Network-association team: a voluntary association of service providers, relating to cross-refer; or to coordinate work with a client, or for other purposes. There is no agreed and binding common policy, and usually each network participant is part of another team, based in a different place and managed by a profession or line manager.

Team leadership positions

Team leadership is helping different disciplines in a team to act towards a common purpose. Formal team leaders have organizational authority to help them. Informal leaders do not – their power to influence people comes from a variety of sources, such as expertise, status, charisma and trust.

Team chairperson (elected)
Responsible for: chairing team meetings.
Some chairpersons are given other responsibilities by the team meeting, for example, to follow up items which other team members do not, to receive items for the team agenda, to 'represent' the team. *Accountable to:* whoever elected them, usually the team meeting. Often there is a time limit to how long one person has the position, and an election or a 'rotating chairperson'. *Authorized to:* deal with members in socially acceptable ways to ensure the best use of time in the team meetings. Chairpersons are not authorized to take action outside of the team meeting unless directed to do so by the meeting.

Team coordinator (appointed)
Responsible for: chairing team meetings, upholding and reviewing the team policy, and for some staff management tasks. *Accountable to:* a manager or group for carrying out the above responsibilities.
Authorized to: take defined actions to uphold the policy, including,
- seeking information about a team member's actions to check if he is following policy,
- ask the member to change his behaviour if it is against policy,
- if he does not, report to the team member's manager and ask for help,
- but not authority to overrule case-decisions for which he is not accountable.
In addition, authority to carry-out whatever staff management tasks are delegated (e.g. taking part in appointments, reviewing work, etc.).

Team manager (fully accountable)
Responsible for: his own work and for delegating work to and managing team members. *Accountable to:* his manager for his performance, and for the performance of his staff team in carrying out their responsibilities. *Authorized to:* refuse to have staff appointed to him who are not acceptable to him, assign and review work, decide team policy, decide training, and initiate disciplinary action.

REFERENCES AND BIBLIOGRAPHY

Adair, J. (1986) *Effective Teambuilding*, Gower, Aldershot.

Anciano and Kirkpatrick (1990) 'CMHTs and clinical psychology; the death of a profession?', *Clinical Psychology Forum*, April, pp. 9–12.

Audit Commission (1986) *Making a Reality of Community Care*, HMSO, London.

Audit Commission (1992) *Community Care: Managing the cascade of change*, HMSO, London.

Basset, T. and Burrel, E. (1992) *Training for Mental Health Issues for Community Care Staff*, Training Pack, Longman, Harlow.

Beardshaw, V. (1991) *Implementing Assessment and Care Management*, Kings Fund College Paper 3, London.

Beardshaw, V. and Towell, D. (1990) *Assessment and Case Management*, Kings Fund College Briefing Paper 10, London.

Belbin, M. (1981) *Management Teams: Why they succeed or fail*, Heinemann, Oxford.

Bion, W. (1968) *Experiences in Groups*, Tavistock, London.

Bradach J. and Eccles R. (1989) 'Price authority and trust from ideal types to plural forms', *Annual Review of Sociology*, 15, pp. 97–118.

British Medical Association (1974) *Primary Health Care Teams*, British Medical Association, London.

British Psychological Society (1986) *Responsibility Issues in Clinical Psychology and Multi-Disciplinary Teamwork*, Division of Clinical Psychology, Working Party Report, BPS, Leicester.

Brown, H. and Craft, H. (1985a) 'Getting a team to pull together', *Health and Social Services Journal*, 19 September, p. 1168.

Brown, H. and Craft, H. (1985b) *Lifestyles Workshop Package*, Pavilion Publications, 6 Pavilion Parade, Brighton, East Sussex BN2 1RA.

Brown, H. and Smith, H. (1992) *Normalisation: A reader for the 90's*, Routledge, London.

Brown, S. and Wistow, G. (1990) *The Role and Tasks of Community Mental Handicap Teams*, Avebury, Aldershot.

Brown, S., Flynn, M. and Wistow, G. (1992) *Back to the Future: Joint work for people with learning disabilities*, National Development Team and Nuffield Institute, Leeds.

Butler, R.J. (1980) 'Control through markets hierarchies and collectives', paper presented at EGOS Conference, Imperial College, London, December.

Butler, R.J. (1983) 'A transactional approach to organizing efficiency', *Administration and Society*, 15(3), pp. 323–62.

Challis, D. et al. (1989) *Supporting Frail Elderly People at Home*, PSSRU, University of Kent.

Challis, D. et al. (1990) *Case Management in Social and Health Care*, PSSRU, University of Kent.
    Client Access to Social Services Files, DHSS Guidance (LAC(83)14), HMSO, London.
Cumberlege (1986) *Neighbourhood Nursing – A Focus for Care*, HMSO, London (Cumberledge Report).
Day, P. and Klein, R. (1987) *Accountabilities*, Tavistock, London.
De Board, R. (1978) *The Psychoanalysis of Organisations*, Tavistock, London.
Department of Health and Social Security (DHSS) (1975) *Better Services for the Mentally Ill* (Cmnd 6233), HMSO, London.
DHSS (1981a) *Growing Old*, White Paper, HMSO, London.
DHSS (1981b) *Care in the Community. A consultative document on moving resources for care in England*, HMSO, London.
DHSS (1981c) *Care in Action. A handbook of policies and priorities for the health and personal social services in England*, HMSO, London.
DHSS (1984) *Implementation of the NHS Management Inquiry Report*, HC (84) 13, HMSO, London.
DHSS (1986a) *Community Care – With Special Reference to Adult Mentally-Ill and Mentally-Handicapped People* (White Paper), HMSO, London.
DHSS (1986b) *Health Services Management – Resource Management (Management Budgeting) in Health Authorities*, Health Notice HN (86) 34, HMSO, London.
Department of Health (DoH) (1987) *Promoting Better Health*, HMSO, London.
DoH (1989a) *Working for Patients*, HMSO, London.
DoH (1989b) *Caring for People: Community care in the next decade and beyond*, HMSO, London.
DoH (1989c) *Working Paper No 1. Self-governing Hospitals*, HMSO, London.
DoH (1989d) *Working Paper No 2. Funding and Contracts for Hospital Services*, HMSO, London.
DoH (1990) *Caring for People: Policy guidance*, HMSO, London.
DoH (1991) *The Health of the Nation*, HMSO, London
Dingwall, R. (1980) 'Problems of teamwork in primary care'. In Lonsdale et al. (1980).
Douglas, T. (1983) *Groups*, Tavistock, London.
Edwards (1987) *Nursing in the Community: A team approach for Wales* (Edwards Report), Welsh Office Information Division, Cardiff.
Essex, B., Doig, R. and Renshaw, J. (1990) 'Pilot study of shared care for people with mental illness', *British Medical Journal*, 300, pp. 1442–6.
Foster, A. (1991) *FHSAs – Today's and Tomorrow's Priorities*, HMSO, London.
Foster, M-C. (1992) 'Power to the people: community health centres in Australia', *Health Services Journal*, 23 January, pp. 24–5.
Galano, J. (1977) 'Increased treatment effectiveness as a function of increased client involvement in therapy'. Cited in Jensen, *To Own Your Life*, Bergen University (1988).
Glennerster, H., Matsaganis, M. and Owens, P. (1992) *A Foothold for Fundholding*, Kings Fund Institute, London.
Good Practice in Mental Health and IAMHW (1985) *Community Mental Health Teams/Centres Information Pack*, GPMH, 380 Harrow Rd, London W9.
Goodwyn, S. (1990) *Community Care and the Future of Mental Health Services Provision*, Avebury, Aldershot.
Grant, Humphries and McGrath, M. (eds) (1987) *Community Mental Handicap Teams: Theory and Practice*, British Institute of Mental Handicap, Kidderminster, Worcs.
Griffiths (1988) *Community Care: Agenda for action* (Griffiths Report), HMSO, London.
Harding, W. and Frost, W. (1981) *The Primary Health Care Team*, Standing Medical Advisory Committee and Standing Nursing and Midwifery Advisory Committee, DHSS, London (Harding Report).

Harrison, T. (1990) 'Multidisiplinary teams and how to survive them'. Paper for Section for Community and Rehabilitation, Royal College of Psychiatrists, November.

Hunter, D. and Wistow, G. (1989) *Accountability and Interprofessional Working for People with Mental Handicaps*, Nuffield Institute, University of Leeds.

Huxley, P. (1990) *Effective Community Mental Health Services*, Avebury, Aldershot.

Jaques, E. (ed.) (1978) *Health Services: Their nature and organisation and the role of patients, doctors, and the health professions*, Heinemann, London.

Jaques, E. (1982) 'The method of social analysis in social change and social research', *Clinical Sociology Review*, 1, pp. 50–8.

Jaques, E. (1990a) 'In praise of hierarchy', *Harvard Buiness Review*, January–Februrary, pp. 127–33.

Jaques, E. (1990b) *Requisite Organisation*, Casson-Hall, Arlington, Virginia.

Johnson et al. (1991) *Care for Elderly People at Home*, OUEE, Milton Keynes.

Johnston, R. and Lawrence, P. (1988) 'Beyond vertical integration', *Harvard Business Review*, 88, p. 94–104.

Lamb, D. and Van Abendorff, R. (1988) 'Community teams for elderly people: some issues in the planning and working of multidisciplinary teams' *Clinical Psychology Forum*, 18, pp. 6–8.

Lewin, K. (1947) 'Frontiers in group dynamics', *Human Relations*, 1 (1).

Lieberman, R. (1990) 'It can be done', *Community Care*, 6th December, pp. 26–8.

Lindesay, R. (ed.) (1991) '*Working Out – Setting Up and Running Community Psychogeriatric Teams*', Research and Development for Psychiatry, 134 Borough High Street, London SE1 1LB.

Lonsdale, S. Lonsdale, Webb, A. and Briggs, T. (eds) (1980) *Teamwork in the Personal Social Services and Health Care*, Croom Helm, London.

Macdonald, I. and Øvretveit J. (1987) 'Organisation of St Ebbas Mental Handicap Hospital', MHU, BIOSS, Brunel University.

Macdonald, I. (ed.) (1990) *The Organisation and Development of the Rhondda Vanguard Service for People with a Mental Handicap*, Mental Handicap Services Unit Working Paper, BIOSS, Brunel University, Uxbridge, Middlesex.

Macneil, I. (1978) 'Contracts: adjustments of long-term relations', *Northwestern Law Review*, 72, pp. 854–906.

McGrath, M. (1991) *Multi-disciplinary Teamwork: Community mental handicap teams*, Avebury, Aldershot.

Neate, J. (1991) 'Putting it into practice', *Community Care*, 28 March, Supplement.

NHS Management Executive (1990) *Access to Health Record Acts 1990. A guide for the NHS*, NHSME, London.

Onyett, S. and Malone, S. (1990) 'Making the teamwork work', *Clinical Psychology Forum*, 28, pp. 16–18.

Ouchi, W. (1980) 'Markets, bureaucracies, and clans', *Administrative Science Quarterly*, 25, pp. 129–41.

Øvretveit, J. (1984) 'Action Research and Social Analysis', MPhil Thesis, Brunel University Library, Uxbridge.

Øvretveit, J. (1985) 'Medical dominance and the development of professional autonomy in physiotherapy', *Sociology of Health and Illness*, 7(1), pp. 76–93.

Øvretveit, J. (1986a) 'Management and democratic teams', *Clinical Psychology Forum*, October.

Øvretveit, J. (1986b) *Organising Multidisciplinary Community Teams*, HSC Working Paper, BIOSS, Brunel University, Uxbridge UB8 3PH.

Øvretveit, J. (1986c) *Improving Social Work Records and Practice*, BASW Publications, Birmingham.

Øvretveit, J. (1987a) 'Aspects of CMHT Organisation and Management', in Grant, et al. (1987).

Øvretveit, J. (1987b) *Volunteers in Drugs Agencies*, HSC Working Paper, BIOSS, Brunel University.

Øvretveit, J. (1988a) 'Management and multidisciplinary teamwork', *Scottish Division of Educational and Child Psychology Newsletter*.

Øvretveit, J. (1988b) *A Peer Review Process for Developing Service Quality*, BIOSS Working Paper, Brunel University, Uxbridge UB8 3PH.

Øvretveit, J. (1988c) 'The Griffiths proposals for community care – a summary and some implications', *Clinical Psychology Forum*, 16, August.

Øvretveit, J. (1990a) *Improving Primary Health Care Team Organisation*, Research Report, BIOSS, Brunel University, Uxbridge UB8 3PH.

Øvretveit, J. (1990b) 'Making the team work', *The Professional Nurse*, 5(6), pp. 284–6.

Øvretveit, J. (1990c) 'What is quality in health services', *Health Service Management*, June, pp. 132–3.

Øvretveit, J. (1991a) *Records and Access in Community Mental Health Teams*, Service Development Unit, Denbigh Hospital, Clwyd.

Øvretveit, J. (1991b) 'Why teams fail'. In Lindesay (1991).

Øvretveit, J. (1991c) 'Quality costs – or does it?', *Health Service Management*, August.

Øvretveit, J. (1991d) 'Case management and psychologists', *Clinical Psychology Forum*, 36, October, pp. 3–7.

Øvretveit, J. (1991e) 'Case management for community nursing', *The Professional Nurse*, October.

Øvretveit, J. (1991f) 'Case management and team-work'. In *Case Management Issues in Practice*, *Conference Proceedings*, Personal Social Services Research Unit, University of Kent at Canterbury.

Øvretveit (1991g) 'Quality through teamwork', from Down & Lisburn Unit, Lisburn Health Centre, Northern Ireland.

Øvretveit, J. (1992a) *Health Service Quality*, Blackwell Scientific Publications, Oxford.

Øvretveit, J. (1992b) *Therapy Services: Organisation, management, and autonomy*, Harwood Academic Press, London.

Øvretveit, J. (1992c) 'Towards market-focused measures of customer/purchaser perceptions', *Quality Forum*, 19(3), pp. 21–4.

Øvretveit, J. (1992d) *Purchasing for Health Gain in 'Internal Markets' for Health Care*, LOS-Sentrum, Bergen.

Øvretveit, J. (1993a) 'Joint Commissioning', Briefing Paper, H&SSMP, Brunel University, Uxbridge, Middlesex.

Øvretveit, J. (1993b) 'Auditing Service Quality', *International Journal of Service Industry Management*, No. 2.

Øvretveit, J. (1993c) *Measuring Service Quality*, Technical Communications Publications, Letchworth, Hertfordshire.

Øvretveit J. and Davies D. (1989) 'Management of mental handicap services in the community', *The Professional Nurse*, August.

Øvretveit, J. and Davies K. (1988) 'Client participation in mental handicap services', *Health Services Management*, August.

Patmore, C. and Weaver, T. (1990a) 'Rafts on an open sea', *Health Service Journal*, 11 October, pp. 1510–12.

Patmore, C. and Waver, T. (1990b) 'United fronts', *Health Service Journal*, 18 October, pp. 1554–5.

Powell, W. (1990) 'Neither market nor hierarchy: network forms of organisation', *Research in Organisation Behaviour*, 12, pp. 295–336.

Research and Development for Psychiatry (1991) *Case Management Project*, RDP, 134 Borough High St, London SE1 1LB.

Rowbottom, R. (1977) *Social Analysis*, Heinemann, London.

Rowbottom, R. and Hey, A. (1977a) *Organisation of Services for the Mentally Ill*, Working Paper, BIOSS, Brunel University, Uxbridge UB8 3PH.

Rowbottom, R. and Hey, A. (1977b) *Organisation of Child Guidance Services*, Working Paper, BIOSS, Brunel University, Uxbridge UB8 3PH.

Sayce, L., Craig, T. and Boardman, A. (1991) 'The development of community health centres in the UK', *Social Psychiatry and Psychiatric Epidemiology*, 26, pp. 14–20.

Searle, R. (1991) 'Community mental health teams; fact or fiction?', *Clinical Psychology Forum*, 31, pp. 15–17.

Spenser, L. and Macdonald, I. (1989) *MESH: A report on the development of mental handicap services in Hillingdon*, BIOSS, MHSU, Brunel University, Uxbridge UB8 3PH.

SSI/SOSWSG (1991a) *Care Management and Assessment: Summary of practice guidance*, HMSO, London.

SSI/SOSWSG (1991b) *Care Management and Assessment: Manager's guide*, HMSO, London.

Stone (1987) *The Darlington Community Care Project for the Elderly*, Darlington Health Authority.

Watson (1990) 'Another perspective on CMHTs and clinical psychology', *Clinical Psychology Forum*, October, pp. 27–8.

Webb, A. and Briggs, T. (eds) (1977) *Teamwork in the Personal Services and Health Care*, Croom Helm, London.

Williamson, E.O. (1975) *Markets and Hierarchies*, Free Press, New York.

Winkler, F. (1987) 'Consumerism in health: beyond the supermarket model', *Policy and Politics*, 15 (1).

INDEX